AF761773

STATE AID AND THE EUROPEAN ECONOMIC CONSTITUTION

Recent years have seen the rise of EU State aid law as a crucial component of the European economic constitution. To date, however, the literature has neglected the contribution of this area of EU law to the internal market. This book seeks to fill this gap in our understanding of the economic constitution by exploring the significance of State aid law in addressing questions that go to the core of the internal market project. It does so by examining the case law relating to three different activities that Member States engage in: market participation, market regulation, and funding for Services of General Economic Interest. Each of these areas offers insights into fundamental questions surrounding the economic constitution, such as the separation between the State and the market, the scope for Member States to engage in regulatory competition, and the tension between market and nonmarket concerns.

Volume 2 in the series Hart Studies in Competition Law

State Aid and the European Economic Constitution

Francesco de Cecco

·HART·
PUBLISHING
OXFORD AND PORTLAND, OREGON
2013

Published in the United Kingdom by Hart Publishing Ltd
16C Worcester Place, Oxford, OX1 2JW
Telephone: +44 (0)1865 517530
Fax: +44 (0)1865 510710
E-mail: mail@hartpub.co.uk
Website: http://www.hartpub.co.uk

Published in North America (US and Canada) by
Hart Publishing
c/o International Specialized Book Services
920 NE 58th Avenue, Suite 300
Portland, OR 97213-3786
USA
Tel: +1 503 287 3093 or toll-free: (1) 800 944 6190
Fax: +1 503 280 8832
E-mail: orders@isbs.com
Website: http://www.isbs.com

© Francesco de Cecco 2013

Francesco de Cecco has asserted his right under the Copyright, Designs and Patents Act 1988, to be identified as the author of this work.

All rights reserved. No part of this publication may be reproduced, stored in a retrieval system, or transmitted, in any form or by any means, without the prior permission of Hart Publishing, or as expressly permitted by law or under the terms agreed with the appropriate reprographic rights organisation. Enquiries concerning reproduction which may not be covered by the above should be addressed to Hart Publishing Ltd at the address above.

British Library Cataloguing in Publication Data
Data Available

ISBN: 978-1-84946-105-4

Typeset by Compuscript Ltd, Shannon
Printed and bound in Great Britain by
Lightning Source UK Ltd

For Vicky, Julia and Emily

Acknowledgements

In chronological order, my thanks go to Professor Derrick Wyatt who was my MPhil supervisor at the University of Oxford and offered excellent advice to me in that capacity. This book is—in large part—based on work carried out during my doctoral research funded by the Helena Normanton Research scholarship at the University of Sussex. My supervisor there, Malcolm Ross, provided constant encouragement, moral support and constructive criticism—I have learnt a great deal from him, well beyond the doctorate.

Yuri Borgmann-Prebil and Niamh Nic Shuibhne examined my thesis, and made constructive comments and suggestions, both during and after the viva. I am especially grateful to Niamh Nic Shuibhne who read parts of this book and offered detailed and extremely useful comments. I am greatly indebted to Eleanor Spaventa, not only for reading and commenting on parts of this book at a crucial stage, but also for having been an exceptionally supportive friend throughout these years. I am also grateful to Patrick O'Callaghan for his insightful comments on Chapter two, and to Richard Hart, Rachel Turner, Mel Hamill and their colleagues at Hart Publishing for their patience and valuable assistance.

This book would never have seen the light of the day without the support of my close family: my parents, my brother, my wife, and my two daughters. However, Vicky, little Julia and Emily, have made the greatest sacrifices for this book, and it is right that I should dedicate it to them as a small, but deeply felt, token of gratitude.

Contents

PART III

Table of Cases

Table of Legislation

Treaties

EU Regulations

EU Directives

EU Decisions

1

Introduction

Subsidies and other forms of public intervention are tools in the politician's toolkit, which governments and local authorities often resort to in pursuit of objectives that they have been elected to achieve. Yet, the presence of the EU rules on State aid control determines the shape, and limits the availability, of such tools. State aid law is an intrusive policy, which places significant constraints on decision-making at every level of government. Moreover, State aid law affects, and to a certain extent is itself the expression of, fundamental political choices; choices which may not be immediately apparent, or may not be systematically articulated, but which underlie an entire spectrum of legal concepts and principles. Such choices concern the respective roles of the State and the market, the desirability or otherwise of competition between jurisdictions, or the appropriate balance between market and nonmarket concerns. To the extent that these choices are crystallised into law, they become part of the EU's economic constitution.

While large sections of internal market law have been examined in their constitutional dimensions, the emergence of academic interest in the constitutional implications of State aid law is a relatively recent development.[1] The special appeal offered by this section of EU law lies in the fact that it represents a microcosm in which many of the themes that colour the debate on internal market law converge, and, at the same time, it is a distinct area characterised by a unique set of rules, principles and concepts, all of which contribute to determine the evolution of the European economic constitution. The book's specific focus is on the case law that defines the boundaries of the legal notion of State aid under Article 107(1) of the Treaty on the Functioning of the European Union (TFEU), a jurisprudence that has been dissected in its manifold aspects, but which continues to present a number of stimulating questions in light of its wider constitutional implications. As the freedom that governments enjoy to mould the economic destinies of their countries is affected by the answers that are given to questions on the boundaries of State aid, these are, plainly, constitutional questions.

The book is divided in three parts. Part I sets the scene by laying out the constitutional framework which informs the rest of the book. Chapter two fleshes

[1] The term 'internal market' is used throughout this book to include State aid law. As made clear by the Protocol on the Internal Market and Competition annexed to the Lisbon Treaty, 'the internal market as set out in Article 3 of the Treaty on European Union includes a system ensuring that competition is not distorted'.

out the concept of economic constitution and explains its usefulness for the book's purposes, while chapter three plots the position of State aid within this constitution by comparing the main features of the State aid regime to the main features of free movement and antitrust law. Part II then moves on to examine some fundamental issues in the interpretation of the notion of State aid. It does this by considering how State aid law takes account of the role of the State as market participant, in chapter four, and of the State as regulator, in chapter five. Part III considers two areas of interpretation that allow us to explore in greater depth some of the themes identified in previous sections of the book: the issue of regional tax autonomy (in chapter six) and the question of public service funding (chapter seven).

The term economic constitution is not used here as a form of homage to the ordo-liberal pedigree of the concept. Instead, it serves two purposes. The first is to emphasise the constitutional nature of the EU's primary economic law. The constraints on public (and private) power that it sets are subject to the constitutional principles that apply across EU law, and are the object of interpretation by the Court of Justice, which gives substance to often anaemic primary law provisions. The second purpose is to bring to light the material aspect of the constitution; in other words, to identify the EU's long-term orientation as to the role of the State in the economy. Whether this constitution expresses a particular philosophy of political economy, an overarching ideology, a neo-liberal *pensée unique*, or, rather, it is an open-ended project that accommodates a plurality of approaches to political economy, is a matter of intense discussion among scholars. This book proceeds from the view that the legitimacy of EU law rests on its ability to deliver a single market which does not undermine the capacity of Member States to pursue redistributive policies, and to preserve the delicate balance between EU law supremacy and national concerns regarding their constitutional spaces. The arduous balance between market and nonmarket values, between EU and national competences and their respective constitutional spaces, is very much a necessity of the current stage of integration, which is characterised by an asymmetry between economic integration on the one hand, and redistributive policies, on the other. The advanced level of economic integration achieved so far through the single market has not been matched by an equivalent level of integration in redistributive policies; this is so because the prospect of political integration, a precondition for progress towards greater integration in such policies, is enveloped in a thick mist.[2] This, however, does not mean that economic integration has no bearing on redistributive policies and on policies that embody nonmarket values. On the contrary, spillover into the latter policies and values is an intrinsic consequence of advanced market integration. The

[2] This is not to diminish the importance of EU social policy, however. For a recent overview, see C Barnard, 'EU "Social" Policy: From Employment Law to Labour Market Reform' in P Craig and G de Búrca (eds), *The Evolution of EU Law*, 2nd edn (Oxford, Oxford University Press, 2011).

EU's legitimacy crucially turns on the manner in which it deals with this kind of spillover.

It may seem surprising that a study on the boundaries of State aid should contemplate questions of legitimacy. After all, when one considers the output legitimacy of State aid and, more generally, of the law of the single market, the arguments in favour of EU action seem compelling.[3] According to a highly influential view, the output legitimacy of economic integration rests on the transnational nature of the problems that it addresses, and on the inadequacy of national political systems to offer solutions to problems with transnational dimensions.[4] On one account, in particular, the EU is a 'regulatory state', as it rectifies market failures that cannot adequately be resolved by 'majoritarian' institutions, but are best dealt with when delegated to agencies that are endowed with independence and technical expertise.[5] Non-majoritarian agencies are better placed to play this role as they are not prone to capture by the short-term interests of the majority, but are able to secure both the long-term interests of the majority, and the interests of minorities. Moreover, the existence of negative cross-border externalities and commitment problems that arise in economic and trade-related matters make the upward delegation to supranational institutions an attractive solution both from the perspective of the EU's legitimacy and of the Member States' own legitimacy, as delegation to the EU cures the legitimacy issues caused by the inability of Member States to offer adequate solutions to problems with transnational dimensions. On this view, legitimacy questions are virtually absent in areas relating purely to economic integration, since decisions taken in these areas do not concern redistribution, but yield, instead, Pareto-efficient solutions, outcomes in which there are some winners, but—crucially—no losers. Given the lack of redistributive outcomes, so goes the theory, such areas have a low level of political salience—public opinion is virtually indifferent to them.[6]

Yet these views, and, in particular, the idea that the areas covered by economic integration lack political salience and elude political contestation, which was never without its challengers, have been seriously undermined by recent events.[7] One need only think of the debate on legislative proposals for a Services Directive, or the fallout from the *Viking* and *Laval* case law,[8] both instances in which the

[3] For an account of legitimacy in the EU and of 'output legitimacy' in particular, see F Scharpf, *Governing in Europe. Effective and Democratic?* (Oxford, Oxford University Press, 1999). Output legitimacy denotes the ability of institutions to deliver outcomes that satisfy citizens' preferences.

[4] GD Majone, 'The Rise of the Regulatory State in Europe' (1994) 17 *West European Politics* 77; A Menon and S Weatherill, 'Transnational Legitimacy in a Globalising World: How the European Union Rescues its States' (2008) 31 *Western Union Politics* 397.

[5] Majone, 'The Rise of the Regulatory State in Europe' (n 4).

[6] A Moravcsik, 'In Defense of the "Democratic Deficit". Reassessing Legitimacy in the European Union' (2002) 40 *Journal of Common Market Studies* 603.

[7] A Follesdal and S Hix, 'Why There is a Democratic Deficit in the EU: A Response to Majone and Moravcsik' (2006) 44 *Journal of Common Market Studies* 533.

[8] Case C-438/05 *Viking Line* [2007] ECR I-10779; C-341/05 *Laval un Partneri Ltd v Svenska Byggnadsarbetareförbundet and others* [2007] ECR I-11767.

interests of free trade, on the one hand, and the rights and interests protected by employment policy and industrial relations law, on the other, came to be seen as antagonists; or, again, the ongoing political repercussions of the euro-zone crisis, which have exposed the consequences of the lack of a comprehensive political debate behind fundamental aspects of monetary union, and have further demonstrated the relevance to public opinion of matters that were previously regarded as lacking salience. As all these events reveal, policies, decisions, or legislation emanating from the EU may, at least at the level of perceptions, create winners and losers, and it is wrong to assume that economic regulation can be completely insulated from the surrounding social and political context.

Still, the fact that EU policy is subject to contestation does not necessarily mean that constitutional adjudication by the European courts should give rise to questions of legitimacy. Unease with certain aspects of EU policy, or disgruntlement with isolated rulings of the Court of Justice does not affect the Court's legitimacy. Regardless of the Court's standing in public opinion, a matter of questionable verifiability, there is little doubt that its jurisprudence, through the elaboration of concepts and principles, such as mutual recognition, that have been central to the success of the single market, has contributed to the output legitimacy of the European project.[9] Yet, if that is the case, then it is plausible to assume that the Court's contribution could also be in the opposite direction. Individual cases are not sufficient to undermine the legitimacy of the Court's constitutional authority; however, the cumulative effect of the Court's interpretation of different treaty provisions may be a gradual erosion of the EU's output legitimacy. If constitutional adjudication is to avoid becoming inextricably linked to the EU's legitimacy crisis, where internal market law intercepts sensitive aspects of national competence, careful judicial handling commends itself to the Court.

Granted, there is little doubt that the Court is ill-placed to address the fundamental limitations which stem from the (above-mentioned) asymmetry between economic, social and political integration that characterises European integration in its current form. Such limitations may only be rectified through the European political process.[10] Moreover, the Court is unable to prevent spillover of economic integration into noneconomic/nonmarket areas. Yet, the Court's role consists in ensuring that its jurisprudence justifies the perception that such spillover effects are contained and managed in accordance with a transparent and predictable set of principles. A certain degree of sacrifice to nonmarket interests and to the exercise of national competences is an inevitable consequence of

[9] On the question of the Court's legitimacy, see D Kelemen, 'The Political Foundations of Judicial Independence in the European Union' (2012) 12 *Journal of European Public Policy* 43.

[10] Which, of course, does not necessarily mean that the European political process is currently capable of doing so. Note that 'European' is used here in all its ambivalence: it means at EU, or at Member State level, or both. Of course, this book makes no claims as to how this particular nut is to be cracked.

market integration; yet to be accepted, sacrifices of this sort should be justified by reasoning that is able to command widespread acceptance.

State aid law is not immune from these considerations. While rulings such as *Azores* or *Altmark* may not have produced controversies with the same resonance in public opinion as *Viking* and *Laval*, they have, nonetheless, caused keen interest among governments and parliaments both at national and at regional levels across Europe.[11] Unsurprisingly so, as they address politically sensitive questions that relate to the extent to which fiscal powers can be devolved from central governments to sub-national governments, or how public services should be run. Both cases, in other words, relate to constitutional questions, as they ultimately concern the relative status of market and nonmarket values in EU law, and the scope for national regulatory autonomy and national constitutional identities under EU law. For these reasons, the constitutional framework sketched out in chapter two is essential to understanding the themes with which the book is threaded.

While chapter two concerns the broader constitutional picture, and leaves State aid law to one side, State aid law makes a first appearance in chapter three, which considers its distinctiveness within the European economic constitution. The chapter compares and contrasts the State aid regime with other areas of internal market law (free movement and 'antitrust law'). It finds that, behind a unity of purpose, and despite the remark that both areas fall within the wider category of 'competition law', State aid appears to share little with antitrust law in the way in which market analysis is approached. The empirical questions that characterise antitrust law are virtually absent in State aid law. In part, this can be attributed to the fact that, unlike antitrust law, much of State aid law concerns regulatory measures which, by their nature, do not lend themselves to (the same type of) market analysis that applies to measures whose effects on individual undertakings may be more readily identifiable. In this latter sense, the absence of an empirical approach is reminiscent of the Court's approach to the concept of distortion of competition in the case law on the preconditions for harmonising legislation under Article 114 TFEU.

Another significant discrepancy emerges from this inquiry. While free movement law, and the principle of mutual recognition in particular, may be said to lay down the conditions for a process of regulatory competition between Member States to emerge, albeit with a number of safeguards for national regulatory autonomy, the State aid provisions have the opposite effect. The effect of the EU's State aid regime is, in fact, to limit the extent to which Member States may employ subsidies or selective regulation (and taxation in particular) to attract business activity to their jurisdiction.

What emerges from this analysis is a body of law which may be described as giving rise to both a form of negative integration and to a form of positive

[11] Case C-88/03 *Portugal v Commission (Azores)* [2006] ECR I-7115; Case 280/00 *Altmark Trans GmbH, Regierungspräsidium Magdeburg v Nahverkergesellschaft Altmark GmbH* [2003] ECR I-7747.

integration. The deregulatory effect associated with negative integration, which derives from the general prohibition of State aid, is accompanied by the exercise on the part of the Commission of a set of powers which are designed to ensure that State intervention is channelled towards objectives that are perceived as priorities from an EU perspective.

Once this framework in place, Part II goes on to address the case law on the definition of State aid through an analytical model which juxtaposes cases involving Member States acting as market participants, and cases involving Member States acting as regulators. This dichotomy throws light on the different legal standards that apply to each of the two categories of State actions and on the significance of these in terms of the values that they appear to further. It also highlights the effects of State aid law on the separation between State and market, and on the extent to which Member States remain free to pursue regulatory (or tax) competition. Chapter four examines cases in which Member States act as market participants. The central notion in this case law is the market operator principle, which acts as a boundary marker between subsidies and normal market transactions. The way in which the principle operates consists in comparing the conduct of a State to that of a private investor, seller, or lender operating under normal market circumstances. Where the conduct of the State deviates from this benchmark of behaviour, it is deemed to create an advantage in favour of the undertaking(s) concerned. This standard of conduct dictated by State aid law prompts Member States to adopt the logic of economic efficiency in areas that would not necessarily be subject to it. In doing so, it appears to reveal EU State aid as a strongly market-orientated policy which is committed to the liberal principle of the separation between the State and the market. Moreover, the chapter questions the apparent neutrality of EU law regarding State versus private ownership of economic activity. It, instead, argues that the approach of EU law is one of substantive equality. Critics who argue that the market operator test embodies a neo-liberal view of the respective role of the State and the market may have a point. However, as the concluding part of the chapter shows, the Court seems prepared to eschew a mechanistic approach to the separation between State and market in cases that display a strong public interest dimension.

The distinction between market participation and regulation is not free from difficulty. While recent case law has attempted to provide some clarity on the scope of the market operator test by employing the concept of economic activity to trace a dividing line, it has not cleared the ground from potential difficulties. Chapter five argues that, in adopting this approach, the General Court appears to have neglected the rationale for excluding regulatory measures from the scope of the market operator principle. The State aid case law has consistently regarded regulation as forming part of the normal costs of an undertaking, and has adopted a presumption that State intervention that alters the regulatory framework in which undertakings operate is distortionary. This is why, where the State acts in its regulatory capacity, the relevant question is not whether its behaviour conforms to the rationality of an investor, or a creditor, but whether regulatory intervention is asymmetric in its effects.

Determining whether regulation has asymmetric effects, whether it is 'selective', is, however, an arduous task. The difficulties derive from the fact that regulation often produces asymmetries, and, therefore, EU law must take a view on which asymmetry is a normal effect of regulation, and which is a distortion caused by State intervention. The case law struggles under the competing demands of pragmatism and of legal certainty. The same difficulties arise in relation to another legal test that has emerged from the Court's case law, which exploits a textual ambiguity in Article 107(1) TFEU in order to create a legal safe-haven for sensitive areas of domestic legislative competence, such as employment law or energy policy. There is a certain degree of formalism involved in tracing bright lines of this sort. Yet, the solutions that have so far been advanced in the literature are perhaps more problematic than a refinement and recalibration of the Court's existing case law.

Part III brings into focus two areas that offer insights into the way in which the relationship between State aid law and (domestic) nonmarket values can be addressed in the case law. Chapter six considers whether, and under which conditions, tax measures that have a regional (sub-national) scope should be treated as State aid. There is no straightforward answer to this question, as, clearly, the regional scope of a measure cannot automatically lead to the conclusion that there is a State aid; to do so would result in suppressing a crucial aspect of regional autonomy, in contravention of the EU Treaty's renewed commitment to national constitutional identity and regional autonomy enshrined in Article 4(2) of the Treaty on European Union (TEU). At the same time, however, the standard approach to the definition of State aid, and EU law orthodoxy, would imply the irrelevance of internal constitutional arrangements. While this chapter finds the Court's approach to be consistent with the view that internal market law should not undermine national constitutional identity, it also argues that this solution is not entirely without consequences as far as tax (and regulatory) competition is concerned.

Chapter seven completes this picture by examining how the Court has attempted to reconcile a thorough application of the State aid rules with EU law's commitment to Services of General Economic Interest (SGEIs). The reasons why this area of EU State aid law commends itself to our attention are obviously linked to the significance of SGEIs to the objective of a 'highly competitive social market economy';[12] they are, in other words, part and parcel of the attempt by EU law to reconcile market integration and the pursuit of efficiency and competitiveness with the pursuit of social aims. Yet, as the chapter makes clear, any attempt to characterise the internal market as an economy endowed with a unified approach to nonmarket values is confronted with a fragmented reality made up of distinct

12 Article 3(3) Treaty on European Union.

approaches to public service values. With its emphasis on domestic competence to define SGEIs, the Lisbon Treaty seems to have taken stock of this reality. Moreover, both the Commission and the EU Courts now appear to recognise that national competence in this area represents a limit to the prescriptive nature of the significant regulatory constraints imposed through the application of State aid law to public service compensation.

Part I

2

The Constitutional Framework

The term 'economic constitution' enjoys widespread currency among EU law scholars. Yet, the original concept with which it is associated is considerably vague, and heavily burdened by ideology. Once this ideological cargo is unloaded, however, the term's explanatory capacity begins to emerge. Its value lies in the ability to evoke, at the same time, the legal structure of the internal market, its political-economic orientation, and the connections between the two. Such connections shine light on the Court of Justice's jurisprudence on the boundaries of EU economic law, which is the central concern of our inquiry. The indeterminacy of much of the law of economic integration, and the role of the Court in giving substance to its provisions create inextricable links between adjudication and the development of a set (though not a system) of values. While this set of values does not amount to a comprehensive ideology that lies ready to hand, it is not immune from contestation, as market integration affects public policy choices, and domestic constitutional spaces. This chapter outlines, first, the relevant features of the concept of economic constitution, and then moves on to address the debate on the orientation of the internal market case law; the final part considers whether, and to what extent, it is possible that the changes introduced by the Lisbon Treaty that recognise both the centrality of the social dimension of market integration and the relevance of domestic constitutional spaces may eventually find their way into the case law.

1. THE CONCEPT OF A EUROPEAN ECONOMIC CONSTITUTION

The term 'economic constitution' has its roots in German 'ordo-liberalism', which, in all of its variants and offshoots, is associated with the school of thought that developed around the belief that a higher-order law could protect individual freedom from abuses of both private and public economic power.[1] In the ordo-liberal

[1] D Gerber, 'Constitutionalising the Economy: German Neo-Liberalism, Competition law and the "New" Europe' (1994) 42 *American Journal of Competition Law* 25; W Sauter, 'The Economic Constitution of the European Union' (1998) 4 *Columbia Journal of European Law* 27; M Poiares Maduro, *We The Court: The European Court of Justice and the European Economic Constitution* (Oxford, Hart Publishing, 1998); DJ Gerber, *Law and Competition in Twentieth Century Europe: Protecting Prometheus* (Oxford, Oxford University Press, 2001) chs 7–8; J Baquero Cruz, *Between Competition and*

manifesto, the economic constitution was defined as 'a general political decision as to how the economic life of the nation is to be structured'.[2] On this view, the role of the constitution was to resolve conflicts between the political and the economic spheres by positing a legally enforceable separation between the State and the market, by giving individual economic rights constitutional recognition, and by setting clear limits to the State's discretion.[3] Ordo-liberals shared with classic liberalism a deep suspicion of the administrative branch of government, and, in particular, of the use of discretion by public powers to pursue general interest goals; instead, they claimed, the general interest would flourish if the legal system was equipped adequately to protect individual rights. Competition law was seen as the fulcrum of their ideal constructs of government. Competition, they believed, allowed the market economy to function effectively.[4] And by competition they meant 'complete competition', a system in which no undertaking in a market would be in a position to exercise market power.[5] Government intervention was regarded as a means of perverting the normal workings of competition in a free market and was treated with suspicion. The role of the constitution was therefore to limit political discretion in economic matters, while the, nonetheless crucial, role of the State was to uphold the constitution.

When ordo-liberals turned their attention to the project of European market integration they saw in it an antidote to the tendency of national governments to expand their sphere of influence at the expense of individual autonomy.[6] The emergence of supranational economic governance was, in fact, viewed as an opportunity to take market regulation away from the hands of politicians and to uphold the separation of market regulation from political intervention.

Free Movement (Oxford, Hart Publishing, 2002); G Marenco, 'The Birth of Modern Competition Law in Europe' in A von Bogdandy, PC Mavroidis and Y Mény (eds), *European Integration and International Co-ordination: Studies in Honour of Claus-Dieter Ehlermann* (The Hague, Kluwer Law International, 2002) 279; C Joerges, 'What is Left of the European Economic Constitution' (2005) 30 *EL Rev* 431; C Ahlborn and C Grave, 'Walter Eucken and Ordoliberalism: An Introduction from a Consumer Welfare Perspective' (2006) 2 *Competition Policy International* 197; G Monti, 'EC Competition Law' (Cambridge, Cambridge University Press, 2007) 23–25; C Joerges, 'A Renaissance of the European Economic Constitution?' in U Neergaard, R Nielsen and L Roseberry (eds), *Integrating Welfare Functions into EU Law* (Copenhagen, DJØF Forlag, 2009). On the concept of 'social market economy', perhaps the most influential legacy of ordo-liberalism: R Sally, *Classical Liberalism and International Economic Order* (London, Routledge, 2002); N Goldschmidt and M Wohlgemuth, 'Social Market Economy: Origins, Meanings and Interpretations' (2008) 19 *Constitutional Political Economy* 261.

[2] F Bohm, W Eucken and H Grossmann-Doerth, 'The Ordo Manifesto of 1936' in A Peacock and H Willgerodt (eds), *Germany's Social Market Economy: Origins and Evolution* (London, Macmillan, 1989) 15–26.

[3] W Sauter, 'The Economic Constitution of the European Union' (1998) 4 *Columbia Journal of European Law* 27, 47.

[4] Gerber, 'Constitutionalising the Economy' (n 1) 43.

[5] Ibid, translating Eucken's term '*vollständiger Wettbewerb*' used in W Eucken, *Grundsätze der Wirtschaftspolitik* (Tübingen, Francke und Mohr, 1952) 228.

[6] It should be noted, however, that support for European integration among ordo-liberals was not uniform, nor homogenous in its articulations. See Sally, *Classical Liberalism and International Economic Order* (n 1) 131–46.

A technocratic supranational body would act as a politically neutral supervisor of the order created by the European economic constitution, while national political systems would remain in charge of formulating policy. Latter-day ordo-liberals described the common market as a 'self-organising system', in which free movement law creates the conditions for 'an unimpeded self-co-ordination of economic actors' and where competition law allows 'the self-control of economic actors through competition', and the Court is charged with the task of enforcing this 'order'.[7]

A. Ordo-liberalism and the *European* Economic Constitution

These ideas exercised *some* influence on the European elites during the initial stages of the common market,[8] and came to greater fruition at a later stage, when the rules on monetary union were fleshed out.[9] However, neither the Treaty of Rome, nor the evolution of European economic integration from EEC into EU, can be said to have been shaped from the ordo-liberal mould. The functional nature of European economic integration, its ultimate pursuit of peace and prosperity through trade, and the different political-ideological backgrounds of the Member States, prevented the common/internal market from becoming wedded to a distinct, well-defined, and comprehensive politico-economic ideology. True, in signing the Treaty of Rome, the Member States committed themselves to the pursuit of free trade; yet that commitment did not carry with it a prescription of a specific model of *domestic* political economy, nor did it encompass a vision of the role of the individual vis-a-vis the State. Indeed, Member States were, for a number of decades, largely unconstrained by the law of the common market in the pursuit of their domestic policies, which involved large-scale State intervention and the significant expansion of their welfare systems. During the post-war decades, a period of extraordinary economic growth, interventionist policies on the domestic front went hand in hand with the progressive opening of national economies to European trade, a combination which is captured in the famous

[7] M Streit and W Mussler, 'The Economic Constitution of the EC from "Rome" to "Maastricht"' (1995) 1 *European Law Journal* 5, 14.

[8] See Gerber, 'Constitutionalising the Economy' (n 1); G Amato, *Antitrust and the Bounds of Power: The Dilemma of Liberal Democracy in the History of the Market* (Oxford, Hart Publishing, 1997) 40–43. However, recent research on the *travaux préparatoires* of the Treaty of Rome has questioned the impact of ordo-liberal ideas on the drafting of the Treaty's competition rules: P Akman, 'Searching for the Long-Lost Soul of Article 82 EC' (2009) 29 *OJLS* 267.

[9] See K Dyson and K Featherstone, *The Road to Maastricht: Negotiating Economic and Monetary Union* (Oxford, Oxford University Press, 2009). The influence of ordo-liberal doctrines on certain sections of the European elites is still felt. For a recent profession of faith in ordo-liberalism, see the speech given by Jürgen Starck, then member of the executive board of the European Central Bank, www.ecb.int/press/key/date/2008/html/sp081118_1.en.html. For an insightful account of ordo-liberal echoes in the current debate regarding the euro-zone sovereign debt crisis see P O'Callaghan, 'Collective Memory in Law and Policy: The Problem of the Sovereign Debt Crisis' (forthcoming).

expression 'Keynes at home and Smith abroad'.[10] Interventionist policies were not only a feature of national economies; they were, and are, also part of the EU's economic order.[11]

Moreover, the project of European integration was never limited to keeping public and private economic power in check, as the ordo-liberal concept of economic constitution, instead, dictated. Article 2 of the Treaty of Rome read: 'The Community shall have as its task, by establishing a common market and progressively approximating the economic policies of member states, to promote throughout the Community a harmonious development of economic activities, a continuous and balanced expansion, an increase in stability, an accelerated raising of the standard of living and closer relations between the states belonging to it'. It was clear that the task of promoting 'a harmonious development of economic activities' or a 'continuous and balanced expansion' could not be achieved without effecting choices that necessitated some degree of political input and the exercise of discretion. This became increasingly evident as integration progressed on a parallel track: on the one hand, market integration advanced with remarkable intensity; on the other, integration embraced ever wider areas beyond trade.

This pursuit was, of course, the result of political choices enshrined in a succession of treaties. The story is well known. The Single European Act gave the process of market integration a more powerful footing, by defining the internal market,[12] by setting a deadline for its establishment, and by introducing qualified majority voting; but it also introduced new competences in nonmarket areas, including regional development, social policy, health and safety, and environmental policy.[13] This parallel expansion of market and nonmarket areas reached its apogee in the Maastricht Treaty.[14] Here the objectives of an 'open market economy with free competition', the pursuit of 'stable prices, sound public finances and sustainable balance of payments' were proclaimed, and the fundamental steps in the process of establishing the single currency were laid down; at the same time, however, European citizenship was introduced and new nonmarket areas of Community competence, such as (amongst others) culture, consumer protection and public health, were added, while existing ones, such as environmental protection and regional development, were expanded. The Treaty of Amsterdam further strengthened the presence of nonmarket values by introducing an employment title, but also by introducing a new provision, Article 16, which acknowledged the

[10] R Gilpin, *The Political Economy of International Relations* (Princeton, Princeton University Press, 1987) 355.

[11] The Common Agricultural Policy being the most obvious example.

[12] Article 13 of the Single European Act, which added Article 8a to the EEC Treaty (subsequently Article 14 EC), whose second paragraph read: 'The internal market shall comprise an area without internal frontiers in which the free movement of goods, persons, services and capital is ensured in accordance with the provisions of this Treaty'.

[13] Economic and Social Cohesion (Article 130a–e EEC); Social Policy; Health and Safety at Work; Research and Technological Development (Article 130f–q EEC); and Environmental Policy (Article130r–t EEC).

[14] Joerges, 'What is Left of the European Economic Constitution' (n 1).

place occupied by Services of General Economic Interest in the shared values of the Union and their role in promoting social and territorial cohesion.

The evolution (to date) culminates in the Lisbon Treaty, in which the, ungainly but potentially significant, concept of a 'highly competitive social market economy' was introduced, and the reference to the pursuit of 'undistorted competition' was removed from the Treaty's definition of internal market, and relegated to a—less visible but equally binding—protocol;[15] moreover Article 16 EC was amended as Article 14 TFEU and a protocol added, so as to emphasise national discretion in relation to Services of General Economic Interest, and to assign exclusive Member State competence over 'Non Economic Services of General Interest'.[16]

B. The Continuing Relevance of the Concept of Economic Constitution

If the case for an ordo-liberal reading of the European internal market appears to be weak, it is worth asking whether the *concept* of a European economic constitution may, instead, offer greater insights. At first sight, the answer seems to be negative. The definition of economic constitution as a formal document that crystallises a *general decision* on the structure of an economic system centred on a comprehensive economic ideology plainly jars with the reality of a legal order, such as the EU, that, in large part, has emerged, layer after layer, from the political initiative of the Member States channelled through successive treaty amendments, and from the Court's interpretation of these treaties, rather than from an original ideological design.[17] Moreover, even if we were to extend the definition to include the case law, the very nature of judicial decision-making in the EU, a system in which jurisprudential evolution often depends on the (heavily context-specific) vagaries of national litigation, would prevent such a characterisation. While some of the Court's seminal judgments may indeed be regarded as decisions containing fundamental choices that affect the structure of the internal market, any description of such case law as an organic and coherent ideological whole, a system, is, at best, aspirational. Of course, the Court's reliance on European integration, on an 'ever closer union among the peoples of Europe', as an objective which justifies recourse to teleology may be characterised as the Court's ideological genetic code, which has informed more than one generation of judges and Advocates General.[18] Yet, this natural commitment to European integration is hardly the comprehensive decision on the structure of the economy that ordo-liberals prescribed.

If ordo-liberalism as a set of ideas and analytical tools is ill-suited to capture the essence of internal market law, why, then, continue to use a term, such as economic

15 Protocol 27 'on the Internal Market and Competition'.

16 Protocol 26 'on Services of General Interest'.

17 See Baquero, *Between Competition and Free Movement* (n 1) 26–29.

18 The reference is to the wording of the Preamble of the Treaty of Rome (now reproduced in the Preamble to the TFEU).

constitution, which is so closely connected to that intellectual framework? If the term is to be not only rescued, but put to good use, as indeed is argued here, two preliminary steps need to be taken. First, we need to obliterate its ideological associations. Secondly, we need to be clear about the meaning of 'constitution'. The point to start from is the contention that the EU exhibits constitutional features, a set of fundamental principles that emanate from the primary sources of EU law as interpreted by the Court of Justice. Of course, the constitutional nature of this body of law turns on the crucial role of the case law in fleshing out basic constitutional doctrines and principles, but also, equally crucially, on the cooperation of, and tolerance by, national courts, legal orders, and political authorities in this process.[19] Naturally, this view cannot be countenanced if one conceives of constitutions as written, codified documents containing the fundamental principles establishing and regulating the powers of political institutions of a State and the relationship between the individual and the State, quite simply because the EU is not a State, and its constitutional laws, principles and doctrines are not codified.[20] Yet, a wider and more sophisticated reading of the term constitution is possible: one that removes statehood as a necessary condition, that contemplates the possibility that foundational principles remain uncodified, and that requires constitutional interpretation to be dynamic and responsive to decentralised inputs.[21] Indeed, this interpretation is today part of the mainstream.[22]

While the ordo-liberal assumption that it is possible to identify a general decision on the structure of the EU's 'economic life' can be disposed of with ease, there is something useful to be retained from the idea of a 'political decision'. It is indeed true, as Baquero Cruz suggests, that the term *economic constitutional law* is sharper than *economic constitution*, as it avoids misleading comparisons with domestic legal orders. Yet, the ordo-liberal term, and its reference to a system of fundamental values inherent in a political-economic order, is useful in throwing light on the link between legal structures and political economy choices and in allowing evaluation to play its part. Granted, analytical propriety requires the legal dimension to be kept separate from the politico-economic aspect of the economic

[19] What Martinico, paraphrasing Dicey, calls the 'efficient secret' of the European constitution, G Martinico, 'Complexity as the "Efficient Secret" of the European Constitution: an Alternative (Explanatory) Proposal' (2011) *EUI Max Weber Working Paper* 1/11, www.cadmus.eui.eu/handle/1814/15461. On constitutional tolerance, see JHH Weiler, 'A Constitution for Europe? Some Hard Choices' (2002) 42 *Journal of Common Market Studies* 563.

[20] The doctrines of supremacy and direct effect being the most conspicuous absences in the Treaties.

[21] E Stein, 'Lawyers, Judges, and the Making of a Transnational Constitution' (1981) *75 American Journal of International Law* 1; K Lenaerts, 'Constitutionalism and the Many Faces of Federalism' (1990) 38 *American Journal of Comparative Law* 205; JHH Weiler, 'The Transformation of Europe' (1991) 100 *Yale Law Journal* 2403; P Craig, 'Constitutions, Constitutionalism and the European Union' (2001) 7 *ELJ* 125; M Kumm, 'The Jurisprudence of Constitutional Conflict: Constitutional Supremacy in Europe before and after the Constitutional Treaty' (2005) 11 *European Law Journal* 262.

[22] But see T Hartley, *Constitutional Problems of the European Union* (Oxford, Hart Publishing, 1999); P Eleftheriadis, 'The Idea of a European Constitution' (2007) 27 *OJLS* 1; and P Eleftheriadis, 'The Structure of European Union Law' in C Barnard and O Odudu (eds), 12 *The Cambridge Yearbook of European Legal Studies 2009–2010* (Oxford, Hart Publishing, 2011).

constitution; but the two are undoubtedly linked, and, for this reason, the ambiguity in the term economic constitution is—arguably—a productive one.

According to Baquero Cruz, another fundamental objection against the use of the term rests on the fragmentation of the legal order that would ensue from the 'restriction of reference' conveyed by the adjective 'economic'. This fragmentation, he argues, is liable to undermine the coherence between different branches of the legal order, and to designate areas that are subject to partial, sectoral constitutions, rather than being constrained by the political constitution. Under this approach, gaps would be filled by relying on sector-specific principles, rather than on generally applicable constitutional principles; the ultimate result would be to subtract an entire area of public life from the democratic processes that emanate from the (political) constitution.[23]

The isolation of market principles from constitutional values and principles is indeed a possible outcome of an interpretation that tends to partition the constitution into substantive areas. Yet this is not a *necessary implication* of the term economic constitution. On the contrary, the fact that the market is constitutionalised implies its subjection to constitutional principles. As Nic Shuibhne has written, '[a] *constitutional* market does not presume crude victory for the economic values or vices of the market-place. Rather, constitutionalism *requires* (not just allows) a more nuanced market to take shape'.[24] While certain economic values are recognised as integral to the constitution, their rank does not command a higher status than other constitutional values. The purchase of the term *economic* constitution lies, therefore, in highlighting the constitutional nature of economic law, and in placing economic law in a wider constitutional framework which includes nonmarket values.

These considerations should be sufficient to allay concerns regarding the emergence of an economic branch of constitutionalism which seeks to secede from general constitutional law and its constraints. If the word 'economic' is intended in its descriptive rather than its normative sense, there is no compelling reason why the legal decisions regarding economic matters should be immune from the constitutional principles that govern non-economic matters. This is not to deny that economic matters are subject to specific legal structures; but recognising this does not entail isolating economic constitutional law, the economic constitution, from constitutional law as a whole.

2. THE ECONOMIC ORIENTATION OF THE INTERNAL MARKET CASE LAW

What has been argued so far may appear to contain an inherent contradiction. On the one hand, the ordo-liberal notion that a constitution sets out the political economic orientation of a polity has been dismissed; on the other, the notion

23 Baquero Cruz, *Between Competition and Free Movement* (n 1) 28.

24 N Nic Shuibhne, 'The Resilience of EU Market Citizenship' (2010) 47 *CML Rev* 1597, 1608–09.

of economic constitution has been retained for its ability to identify links and associations between the substantive law of the internal market and fundamental political economy choices. Yet, what has been dismissed in the previous section is the idea of a specific ideological design, not the suggestion that fundamental economic political economy choices may result from the evolution of EU internal market law. More precisely, the judicial construction of certain legal principles produces effects that may be ascribed to the state of affairs that a certain view of political economy seeks to bring about. Yet, the interpretation of the case law on the internal market elicits widely differing views, which is part of the reason why the EU's economic orientation is so hard to pin down. It is to this debate that we now turn.

A. The Role of Economic Liberalism

Given the nature of the project, it is hardly surprising that there is a wide consensus on the contention that market integration embodies some form of economic liberalism. Yet, this consensus is a superficial one, as differences emerge as soon as the extent to which economic liberalism informs European integration is examined. On one side of the debate is the view that, drawing from an early account of the Court's contribution to market integration, we could describe as 'instrumentalist liberalism'. The term was used in the 1970s by Mertens de Wilmars. Mertens held that the kind of economic liberalism that found expression in the rules of the Treaty of Rome was of liberalism of an instrumentalist kind, insofar as it was a means to economic integration; yet, he added, it did not purport to act as an organising principle for the integrated economies.[25] Later accounts have emphasised that the kind of economic liberalism that finds its way through the internal market case law does not amount to an endorsement of the view that the objective of the free movement provisions should be to protect economic freedom per se; instead, constraints on States based on economic free movement are justified for their link to market integration. Free movement rights, in other words, are not conceived as freedom from State interference in economic activity, but as freedom to pursue trade within an internal market context.[26]

Maduro's work on the economic constitution takes this position further. He rejects the view that the internal market case law endorses a single model of

[25] 'Les conceptions économiques qu'expriment nombre de règles du traité correspondent à une conception instrumentaliste du libéralisme économique non à l'idée qu'il est l'*Ordnungsprinzip* des économies intégrées', J Mertens de Wilmars 'La Jurisprudence de la Cour de Justice comme Instrument de l'Intégration Communautaire' (1976) 1 *Cahiers de Droit Européen* 135. Judge Mertens de Wilmars was one of the main protagonists of the so-called 'heroic' period of the ECJ's jurisprudence.

[26] Opinion of Advocate General Tesauro in Case C-292/92 *Hünermund and Others* [1993] ECR I-6787. See also Opinion of Advocate General Tizzano in *Case* C-442/02 *France v Ministère de l'Économie, des Finances et de l'Industrie* [2004] ECR I-8961, paras 68–78.

economic constitution. He believes—instead—that multiple models are at work.[27] He identifies three such models: the 'centralised' model, which favours market re-regulation at the European level to complement negative integration; the 'competitive model', which he attributes to ordo-liberal and neo-liberal accounts of the economic constitution,[28] and which holds that the optimal level of market regulation should emerge spontaneously through mutual recognition and regulatory competition; and, finally, the 'decentralised model', which allows Member States to retain regulatory powers but requires them not to discriminate against foreign products/persons. While each of these models presents institutional malfunctions, all three play a role in shaping the EU's economic constitution.[29]

Maduro, however, rejects the view that the economic constitution, and, in particular, the free movement case law, contains a neo-liberal bias. Writing on the scope of Article 34 TFEU, he notes that even where the Court has adopted a wide interpretation of the scope of that provision, it has not done so in adherence to an ideological belief in the need to place constitutional limits on public intervention in the market; there is, he adds, no evidence from the more activist case law that the Court has 'a certain "free market" conception of the economic constitution of the European Union which is to be protected as a constitutional right and which the Court considers legitimate to impose on public authorities'.[30] The Court is more concerned with '*State* intervention than with *public* intervention in the market': its focus is on national decisions affecting the internal market, not necessarily on public ones.[31]

Others are more sanguine about the liberal mould of the case law. According to these authors, nonmarket values are given a narrow interpretation whenever they interact with market values. This, they argue, is borne out by a long-standing interpretation in the case law which treats nonmarket interests as narrowly-construed exceptions to fundamental freedoms (or to other internal market provisions). On this view, the European economic constitution contains an inbuilt neo-liberal bias.[32] According to Baquero Cruz, the EU's economic constitutional law is not neutral; it is, in fact, more specific than national constitutional laws regarding the 'constitutional determinations of economic structure and process' and endorses an economic order that is closer to a liberal market economy than to a mixed economy model.[33] The 'neo-liberal economic ethos of the Community',

27 Maduro, *We the Court* (n 1) 103–50; A Somek, 'Equality and Constitutional Indeterminacy: An Interpretative Perspective on the European Economic Constitution' (2001) 7 *European Law Journal* 17.

28 In this category Maduro bundles together ordo-liberal theorists and neo-liberal ones, such as Hayek, Buchanan and Petersmann.

29 Maduro, *We the Court* (n 1) 150.

30 Ibid 67. It is worth noting, however, that, since the book was published (1998) the free movement case law has seen some considerable developments (see discussion and n 39 below).

31 Ibid 68.

32 Baquero Cruz, *Between Competition and Free Movement* (n 1) 79.

33 Ibid 77.

he argues, which confers constitutional pride of place on free movement and competition, is at the heart of the EU's legal system.[34]

The liberal orientation of the internal market case law is also at the centre of critical accounts of the economic constitution. At the radical end of this spectrum, Nicol, for instance, argues that the EU Treaties contain a 'structural bias' in favour of a distinct economic ideology characterised by the separation of the market from the State, which facilitates the gradual takeover of traditional public tasks by private sector organisations.[35] On this view, the economic constitution ensures that economic activity is insulated from politics and that, therefore, fundamental economic policy choices are taken outside the domain of national democracies. That is also the concern expressed by Scharpf and others.[36] While Scharpf does not make the claim that the Court is ideologically driven towards neo-liberalism, he believes that the economic constitution inevitably yields outcomes that map on to neo-liberal templates of economic policy. His argument is that the tension between trade liberalisation and competing concerns is a tension between transnational economic interests and domestically-entrenched nonmarket values. The central assumption behind this reasoning is that redistributive policies remain rooted in the nation-state, where their legitimacy finds its source. Moreover, since redistributive policies and welfare systems vary considerably across Europe, especially as a consequence of the accession to the EU of central and eastern European countries, heterogeneous preferences inhibit agreement on common standards, such that the pursuit of redistributive policies through positive integration becomes unrealistic. At the same time, however, negative integration continues to encompass ever wider domains, often at the expense of national policy autonomy. The impact of this expansion is, according to Scharpf, asymmetrical: Member States that place greater emphasis on public-interest regulation of market forces and on social welfare policies are affected to a greater extent by negative integration than countries whose political economies are oriented towards market liberalism.[37]

B. The Balance Between Internal Market and Social Rights

Any attempt to capture the internal market case law along ideological fault lines is an exercise fraught with difficulty, which is bound to lead to—at least

[34] Ibid 79. It goes without saying that Baquero Cruz's remarks predate, and therefore do not take account of, the Lisbon Treaty's reference to a highly competitive social market economy.

[35] D Nicol, 'The Constitutional Protection of Capitalism' (Oxford, Hart Publishing, 2010).

[36] FW Scharpf, 'The Double Asymmetry of European Integration' *Max-Planck-Institut für Gesellschaftsforschung Working Paper* 09/12, www.mpifg.de/pu/workpap/wp09-12.pdf. M Höpner and A Schäfer, 'Polanyi in Brussels? Embeddedness and the Three Dimensions of European Economic Integration' (2010) *Max-Planck-Institut für Gesellschaftsforschung Working Paper* 10/8.

[37] On the difference between organised and liberal market economies, see PA Hall and D Soskice (eds), *Varieties of Capitalism: The Institutional Foundations of Comparative Advantage* (Oxford, Oxford University Press, 2001).

partially—arbitrary findings. A number of factors need to be taken into account. The differences among areas of internal market law provisions make it hard to come up with a unified account of the case law on the four freedoms. Moreover, it is often impossible to separate the domestic repercussions of EU trade law from its cross-border effects, as opening up sections of national economies to cross-border trade may inevitably produce a deregulatory effect at national level. And, of course, one should not lose sight of the institutional peculiarities of the Court of Justice, the variable composition of its chambers, the differences in cultural background of the judges, all of which are factors that conspire to make it unlikely for a fixed ideological commitment to emerge.

Historical, political and economic context are also important factors. The fact that Community law did not (initially) intersect with politically sensitive areas of national regulatory competence ensured relatively painless interactions between domestic regulation and Community law, and explains the 'benign neglect' of politicians and public opinion towards the Court.[38] Yet, the progressive expansion of the reach of internal market law, which, however, went hand in hand with the recognition, as a matter of EU law, of nonmarket interests as legitimate grounds that delimit the scope of the free movement provisions, dramatically increased the opportunities for tensions between competing values to emerge. Moreover, the introduction of EU citizenship and the recognition of the increasing economic relevance of the services sector as opposed to manufacturing may explain the greater willingness on the part of the Court to expand the scope of the free movement of persons and services provisions vis-a-vis the free movement of goods.

Nonetheless, with these caveats in place, some fundamental points that emerge from the internal market case law merit consideration. The significant expansion in scope of (nearly) all the free movement provisions from the 1990s onwards has exposed ever wider aspects of national regulatory competence to supranational scrutiny.[39] Such jurisprudential developments have gradually attenuated the connection to cross-border movement, thus lending credence to the suggestion that the free movement case law has taken a distinctly liberal turn. And while any expansion of such a nature is to be placed into the context of a growth in the

[38] According to the celebrated description in E Stein, 'Lawyers, Judges and the Making of a Transnational Constitution' (1981) 75 *American Journal of International Law* 1.

[39] See generally, E Spaventa, 'From *Gebhard* to *Carpenter*: Towards a (non-)Economic European Constitution' (2004) 41 *CML Rev* 743. The exception is free movement of goods, where the *Keck* ruling produced the opposite effect. Joined Cases C-267/91 and C-268/91 *Keck and Mithouard* [1993] ECR I-6097. Recent case law on Article 34 TFEU, however, has re-opened the question on the scope of that provision: Case C-110/05 *Commission v Italy (Trailers)* [2009] ECR I-519; Case C-142/05 *Åklagaren v Percy Mickelsson and Joakim Roos* [2009] ECR I-4273 and Case C-265/06 *Commission v Portugal (tinted film)* [2008] ECR I-2245. While this case law injects some uncertainty around the scope of the notion of measures having equivalent effect to quantitative restrictions on imports, subsequent rulings have made it clear that the notion of selling arrangements has not been made redundant: Case C-531/07 *Fachverband der Buch- und Medienwirtschaft v LIBRO Handelsgesellschaft mbH* [2009] ECR I-3717. On this case law see P Oliver, 'Of Trailers and Jet Skis: Is the Case Law on Article 34 Hurtling in a New Direction?' (2011) 33 *Fordham International Law Journal* 1423.

variety of noneconomic justifying factors (mandatory, overriding, or imperative requirements), the very balance between free movement and noneconomic values has been one of the most controversial aspects of the Court of Justice's internal market case law. It is in this context that the claim that the Court displays bias in favour of the interests of the market has found greater empirical support.

The *Viking* and *Laval* judgments, in particular, lend themselves to such critique.[40] In *Viking*, the Court was asked whether trade union action to prevent the adoption of an Estonian flag of convenience by a Finnish ferry operator amounted to a breach of Article 49 TFEU on freedom of establishment and whether it could be justified. In *Laval*, a trade union blockade against a Latvian firm that employed posted workers on a Swedish building site, adopted after the breakdown of negotiations on the extension of the Swedish collective agreement to the Latvian firm's Swedish arm, was found to breach Article 53 TFEU on the free movement of services. In both cases, the Court identified the breach in the fact that collective action made it less attractive or more difficult for the company to take advantage of its internal market freedoms. In both cases, the Court recognised the nature of the right to collective action as a fundamental right. Yet, at the same time, the Court seemed to ignore that according to the division of jurisdiction between the EU judicature and national courts, it is in principle for the national court to determine whether, on the facts, a measure restricting one of the fundamental freedoms is proportionate to its aim; instead, it went to great lengths to explain why the trade union's actions were disproportionate. And, finally, in both cases, the Court addressed proportionality in a way that seemed to ignore the essence and purposes of collective bargaining, and of the right to strike.[41]

These rulings raise a broader question, however, which relates to the status of social rights. The Court characterised social rights as fundamental rights, and was anxious to convey the impression, as it did in *Schmidberger*, that fundamental rights and 'fundamental freedoms' (ie free movement rights) are ascribed the same value as a matter of EU law.[42] The Court therefore seemed to depart from the rule-exception paradigm, whereby mandatory requirements were narrowly-tailored exceptions to the free movement rule that characterised earlier case law. Yet, in prompting the referring courts to enquire whether the trade unions had exhausted all possible, less restrictive alternatives before resorting to the incriminated actions, the Court seemed to contradict its previous statement as to the 'parity of esteem' of free movement and social rights. Clearly, if the solution entails a duty on trade unions to adopt the action that is least restrictive of free

[40] Case C-438/05 *The International Transport Workers' Federation and The Finnish Seamen's Union* [2007] ECR I-10779; Case C-341/05 *Laval un Partneri* [2007] ECR I-11767.

[41] See among others A Davies, 'One Step Forward, Two Steps Back? The *Viking* and *Laval* Cases in the ECJ', (2008) 37 *Industrial Law Journal* 126; S Sciarra, 'Viking and Laval: Collective Labour Rights and Market Freedoms in the Enlarged EU' (2007–2008) 10 *Cambridge Yearbook of European Legal Studies* 563; L Azoulai, 'The Court of Justice and the Social Market Economy: The Emergence of an Ideal and the conditions for its Realization' (2008) 45 *CML Rev* 1335.

[42] Case C-112/00 *Schmidberger v Austria* [2003] ECR I-5659.

movement rights, but does not entail an equivalent duty on the national court to interpret free movement in the manner which is the least restrictive of the fundamental right to take collective action, the conclusion must be that there is a hierarchy of values in internal market law. What is more, as Spaventa has argued, the very premise that fundamental freedoms and fundamental rights are subsumed under the same category is questionable.[43] There is a crucial difference between the two sets of rights: while free movement rights are instrumental to a political project, the internal market, and are only enjoyed as a matter of EU law, fundamental rights are universal in aspiration and also exist outside the treaty framework. Moreover, the idea that fundamental rights may represent legitimate interests that allow restrictions to be placed on free movement rights appears to suggest a reversed hierarchy.[44]

3. THE LIMITS OF CONSTITUTIONAL ADJUDICATION

The brief critical overview carried out so far confirms the following points. The current stage of market integration entails far greater scope for tensions between the single market provisions and non-economic rights or interests than was originally the case. These tensions stem from the parallel expansion of the scope of the internal market provision and of the non-economic interests that can be invoked as justifying factors. Yet, despite the increased relevance of nonmarket concerns as a matter of EU law, when tensions between market and nonmarket interests have arisen, they have often given rise to the perception that the former enjoy priority of place vis-a-vis the latter. This perception is particularly significant in view of the fact that the EU single market provisions are pitched against national competences, a fact that goes to the heart of the fundamental asymmetry highlighted by Scharpf between economic integration and public policy.

In the presence of such an asymmetry between market integration and non-market policies, and in the absence of a firm political basis for supranational action to address it, the legitimacy of the internal market crucially depends on the extent to which it is perceived not to undermine the Member States' scope for action in pursuing redistributive policies; internal market law may only achieve this outcome on the strength of the Court's ability to strike the appropriate balance between the competing values and objectives of the internal market, on the one hand, and of domestic political and constitutional domains, on the other. The Lisbon Treaty has provided the Court with new or revised legal material with which such a balance may be pursued: Article 4(2) TEU, which refers to the

[43] E Spaventa, 'Federalisation Versus Centralisation: Tensions in Fundamental Rights Discourse in the EU' in M Dougan and S Currie (eds), *50 Years of the European Treaties: Looking Back and Thinking Forward* (Oxford, Hart Publishing, 2009) 343.

[44] Ibid.

duty on the Union to respect 'national identities, inherent in their fundamental structures, political and constitutional, inclusive of regional and local self-government'; and Article 3(3) TEU, which introduces the objective of a 'highly competitive social market economy'.

A. National Identity and the Social Market Economy in the Court

The case law on Article 4(2) TEU shows a certain willingness on the part of Advocates General to rely on the concept of national constitutional identity, which the Court seems, partly, to share. In *Michaniki*, Advocate General Maduro held that constitutional identity could be invoked as an autonomous ground for derogation from the fundamental freedoms.[45] In *Sayn-Wittgenstein*, national constitutional identity played a role in the Court's application of proportionality. The case concerned the compatibility with Article 21 TFEU of the decision to change the surname of an Austrian citizen residing in Germany, in compliance with the Austrian ban on the use of aristocratic titles. Although the Court ultimately relied on public policy, it held that 'it must be accepted that, in the context of Austrian constitutional history, the Law on the abolition of the nobility, as an element of national identity, may be taken into consideration when a balance is struck between legitimate interests and the right of free movement of persons recognized under European Union law'.[46] It may well be, as von Bogdandy and Schill argue, that Article 4(2) TEU acts as a 'new conceptual frame and an explicit legal basis' which 'feeds into the proportionality test generally applied by the ECJ to balance fundamental freedoms and conflicting rights'.[47] However, as they add, the Court has not so far recognised that Article 4(2) TEU may provide an independent ground of justification for restrictions on free movement. In other contexts, the Court has omitted altogether any reference to the provision, despite its clear relevance. In *UGT-Rioja*, while the Advocate General emphasised the importance of regional autonomy and self-government to national constitutional identity under Article 4(2) TEU, the Court did not refer to the provision. As we shall see in chapter six, while the omission does not have any immediate practical significance, as the Court followed the Advocate General's Opinion in every other respect, it does, nonetheless, have an impact on the overall coherence of the Court's reasoning.

It is, for course, still too early to tell what the Court makes of the 'social market economy' concept introduced at Lisbon.[48] The question to consider, however, is

[45] Case C-213/07 *Michaniki AE v Ethniko Simvoulio Radiotileorasis* [2008] ECR I-9999, Opinion of Advocate General Maduro, paras 31–33.

[46] Case C-208/09 *Sayn-Wittgenstein*, para 83.

[47] A von Bogdandy and S Schill, 'Overcoming Absolute Primacy: Respect for National Constitutional Identity under the Lisbon Treaty' (2011) 48 *CML Rev* 1417, 1441–42.

[48] On which see the essays in D Schiek, U Liebert, H Schneider (eds), *European and Social Constitutionalism after the Treaty of Lisbon* (Cambridge, Cambridge University Press, 2011).

whether the notion carries the potential to prompt a reorientation of the case law. For its part, the Monti report offers the suggestion that the 'new legal context' will engender greater attentiveness on the Court's part to the concerns raised about the *Viking* and *Laval* judgments by trade unions.[49] There are signs that the Court may be already set on the path to a rebalancing of the status of economic and social rights. In *Commission v Germany*, Advocate General Trstenjak suggested that the approach taken in *Viking* and *Laval* 'sits uncomfortably alongside the principle of equal ranking for fundamental rights and fundamental freedoms'.[50] She went on to add that 'such an analytical approach suggests ... the existence of a hierarchical relationship between fundamental freedoms and fundamental rights in which fundamental rights are subordinated to fundamental freedoms and, consequently, may restrict fundamental freedoms only with the assistance of a written or unwritten ground of justification'.[51] Instead, she recommended the adoption of an approach that presupposes the parity of status of the two sets of freedoms and rights by relying on a particular conception of proportionality, which looks in two directions. In case of conflict between a fundamental freedom and a fundamental right, on the one hand, 'the restriction by a fundamental right on a fundamental freedom is not permitted to go beyond what is appropriate, necessary and reasonable to realise that fundamental right'; on the other, the restriction on a fundamental right by a fundamental freedom must not go beyond what is appropriate, necessary and reasonable to realise the fundamental freedom.[52]

In *Santos Palhota*, Advocate General Cruz Villalón also gave significant weight to this new legal context.[53] The entry into force of the Treaty of Lisbon, he argued, had made it necessary to take into account provisions of 'primary social law which affect the framework of the fundamental freedoms'.[54] In particular, he attributed significance to the link between Article 3(3) TEU and Article 9 TFEU, which lays down a 'cross-cutting' social protection clause and, according to the Advocate General, obliges the institutions 'to take into account requirements linked to the promotion of a high level of employment, the guarantee of adequate social protection, the fight against social exclusion, and a high level of education, training and protection of human health'.[55] That requirement, according to the Advocate General is consistent with the declaration in Article 3(3) TEU that the construction of the internal market is to be realised by means of policies based on 'a highly competitive social market economy, aiming at full employment and social progress'.[56]

[49] M Monti, 'A new strategy for the single market: at the service of Europe's economy and society', Report to the President of the European Commission (2010) 70, A7-0132/2010.

[50] Case C-271/08 *Commission v Germany* [2010] ECR I-7091, Opinion of Advocate General Trstenjak, para 183.

[51] Ibid para 184.

[52] Ibid para 190.

[53] Case C-515/08 *dos Santos Palhota and Others*, Opinion of Advocate General Cruz Villalón (5 May 2010).

[54] Ibid para 51.

[55] Ibid.

[56] Ibid.

The Advocate General went on to add that, as a consequence of this new constitutional environment, which was strengthened by the presence of new primary law provisions such as Article 31 of the Charter of Fundamental Rights, when working conditions constituted an overriding reason relating to the public interest justifying a derogation from the freedom to provide services, they were no longer to be interpreted strictly.[57] Given that the protection of workers is mandated by the Treaties themselves, this was 'not a simple derogation from a freedom, still less an unwritten exception inferred from case-law'.[58] Therefore, he concluded, '[t]o the extent that the new primary law framework provides for a mandatory high level of social protection, it authorises the Member States, for the purpose of safeguarding a certain level of social protection, to restrict a freedom, and to do so without European Union law regarding it as something exceptional and, therefore, as warranting a strict interpretation'.[59]

It would be, perhaps, unwise to overrate the expansive potential of Article 3(3) TEU solely on the basis of these statements, especially given that, in its ruling, the Court ignored the Advocate General's considerations regarding the significance of the changes introduced by the Lisbon Treaty.[60] Advocate General Cruz Villalón's Opinion may demonstrate that the significance of the potential is limited to bolstering the interpretation of *other primary* law provisions. In other words, the social market economy does not appear to strengthen the protection of *domestic* nonmarket values as such; instead, it seems to give weight to European primary law provisions that incorporate social values.

In principle, nonetheless, there is potential for a greater reliance on the social market economy objective and for greater respect for the principle of constitutional identity. Arguably, teleology may offer an opportunity for a more balanced and coherent approach. During the 'heroic' period of 'integration through law', teleological interpretation yielded the most celebrated doctrines and principles of EU constitutional law, and, because of the perceived urgency of market integration, commanded widespread acceptance.[61] Today, the *télos* of integration has changed in a significant way, and a different, more nuanced, version of teleology could emerge, which could accommodate the complexity of the EU's goals as a 'highly competitive social market economy', and its commitment to respecting national constitutional identities.[62]

Teleological interpretation of EU law, as Maduro has written, 'refers to a particular systemic understanding of the EU legal order that permeates the

[57] Ibid para 53.
[58] Ibid.
[59] Ibid.
[60] Case C-515/08 *dos Santos Palhota and Others* (7 October 2010).
[61] J Mertens de Wilmars, 'Réflexions sur les méthodes d'interprétation de la Cour de justice des Communautés européennes' (1986) *Cahiers de Droit Européen* 5.
[62] The respect of which is now enjoined by Article 4(2) TEU. See C Semmelmann, 'The European Union's Economic Constitution under the Lisbon Treaty: Soul-Searching among Lawyers Shifts the Focus to Procedure' (2010) 35 *EL Rev* 516.

interpretation of all its rules'.[63] The question that classic teleological interpretation typically addresses is whether, in the absence of a certain doctrine or a principle of EU law, the pursuit of market integration, and of an ever closer union, would be undermined, or whether a similar effect would be produced by the presence of a certain rule or principle of national law. Yet, it is submitted, this question could *also* be turned around, and the Court could consider whether the *effet utile* of a rule/doctrine/principle that is integral to domestic social policy or to constitutional identity would be frustrated if an extensive interpretation of EU law was to be adopted. Arguably, had a careful examination of the purpose of collective action and of the right to strike taken place in *Viking* and *Laval*, the balance struck in those cases would have been different, and, perhaps, more satisfactory. This suggestion need not represent a challenge to the supremacy of EU law. The example of *Omega* is instructive in this regard. The judgment, though not entirely flawless, stands out as an example of how constitutional adjudication can exhibit sensitivity to the plurality of values within the EU's economic constitution without, in doing so, undermining the primacy of EU law.[64] In *Omega*, the Court took its commitment to the 'internal constitutional space' of the Member States seriously, by incorporating it into the heart of its proportionality review.[65] And yet, deference towards national constitutional diversity did not come at the expense of primacy, as domestic constitutional values were taken into account *as a matter of EU law*.

B. Varieties of Capitalism and Market Integration

The reason for exploring the potential for national identity and the social market economy to act as brakes on the destabilising effect of negative integration on national systems of social protection and on redistributive policies is that these concepts capture two of the most important aspects of the legitimacy question that confronts EU law. Yet, they are only part of the picture. The challenges that the internal market poses to national nonmarket values are not limited to national constitutional identities or to social rights. In particular, there is little that either Article 3(3) TEU or Article 4(2) TEU can offer to prevent differences between national models of

[63] M Poiares Maduro, 'Interpreting European Law: Judicial Adjudication in a Context of Constitutional Pluralism' (2007) 1 *European Journal of Legal Studies*; M Poiares Maduro, 'Courts and Pluralism' in JL Dunloff and JP Trachtman (eds), *Ruling the World?* (Oxford, Oxford University Press, 2009) 356–79.

[64] For a critique, see in particular J Morijn, 'Balancing Fundamental Rights and Common Market Freedoms in Union Law: *Schmidberger* and *Omega* in the Light of the European Constitution' (2006) 12 *European Law Journal* 15.

[65] N Nic Shuibhne 'Margins of Appreciation: National Values, Fundamental Rights and EC Free Movement Law' (2009) 34 *EL Rev* 230. One may note that the reference issued from a country that has repeatedly made clear that its acceptance of the supremacy of EU law is a qualified one, and that that qualification rests, among other things, on the role of fundamental rights in the German constitutional order. One may also wonder whether the Court will simply show deference towards those Member States that are most vociferous in their defence of their constitutional spaces.

capitalism from being gradually worn down by the effects of negative integration. Differences among Member States in the way in which capitalism is regulated are explored by the 'varieties of capitalism' literature, which taxonomises national political economies along two models: 'liberal market economies', and 'coordinated market economies'.[66] In the former, the behaviour of companies is generally the outcome of a competitive process, and the State's role is to provide the legal infrastructure in which disputes are resolved. Instead, in coordinated economies, companies depend more heavily on nonmarket relationships, and the State plays a more interventionist role. Of course, the two categories are the result of necessary simplifications, and a number of countries simultaneously exhibit features from each of the two ideal-types. Yet, these categories highlight important differences among countries within the EU, which is a reason for the theory's popularity among social scientists.

There is a view that the process of market integration causes a gradual dilution of national regulatory diversity, and gives rise to a progressive emergence of liberal market economies as the dominant model. On this view, as a result of market integration, coordinated market economies face the risk of becoming extinct.[67] Others believe these concerns to be exaggerated. Amongst them is Snell, one of the few EU lawyers to have entered the varieties of capitalism debate.[68] His views, which are confined to EU law, are cautiously optimistic as to the survival of variety. The set-up of law-making in the EU, he argues, and the web of vetoes and compromises that it engenders, make the likelihood of a radical reshaping of domestic models of economic governance very remote. As to the Court's case law, its highly fact-specific character, and the very nature of the preliminary reference procedure, suggest that it is unlikely to take positions that will cause 'fundamental disruptions to key national institutions'.[69] Moreover, the Lisbon Treaty's reference to the 'social market economy', the removal of 'undistorted competition' from the Treaty and its relocation to an annexed Protocol, combined with the binding character of the Charter of Fundamental Rights, which contains a solidarity chapter, may well prompt the Court to adopt a 'more restrained interpretation' of EU economic law.[70]

The belief that the changes introduced by the Lisbon Treaty will cause a reorientation in the Court's jurisprudence, and that *Viking* and *Laval* will soon be treated as outliers, may perhaps turn out to be justified. However, since models of capitalism arise from a mixture of economic, social and cultural factors that do not always find express protection in EU primary law, there are limits to the extent to which the concept of a social market economy may act as a safety net. Although decided before the Lisbon Treaty entered into force, the Court's judgment concerning the so-called

[66] See generally, Hall and Soskice (eds), *Varieties of Capitalism* (n 37).

[67] See Scharpf, 'The Double Asymmetry of European Integration' (n 36); M Höpner and A Schäfer, 'A New Phase of European Integration: Organised Capitalisms in Post-Ricardian Europe' (2010) 33 *West European Politics* 344.

[68] J Snell, 'Varieties of Capitalism and the Limits of European Economic Integration' (2010–2011) 13 *Cambridge Yearbook of European Legal Studies* 415.

[69] Ibid 428.

[70] Ibid 429.

'Volkswagen law' may help to illustrate this point.[71] The law in question was introduced in 1959 in derogation to German company law. As the Advocate General recalled in his Opinion, the statute arose from a compromise between Volkswagen employees and the Land of Lower Saxony: the employees agreed to forgo any ownership claims that they had previously put forward on Volkswagen in exchange for protection from the State against dominance by a single shareholder.[72] The compromise was translated into a set of special rules, which consisted in a 20 per cent cap on the voting rights of every shareholder; a majority requirement of over 80 per cent of the capital for the most important decisions to be approved; and the right of the Federal State and of the Land of Lower Saxony to appoint two supervisory board members. The upshot of these provisions was that the Land, which held 20 per cent of the shares, had an indirect veto power over important decisions.

The Court considered the *Volkswagengesetz* to be a restriction on the free movement of capital within the meaning of Article 63 TFEU. It held that 'by limiting the possibility for other shareholders to participate in the company with a view to establishing or maintaining lasting and direct economic links with it which would make possible effective participation in the management of that company or in its control', the arrangements contained in the statute were liable to deter direct investors from other Member States.[73] As to Germany's attempt to justify the law on the basis of the protection of the employees' interests, the Court held that the Member State had been unable to explain, beyond setting out general considerations regarding the need for protection against a large shareholder which might, by itself, dominate the company, why, in order to meet the objective of protecting Volkswagen's workers, it was appropriate and necessary for the Federal and State authorities to maintain a strengthened and irremovable position in the capital of that company.

The fact that the Court dismissed arguments based on the desire to prevent dominance by a large shareholder in a company seems to show unwillingness to contemplate the pursuit of an alternative model of corporate governance, one which places value on the triangular connection between the interests of the State, of the employees, and of private capital. While the details of the case are irrelevant for present purposes, what is striking is the extent to which free movement may, *in principle*, undermine long-standing corporate governance arrangements that are deeply embedded in domestic political economies.[74] Given such a wide interpretation of the scope of free movement of capital, it is not unthinkable that the Court may one day find that other features of the Rhenish model of capitalism, such as codetermination, are obstructions to free movement.[75]

[71] Case C-112/05 *Commission v Germany* [2007] ECR I-8995.

[72] Ibid, Opinion of Advocate General Ruiz Jarabo Colomer, paras 25–29.

[73] Para 52 of the judgment.

[74] However, as Ringe points out, *in practice*, many of the arrangements crystallised in the Volkswagen law have been reintroduced by the parties in question through private law instruments which now replace the statute. W-G Ringe, 'Company Law and Free Movement of Capital' (2010) 69 *CLJ* 378.

[75] C Gerner-Beuerle, 'Shareholders between the Market and the State. The VW Law and other Interventions in the Market Economy' (2012) 49 *CML Rev* 97.

Nonetheless, in the absence of comprehensive empirical evidence to that effect, it is premature to conclude that the Court's internal market case law inevitably results in a gradual suppression of variety in the landscape of European capitalism, and that the effect of this case law is to produce a sort of harmonisation by stealth of national models of economic governance along the liberal model. At the same time, such concerns may not be easily brushed aside. Even if the Court is to take the Lisbon Treaty's commitment towards the social market economy objective as a blueprint for a jurisprudential reorientation, in the absence of a clear link to social or employment policy, justifications based on the peculiarities of a national model of capitalism are unlikely to succeed. It goes without saying, moreover, that Article 4(2) TEU is even less likely to offer any form of protection to national models of capitalism, unless central features of these were enshrined in constitutional law *and* the Court was prepared to accept them as integral to national constitutional identity.

4. CONCLUSION

Despite the redundancy of its ideological matrix, there is still life in the concept of economic constitution, as far as the EU's internal market is concerned. Its ambiguity, its capacity to evoke at the same time the constitutional structure as well as the economic orientation of the internal market, is also its value. Granted, the multitude of tasks, objectives and values that crowd the internal market, and the sometimes mercurial nature of the case law, make capturing that orientation an elusive task. Moreover, associations between jurisprudential trends and ideological undercurrents always contain an element of approximation and arbitrariness. Yet, jurisprudential trends have the potential to influence the long-term orientation of the EU. The claim, advanced by a number of authors, that the growing gap between market integration and public policy, social policy in particular, for which the Court's internal market case law is in part responsible, undermines the legitimacy of the EU's action appears to have been, in part, vindicated. The acceptance of this premise, however, does not necessarily rule out the emergence in future case law of a different balance between market and nonmarket concerns. A reorientation of the case law in this direction is, arguably, possible if the pursuit of non-economic goals in the context of a social market economy, and the protection of national identities, are regarded as *téloi* along similar lines as market integration. Yet, even if such an approach were followed, this would not be sufficient to prevent the latent potential for internal market law to erode the distinctiveness of national models of capitalism.

3

The Distinctive Nature of State Aid Law

A recurring question among those who write on State aid law concerns 'family resemblances': whether State aid bears greater similarities to antitrust or to free movement law.[1] The process of answering this question is an exercise that is well worth engaging in for two reasons. First, an examination of the analogies and differences between State aid and other areas of internal market law allows us to elucidate the role and purpose of State aid law in the context of the internal market. Once we are able to plot the position of State aid in relation to antitrust and free movement law, the functional connections between these areas emerge with greater clarity. Secondly, an appreciation of the distinctive features of State aid control sharpens our understanding of the European economic constitution.

It has been said that the EU State aid regime represents the most original of the EU's competition policies.[2] The claim can be taken a step further. This chapter seeks to show how certain essential features of this regime make State aid control an integral, yet distinctive part of the law of the internal market. The originality of State aid control, in other words, is best appreciated if it is viewed in the context of the internal market, broadly defined, rather than purely as a part of the EU's competition policies.

This chapter begins by considering how the parameters and purposes of State aid law relate to the parameters and purposes of antitrust and free movement law. It then goes on to examine how the purpose and function of State aid control is reflected in its institutional set-up. The concluding part links these findings to the discussion in the previous chapter regarding different models of economic constitution.

1 There is no philosophical allusion here (the term 'family resemblances' is not intended as a reference to Wittgenstein's *Philosophical Investigations*).

2 M Cini and L McGowan, *Competition Policy in the European Union* (Basingstoke, Macmillan, 1998) 135.

1. FAMILY RESEMBLANCES

A. State Aid and Antitrust

On first glance, the Treaty appears to provide an immediate answer to the question regarding family resemblances: State aid control belongs to the competition law family as much as antitrust.[3] Both share the same broad Treaty umbrella (Chapter 1 of Title VII TFEU, entitled 'rules on competition'). Moreover, both Article 107(1) and Article 101 TFEU refer to the concept of distortion of competition. And the analogies do not stop at the textual level: according to the Court, since State aid and antitrust pursue the same aim of securing undistorted competition in the internal market, the interpretation of the two sets of provisions should not lead to mutually incompatible outcomes.[4]

This impression takes further strength when one considers the 'State Aid Action Plan'.[5] Here, in setting out its reform agenda for State aid, the Commission states that distortions occur where Member States afford 'unwarranted selective advantages to some firms, preventing or delaying the market forces from rewarding the most competitive firms'.[6] State aid, adds the Commission, 'may also lead to a build-up of market power in the hands of some firms, for instance when companies that do not receive State aid (e.g. non-domestic firms) have to cut down on their market presence, or where State aid is used to erect entry barriers'.[7] The result of such distortions of competition, concludes the Commission, is that 'customers may be faced with higher prices, lower quality goods and less innovation'.[8] *Efficiency* in all of its forms (productive, allocative and dynamic) seems to be the central concern of this thinking.

Yet, when one considers the actual application of distortion of competition as a criterion that demarcates the substantive scope of the respective treaty provisions on State aid and antitrust, a hiatus emerges. Although the early days of

[3] The term antitrust is used here to refer to the treaty provisions on competition that apply to undertakings.

[4] Case C-225/91 *Matra v Commission* [1993] ECR I-3203, para 42; Case T-49/93 *Société Internationale de Diffusion et d'Edition (SIDE) v Commission of the European Communities* [1995] ECR II-2501, para 72; Case T-156/98 *RJB Mining v Commission* [2001] ECR II-337, para 113.

[5] Commission, 'State Aid Action Plan: Less and Better Targeted State Aid: A Roadmap for State Aid Reform 2005–2009' COM(2005) 107 final, 7 June 2005. For commentary see L Hancher, 'Towards an Economic Analysis of State Aids' (2005) 3 *European State Aid Quarterly* 23; D Hildebrand and A Schweinsberh, 'Refined Economic Approach in European State Aid Control—Will it Gain Momentum? (2007) *World Competition*; JL Buendía Sierra and B Smulders, 'The Limited Role of the "Refined Economic Approach" in Achieving the Objectives of State Aid Control: Time for Some Realism' in JL Buendia Sierra and others, *Liber Amicorum Francisco Santaolalla Gadea* (The Hague, Kluwer, 2008) 1–26; T Kleiner, 'Modernization of State Aid Policy' in E Szyszczak (ed), *Research Handbook on State Aid* (Cheltenham, Edward Elgar, 2011) 1–27.

[6] Commission, 'State Aid Action Plan: Less and Better Targeted State Aid: A Roadmap for State Aid Reform 2005–2009' (n 5) para 7.

[7] Ibid.

[8] Ibid.

competition law were marked by a formalistic and broad-sweeping interpretation of Articles 101 and 102 TFEU,[9] which was determined by the need to push the common market imperative forward, and by the need to introduce undertakings and national regulators to what was for most countries an entirely novel legal mentality, from an early stage the Court introduced the notion of 'appreciability' with regard to the effects of agreements on competition. In *Volk*, it held that those agreements which, by reason of the negligible market-share held by the parties, had an insignificant effect on competition, would fall through the net.[10] Furthermore, from *Delimitis* onwards,[11] the Court made clear that determining the effect of agreements on competition is an empirical matter,[12] which requires a detailed market analysis. The potential existence of a restriction or distortion of competition forms, therefore, an *independent* element in the definition of Article 101 TFEU and the impact that an undertaking is capable of producing *on a specific market* is integral to this analysis.[13]

Judicial review of Commission State aid decisions in relation to the effects of a measure on competition has, instead, been remarkably light-handed. While one might notice a gradual increase in the intensity of review, it does not appear that the nature of the analysis required is, even today, such as to prompt an enquiry similar to the one at work in antitrust. An initial attempt to import the latter type of scrutiny into State aid control was dismissed in *Philip Morris*.[14] The applicants had argued that a finding of aid under Article 107(1) TFEU required a delineation of the relevant product and geographical markets, and an examination of the relationship between the beneficiary and its competitors therein. However, according to the Court, this type of analysis was unnecessary, as the decision contained sufficient information to conclude that the aid measure was able to affect competition: the planned measure was in fact a form of assistance which facilitated the increase of the beneficiary's production capacity; and the simple fact that the measure relieved the beneficiary of part of the costs arising from the increase in its production capacity, costs that its competitors would normally have to bear in full, demonstrated that the aid had an effect on competition and inter-State trade. For the Court, '[w]hen State financial aid strengthens the position of an undertaking compared with other undertakings competing in intra-Community

[9] B Hawk, 'System Failure: Vertical Restraints and EC Competition Law' (1985) 32 *CML Rev* 973.

[10] Case 5/69 *Volk v Vervaecke* [1969] ECR 295.

[11] Case C-234/89 *Delimitis v Henninger Bräu AG* [1991] ECR I-935.

[12] R Whish and D Bailey, *Competition Law*, 7th edn (Oxford, Oxford University Press, 2012) 126.

[13] The Court's approach is distilled in the following paragraph: '[i]t is settled case-law that, in defining the criteria for the application of Article [101(1) TFEU] to a specific case, account should be taken of the economic context in which undertakings operate, the products or services covered by the decisions of those undertakings, the structure of the market concerned and the actual conditions in which it functions.' Case C-399/93 *Oude Luttikhuis and Others v Commission* [1995] ECR I-4515, para 10. See D Baley, 'Scope of Judicial Review under Article 81 EC' (2004) 41 *CML Rev* 1328.

[14] Case 730/79 *Philip Morris* [1980] ECR 2671.

trade, the latter must be regarded as affected by that aid'.[15] That conclusion could be reached without engaging in the kind of economic analysis required by the Court in *Delimitis*.[16]

In State aid law, the anti-competitive impact of public intervention consists in the increase in economic strength of its beneficiary relative to others. The Court considers the fact that competing undertakings may have benefited from equivalent support in their respective jurisdictions to be irrelevant, as is the fact that State aid simply redresses a competitive disadvantage stemming from the more favourable regulatory arrangements existing in other jurisdictions.[17] What matters is that, prima facie, the aid measure allows the undertaking benefiting from it to enjoy an improvement in its competitive strength. What is more, the EU Courts have periodically claimed that even aid of a relatively small amount to an undertaking operating in a market where there is strong competition is liable to distort competition *and* affect trade between Member States.[18]

All such considerations led some commentators to doubt whether the Court views the criterion of a State measure's anti-competitive effect as enjoying conceptual autonomy.[19] In the *Wam* case, however, the General Court appeared to endorse a more economics-informed approach of the criterion.[20] The case concerned a subsidised loan to an Italian undertaking to facilitate its entry into non-EU markets. In its reasoning, the Commission had simply stated that, although the measure was intended to promote exports to non-EU countries, it was nonetheless liable to distort competition and affect *European* trade. The General Court annulled the decision on grounds of insufficient reasoning. The finding that an aid had improved the financial position of an undertaking was

[15] Ibid para 14. The proposition regularly reappears in the Court's case law, eg Joined Cases C-78/08 to C-80/08 *Paint Graphos* (8 September 2011), para 79.

[16] D Hildebrand and A Schweinsberg, 'Refined Economic Approach in European State Aid Control—Will it Gain Momentum?'(2007) 30 *World Competition* 449. For a proposal on how to approach market definition in State aid cases, see J Fingleton, F Ruane and V Ryan, 'Market Definition and State Aid Control' [1999] *European Economy* 3.

[17] Joined Cases 6/69 and 11/69 *Commission v France* [1969] ECR 523 paras 20–21; Case C-6/97 *Italy v Commission* [1999] ECR I-2981, para 21; Case C-372/97 *Italy v Commission* [2004] ECR I-3679 para 67.

[18] Case C-351/98 *Spain v Commission* [2002] ECR I-8031, para 63; Case C-298/00P *Italy v Commission* [2004] ECR I-40107, para 54; Joined Cases T-254/00, T-270/00 and T-277/00 *Hotel Cipriani Spa* [2008] ECR II-3269, para 247. Although the potential distortion of competition and effect on inter-state trade are two separate conditions, the EU Courts tend to examine the two together. The latter condition is very rarely found not to be fulfilled. However, the Commission has introduced a de minimis threshold with its de minimis Notices: in 1992 [1992] OJ C213/2, and in 1996, [1996] OJ C68/9. After the Commission was given the power to enact regulations, two de minimis Regulations were introduced: Regulation 69/2001, [2001] OJ L 10/30 and Regulation 1998/2006, [2006] OJ L379/5.

[19] C Ahlborn and C Berg, 'Can State Aid Control Learn from Antitrust? The Need for a Greater Role for Competition Analysis under the State Aid Rules' in A Biondi, P Eeckhout and J Flynn (eds), *The Law of State Aid in the European Union* (Oxford, Oxford University Press, 2003); M Farley, 'The Role of Economics-based Approaches when Analysing Effects on Trade and Distortions of Competition after *Wam*' (2010) *European State Aid Law Quarterly* 369.

[20] Joined cases T-304/04 and T-316/04 *Italian Republic and Wam SpA v Commission* [2006] ECR II-64.

not evidence of an effect on trade or distortion of competition. Instead, the Commission should have carried out a detailed examination of the likely effects of the aid on trade and competition. The appeal judgment, however, made clear that the level of detail prescribed in order to satisfy the requirements of Article 296 TFEU turned on the level of immediacy and discernibility of the impact of the measure on competition and trade. Thus, while in certain circumstances in which the cross-border anti-competitive effect was apparent the Commission was entitled to rely on presumptions, where such an effect was less immediate, a more rigorous reasoning was required.[21] The ruling, therefore, simply confirmed the existence of a duty incumbent on the Commission to state more clearly in its reasoning, and in a more detailed manner, how the criterion was fulfilled; it was plainly not a Copernican moment.

It is not simply the legal criterion, but also the very notion of competition that lies at the heart of State aid policy, that has attracted criticism in the literature. Critics argue that State aid seems more preoccupied with ensuring that all market players compete *on equal terms* than with the protection of competition and of consumer welfare.[22] The lack of a detailed market analysis, they argue, is simply the consequence of a fundamental belief in the wisdom of ensuring fair competition rather than effective competition, in other words, protecting competitors rather than competition. If, instead, the point of State aid was to protect competition, they surmise, the focus of the exercise of assessing State aid measures' competitive impact would be on preventing inefficient undertakings from surviving or increasing their market power, rather than merely assuming that the improvement in the economic situation of *any* undertaking automatically harms competition.[23] Moreover, as Besley and Seabright point out, the nature of the market in which the aid beneficiary operates should be taken into account, for a subsidy is more likely to harm competition where there is *imperfect* competition in the market concerned.[24]

The distance between State aid and competition law further increases if one considers the type of measures that are caught by Article 107(1) TFEU, and their impact on competition. State aid, in fact, catches not only subsidies to individual undertakings, which are assessed in light of an efficiency test,[25] but also regulatory measures that favour a large number of undertakings or even an entire economic sector.[26] While in the first type of cases it is possible, and perhaps desirable, that

[21] Case C-494/06 P *Commission of the European Communities v Italian Republic and Wam SpA* [2009] ECR I-3639. See Farley, 'The Role of Economics-based Approaches when Analysing Effects on Trade and Distortions of Competition after *Wam*' (n 19).

[22] E Fox, 'State Aids Control and the Distortion of Competition—Unbundling "Distortion"' *Annual Proceedings Fordham Corporate Law Institute Conference*, 28th vol (The Hague, Kluwer, 2001) 91.

[23] Ahlborn and Berg, 'Can State Aid Control Learn from Antitrust? The Need for a Greater Role for Competition Analysis under the State Aid Rules' (n 19).

[24] T Besley and P Seabright, 'The Effects and Policy Implications of State Aids to Industry: An Economic Analysis' (1999) 34 *Economic Policy* 13.

[25] See chapter four.

[26] See chapter five.

the analytical toolbox of competition law be *adapted* to State aid, in the second category of cases, market analysis seems unlikely to develop into a sophisticated *yet accessible* set of concepts.[27] The analysis of the likely impact on competition of regulatory intervention is in fact necessarily a rather blunt judgment, which relies on presumptions rather than on empirical evidence and market analysis, as it is virtually impossible for any court to carry out a detailed analysis of the potential effects of a planned measure which benefits a variety of undertakings from different economic sectors.

The analogy that one is drawn to in this respect is that between the competitive analysis required under State aid law and the case law reviewing the EU legislature's use of the concept of distortion of competition to justify reliance on an internal market legal basis (Article 114 TFEU, in particular). In the past, the potential for legislative disparities among Member States to create obstacles to free movement and to trigger (loosely conceived) distortions of competition was often presented as a justification for harmonising legislation under those provisions.[28] That avenue seemed to be somewhat restricted in *Tobacco Advertising*, where the Court held that the deployment of (then) Article 95 EC (now Article 114 TFEU) could only be based on the need to remove obstacles to inter-State trade or to address *appreciable* distortions of competition.[29]

However, the introduction of an appreciability condition does not seem to have amounted to a requirement for empirical evidence to support the case for regulatory intervention, nor has there been a wholesale transplant of competition law tools. The precise significance of an appreciable distortion seems hard to pin down: in *Tobacco Advertising*, the Court suggested that such a distortion would arise if differences between national rules caused economic actors to choose the location of their economic activity in order to avoid legal restrictions in a particular Member State.[30] One need only consider subsequent case law to appreciate the amount of discretion left to the EU legislature in this regard. In *Leitner*, the Court held that the existence in some Member States, but not in others, of an obligation to provide compensation for 'non-material damage' in the field of package holidays would cause significant distortions of competition given that such damage

[27] As will become clearer in the second part of this chapter, it is crucial that the legal test under Article 107(1) TFEU be formulated in such a way as to make it accessible to national courts, as the latter are under an obligation to enforce the procedural obligations under Article 108 TFEU, an exercise which implies a prima facie assessment of the measure in issue in the light of Article 107(1) TFEU.

[28] See S Weatherill, 'Supply and Demand for Internal Market Regulation: Strategies, Preferences and Interpretation' in N Nic Shuibhne (ed), *Regulating the Internal Market* (Cheltenham, Elgar, 2006); D Wyatt, 'Community Competence to Regulate the Internal Market' in M Dougan and S Currie (eds), *50 Years of European Treaties: Looking Back and Thinking Forward* (Oxford, Hart Publishing, 2009).

[29] Case C-376/98 *Germany v Parliament and Council* [2000] ECR U-8419, para 106. The two conditions are interpreted as being alternative, see S Weatherill, 'The Commission's Options for Developing EC Consumer Protection and Contract Law: Assessing the Constitutional Basis' (2002) 13 *European Business Law Review* 497.

[30] Ibid para 110.

was a frequent occurrence in the field.[31] In (the rather different context of) *Kadi*,[32] the Court found that differences between the measures unilaterally taken by the Member States in relation to the assets of individuals believed to be associated with international terrorism 'could operate to the advantage or disadvantage of the competitive position of certain economic operators' and thus distort competition.[33] More recently, in *Vodafone*, in addressing a challenge to the validity of the Roaming Regulation, which was based on Article 114 TFEU and imposed maximum prices for roaming across mobile phone networks, the Court, ignoring the Advocate General's views that stigmatised the Commission's approach of inferring the potential for distortions of competition from the existence of cross-border price differences, held that 'the divergent development of national laws seeking to lower retail charges' would be 'liable to cause significant distortions of competition'.[34]

State aid differs from this case law in its approach to distortions of competition in that it does not target general measures, but selective ones.[35] Yet, the way in which distortions are deemed to arise bears *some* similarity to the reasoning displayed in the justification for Union harmonisation. Where State intervention takes the form of regulation, the reasoning focuses on the concept of selectivity, and, in particular, on whether regulatory intervention has an asymmetric impact on market actors across a Member State (as opposed to across the EU). Where that asymmetry can be proved, and provided that the other cumulative conditions that make up the notion of State aid are present, the measure is deemed (at least potentially) to distort competition. The crucial similarity, admittedly amongst a host of important differences, lies in the absence of scrutiny regarding the conditions of the market where undertakings that stand to win or to lose from State intervention operate, and of the position of those undertakings on that market. It would of course be absurd to require such scrutiny where regulation is concerned, as regulation is not typically tailored upon individual circumstances, but covers a spectrum of situations and positions. When aid in the form of regulatory intervention benefits an entire economic sector, it is difficult to see how a detailed assessment of the impact of that measure on individual undertakings can be carried out. Similarly, the exercise of determining the existence of appreciable distortions of competition

[31] Case C-168/00 *Simone Leitner v TUI Deutschland Gmbh* [2002] ECR I-2631, para 21.

[32] Joined Cases C-402/05 P and C-415/05 P *Kadi and El Bakarat v Council and Commission* [2008] ECR I-6351. It should be noted, however, that the legislation in question in *Kadi*, Council Regulation (EC) No 881/2002 [2002] OJ L139/2 was not based on then Article 95 EC, but on the joint bases of then Articles 60, 301, and 308 EC.

[33] Ibid para 230. See T Tridimas, 'Terrorism and the ECJ: Empowerment and Democracy in the EC Legal Order' (2009) 34 *EL Rev* 103; see also A Dashwood, 'Article 308 and the Outer Limit of Expressly Conferred Community Competence' in C Barnard and O Odudu (eds), *The Outer Limits of European Union Law* (Oxford, Hart Publishing, 2009). Case C-58/08, *Vodafone Ltd and Others v Secretary of State for Business, Enterprise and Regulatory Reform* [2010] ECR I-4999.

[34] Case C-58/08 *Vodafone Ltd and Others v Secretary of State for Business, Enterprise and Regulatory Reform* [2010] ECR I-4999, Opinion of Advocate General Maduro, paras 31 and 47 of the judgment.

[35] As only aid that benefits 'certain undertakings' is caught under Article 107(1) TFEU.

for the purpose of Article 114 TFEU can never amount to a precise evaluation of the effect of regulation on individual competitors. No matter how refined the economic approach, where regulation is concerned, the micro-level analysis that applies to antitrust law will always amount to a blunt tool as far as regulation is concerned, and as far as much of State aid law is concerned.[36]

B. State Aid and Free Movement

If, as has been argued, the distance between State aid and antitrust is greater than the structure of the Treaty would appear to entail, it may be wondered whether it is the case that, as Buendía Sierra and Smulders have argued, the 'State aid DNA shares more chromosomes with free movement than with antitrust rules'.[37] The fact that the State aid and free movement provisions are potentially applicable to the same material facts suggests at least an element of functional overlap between the two.[38] State aid control is, like free movement, and unlike antitrust law, a policy that finds in the internal market its paramount rationale, which explains why there are no national correlatives of either State aid control or free movement rules but there are EU and domestic systems of antitrust law.[39] The State aid provisions, in other words, complement the free movement rules in securing free and undistorted trade across the Member States.

Yet, there is an important difference between State aid and free movement.[40] Free movement epitomises negative integration, as it seeks to remove obstacles to trade 'in order to merge the national markets into a single market bringing about conditions as close as possible to those of a genuine internal market'.[41] State aid has, of course, a negative component: it prohibits certain kinds of conduct by the Member States which are adverse to the logic of the internal market. To this extent

[36] As far as Article 114 TFEU is concerned, one may wonder whether the *Tobacco Advertising* appreciability condition may actually be a red herring, which, in practice, leads either to a *probatio diabolica*, or (more likely) to a box ticking exercise.

[37] JL Buendía Sierra and B Smulders, 'The Limited Role of the "Refined Economic Approach" in Achieving the Objectives of State Aid Control: Time for Some Realism' (n 5) 9.

[38] Case 249/81 *Commission v Irish ('Buy Irish')* [1982] ECR 4005.

[39] A Biondi and P Eeckhout, 'State Aid and Obstacles to Trade' in A Biondi, P Eeckhout and J Flynn (eds), *The Law of State Aid in the EU* (Oxford, Oxford University Press, 2003) 109. See also A Biondi and M Farley, 'The Relationship between State Aid and the Single Market' in E Szyszczak (ed), *Research Handbook on State Aid* (Cheltenham, Edward Elgar, 2011) 277–92. It is worthy of note that some Member States have introduced national or regional systems of State aid control as a matter of domestic law. See on this, V Di Bucci, 'Quelques Aspects Institutionnels du Droit des Aides d'État' in JL Buendía Sierra and others, *Liber Amicorum Francisco Santaolalla Gadea* (The Hague, Kluwer, 2008).

[40] M Blauberger, 'From Negative to Positive Integration?' (2008) Max Planck Institute for the Study of Societies Discussion Paper 08/4, www.mpifg.de/pu/mpifg_dp/dp08-4.pdf; see also C Baudenbacher and F Bremer, 'European State Aid and Merger Control in the Financial Crisis—From Negative to Positive Integration' (2010) 1 *Journal of European Competition Law and Practice* 267.

[41] Case 15/81 *Gaston Schul Douane Expediteur BV v Inspecteur der Invoerrechten en Accijnzen, Roosendaal* [1982] ECR 1409, para 33.

it may be classed as a form of negative integration, alongside free movement and competition law. Yet, there is another side to this policy: its de-regulatory dimension is accompanied by a distinct re-regulatory dimension.[42] The State aid regime does not limit itself to prohibiting protectionist measures; it also formulates common policy objectives at the supranational level, and creates institutional mechanisms and procedures to ensure compliance with those objectives. By enacting common rules on areas such as environmental or regional aid, new regulatory constraints are placed on Member States and sub-national entities. State aid law, therefore, can be said to give rise to a form of positive integration, in that it promotes the emergence of new regulatory realities, or it subjects previously unregulated areas of national concern to a common regulatory process.

An even cursory examination of the State Aid Action Plan clearly indicates the existence, alongside the aim to eliminate distortions of competition, of a stated belief in the need to draw up common approaches to pursuing objectives such as 'competitiveness', 'innovation', '*high quality* Services of General Economic Interest', 'economic and social cohesion'.[43] The details of the Action Plan confirm the first impression. Consider, for instance, the following statement regarding the issue of regional aid policy:

> Past enlargements have shown that there is scope for win-win development between richer and poorer regions. State aid policy can contribute to such a positive outcome, by preventing a damaging subsidy race between regions, and by *creating the right incentives for growth and jobs*, in the least-developed regions and elsewhere.[44]

Naturally, as the Action Plan's refrain is 'less and better targeted State aid', the promotion of State aid exclusively concerns those areas where the Commission considers aid to be an effective tool of policy, where, that said, State aid is able to address genuine market failures. The Commission aims to achieve an overall reduction in aid, but, at the same time, seeks to find ways of influencing national regulatory processes in such a manner as to achieve aims that the EU regards as virtuous. What is also clear is that the Commission not only decides which State aid measures serve desirable purposes, and which kinds of intervention are less efficient, but it also seeks to combine State aid with a range of different regulatory objectives. For instance, the Action Plan refers to the need to reflect on 'ways and means to better address the challenges and opportunities that sustainable development creates, as set out in the Lisbon and Sustainable Development Strategies, especially with the aim of ensuring a full internalisation of environmental costs.' In particular, the Commission undertakes to 'attempt *to encourage eco-innovation*

[42] Since State aid measures are a form of regulation in that they are used to influence the behaviour of undertakings, the prohibition of State aid may be regarded as producing a de-regulatory effect.

[43] Commission, 'State Aid Action Plan: Less and Better Targeted State Aid: A Roadmap for State Aid Reform 2005–2009' (n 5) para 31.

[44] Emphasis added.

and improvements in productivity through eco-efficiency in line with the Environmental Technologies Action Plan (ETAP)'.[45]

Moreover, the recent financial crisis has made it abundantly clear that, in cases involving State aid to the financial sector, financial stability is as much a regulatory objective of State aid control as is the avoidance or limitation of distortions of competition.[46] This was recently confirmed in a speech by Comissioner Almunía who pointed out that the Commission had 'used State aid control to preserve the integrity of the internal market and to ensure financial stability'.[47] The quote captures the two dimensions of State aid: the negative integration role which complements free movement, but also the instrumental character of the policy, which is 'used' to pursue goals that are not directly connected to the promotion of undistorted competition across the internal market.

C. Competition Between States

State aid and free movement law also appear to part company in another respect. It has often been argued in the literature that, through the principle of mutual recognition, the free movement jurisprudence facilitates the process of 'regulatory' or 'locational' competition,[48] where regulators compete amongst each other to attract economic activity to their jurisdiction.[49] State aid law, instead, pulls

45 Commission, 'State Aid Action Plan: Less and Better Targeted State Aid: A Roadmap for State Aid Reform 2005–2009' (n 5) para 46; Commission, 'Stimulating Technologies for Sustainable Development: An Environmental Technologies Action Plan for the European Union' COM(2004) 38 final.

46 Communication on the application of State aid rules to measures taken in relation to financial institutions in the context of the current global financial crisis [2008] OJ C270/ 8; Communication on the recapitalisation of financial institutions in the current financial crisis: limitation of aid to the minimum necessary and safeguards against undue distortions of competition [2009] OJ C10/ 2; Communication from the Commission on the treatment of impaired assets in the Community banking sector [2009] OJ C72/1; Communication on the return to viability and the assessment of restructuring measures in the financial sector in the current crisis under the State aid rules [2009] OJ C195/9. See H Gilliams, 'Stress Testing the Regulator: Review of State Aid to Financial Institutions after the Collapse of Lehman' (2011) 36 *EL Rev* 3; M Ojo, 'The Changing Role of Central Banks and the Role of Competition in Financial Regulation during (and in the Aftermath of) the Financial Crisis' (2011) 17 *ELJ* 513.

47 Speech of Commissioner Almunía entitled 'State aid control as a resolution tool in the EU' delivered on 15/09/2011, www.europa.eu/rapid/pressReleasesAction.do?reference=SPEECH/11/577&format=HTML&aged=0&language=EN&guiLanguage=en.

48 For want of a more attractive term …

49 See, among others, C Barnard and S Deakin, 'Market Access and Regulatory Competition' in C Barnard and J Scott (eds), *The Law of The Single European Market: Unpacking the Premises* (Oxford, Hart Publishing, 2002) 197–224. There is controversy about the nature and extent of regulatory competition within the internal market. The debate is particularly intense in relation to corporate establishment. See A Johnston and P Syrpis, 'Regulatory Competition in European Company Law after Cartesio' 34(3) *European Law Review* (2009) 378; W-G Ringe, 'Sparking Regulatory Competition in European Company Law—The Impact of the *Centros* Line of Case-Law and its Concept of "Abuse of Law"' in R de la Feria and S Vogenauer, *Prohibition of Abuse Law—a New General Principle of EU Law* (Oxford, Hart Publishing, 2010).

in the opposite direction: by limiting the degree to which Member States may adapt their regulation to the preferences of selected economic actors, these rules limit the extent to which Member States may engage in regulatory competition. True, as chapters five and six will make clear, where State aid law limits regulatory autonomy, it does so by focusing exclusively on selective regulation, and does not concern itself with general regulatory measures. This means that State aid is incapable of targeting strategic regulatory differentiation *among* Member States, but can only target asymmetric regulation *within* individual Member States. Yet, in the perspective of locational competition, the latter type of differentiation may often be a more effective and financially less onerous tool to achieve the result sought by the former sort of regulatory differentiation. Selective regulatory incentives are, in fact, more effective in that they target those undertakings that are more likely to respond to the appeal of public incentives, or undertakings that belong to a specific sector that the Member State seeks to attract to its jurisdiction; moreover, selective regulation also reduces the impact on public finances, in that it does not cover all undertakings across sectors, but only those undertakings that it seeks to attract.[50]

The link between State aid control and competition between States, however, is not simply a relationship of cause and effect, where the effect is merely a consequence of applying Article 107(1) TFEU. Instead, the desire to constrain locational competition is precisely the *rationale* for the existence of State aid law and policy. The reasons for controlling State aid are clearer when one considers the reasons for the existence of State intervention. It is well known that governments often use subsidies and other forms of State aid as a regulatory tool, as a means of addressing a 'market failure'.[51] A typical example is environmental pollution.[52] The logic of the market does not contemplate accounting for the costs to society arising from the environmental consequences of economic activity (in other words, market players do not, of their own free will, internalise the negative 'externalities' to society from such activities). One of the possible regulatory responses to this problem is for States to provide financial assistance to undertakings in order to encourage their compliance with environmental objectives. State intervention may also aim to achieve economic objectives that market mechanisms are typically unable to deliver, such as redistribution (for instance by providing incentives

[50] The area of fiscal State aid, examined in chapters five and, especially, six, provides an eloquent illustration of the significance of State aid in relation to tax competition.

[51] HW Friederiszick, L-H Röller and V Verouden, 'European State Aid Control: An Economic Framework' in P Buccirossi, *Advances in the Economics of Competition Law* (Cambridge Mass, MIT Press, 2008). In its classic formulation, market failure indicates the failure of a system of market institutions 'to sustain "desirable" activities or to estop "undesirable" activities'. See FM Bator, 'The Anatomy of Market Failure' (1958) 72 *Quarterly Journal of Economics* 351, 351.

[52] Eg S Bilal and P Nicolaides, 'State Aid Rules: Do They Promote Efficiency?' in S Bilal and P Nicolaides (eds), *Understanding State Aid Policy in the European Community: Perspectives on Rules and Practice* (The Hague, Kluwer, 1999).

for firms to invest in economically disadvantaged areas) or to pursue purely non-economic objectives (for instance, the protection of national heritage).[53]

Despite all such good intentions,[54] government intervention may result in a series of unintended consequences. A decision by a Member State to offer aid often prompts others, eagerly or reluctantly, to follow suit, often by increasing the amount of the original subsidy so as to influence the undertakings' choice of location. The outcome of this series of events sparked by the initial decision by a Member State to address what may well have been a legitimate concern may therefore be an expensive and damaging subsidies-war, a competitive process in which a set of actions and reactions ultimately results in a decrease in overall welfare. As a result of the decrease in prices resulting from parallel subsidies, overall profits fall, while Member States' finances are drained of resources that could have been put to more productive use.[55] Moreover, where State aid is handed out to inefficient undertakings, the departure from the logic of reward typically associated with a market economy may lead in the long term to harm to consumer welfare, as more innovative undertakings are forced out of the market, and, eventually, higher prices and poorer quality products/services ensue.[56]

What is clear, then, is that State aid policy is concerned with distortions of competition between undertakings, but also, and arguably predominantly, with competition between Member States. This is clear from the very first Commission 'Report on Competition Policy': 'It is inevitable that Member States will be better informed of nationally anticipated "gains" arising from their own decisions [to grant aid] rather than from their negative counterpart at Community level, and that they will tend to underestimate any reaction which their decisions may trigger off on the part of their partners'.[57] 'The ultimate objective of Community aid action is', the Commission goes on to add, 'to reintroduce this Community perspective and to *ensure that the aims of each Member State take its partners' interests into account*' (emphasis added).[58]

Such reasons also emerge from another early document, formulated in the midst of a period of acute recession, in which the Commission emphasises the negative impact that competition between States in granting aid, subsidies races, or 'beggar thy neighbour' policies, produce on Member States and on the European economy as a whole. Compliance with the State aid rules, argues the Commission, is a necessary condition for public intervention to achieve its aims in a rapid

[53] AV Deardorff, 'The Economics of Government Market Intervention, and its International Dimension' in M Bronkers and R Quick (eds), *New Directions in International Economic Law* (The Hague, Kluwer, 2000).

[54] Intentions which, of course, may well be absent from national decisions to grant State aid, for instance, if State aid is the product of corruption or regulatory capture.

[55] T Besley and P Seabright, 'The Effects and Policy Implications of State Aids to Industry: An Economic Analysis' (1999) 34 *Economic Policy* 13.

[56] This, of course, is a highly stylised account of hypothetical scenarios. It should not be read as an inexorable chain of events.

[57] Commission, 'First Report on Competition Policy' (1972) para 134.

[58] Ibid.

and cost-effective manner. In the absence of an effective State aid regime, the Commission makes clear, Member States would engage in mutual over-bidding, which would entail 'the neutralizing of the effects of those national policies which are most justified, the exporting of unemployment from one Member State to another and, finally, the aggravation of the Community situation as a whole'.[59]

In laying down common rules on State aid and an ex ante monitoring mechanism, EU law does not eliminate the possibility of State intervention, but subjects the process to supranational scrutiny in order to reduce its negative repercussions on other Member States and on the internal market. What seems plain is that the emphasis is more on the macro level, that is to say, on the potential impact of State aid on the internal market, than on the micro level, which instead considers the effects of State aid on competition in a specific market. True, the type of analysis that the Commission deploys today in determining the *compatibility* of individual measures with the internal market benefits from sharper microeconomic analysis than was previously the case. Yet, the *definition* of State aid remains largely untouched by the 'refined economic approach' encapsulated in the State Aid Action Plan, and necessarily so. If the objective of State aid control is to prevent the emergence of competitive spirals, a micro-level analysis inevitably fails to assess the potential for other Member States to replicate the subsidy within their jurisdictions.[60]

2. CENTRALISATION AND ITS RATIONALE

The economic rationale of State aid control explains the Treaty's choice in favour of a centralised system of ex ante control, which the drafters preferred to alternative, lighter touch solutions, such as a set of rules of cooperation among Member States. There is a close link between the EU system of State aid control and the pursuit of market integration. Not only is integration *an objective* that justifies the existence of State aid control, but the achievement of the single market constitutes *a reality* the existence of which justifies strict enforcement of this regime. As a normative objective, market integration justifies the choice in favour of a supranational regime, in that weaker forms of cooperation would be prone to a series of regulatory failures.[61] First of all, information as to the effects of State aids across markets may not be readily available to national authorities cooperating with each other. Secondly, there may be mutual distrust, as Member States doubt

[59] Commission 'Fourth report on Competition Policy' (1974) para 148.

[60] Naturally, a de minimis threshold is, for reasons of efficient administrative resource management, indispensable. This, too, however, is a blunt instrument, since, as Buendía Sierra and Smulders have pointedly remarked, there is no plausible *economic* argument for fixing a de minimis threshold at a particular level. JL Buendía Sierra and B Smulders, 'The Limited Role of the "Refined Economic Approach" in Achieving the Objectives of State Aid Control: Time for Some Realism' (n 5) 12.

[61] Bilal and Nicolaides, 'State Aid Rules: Do They Promote Efficiency?' (n 52).

the seriousness of other Member States' commitment towards the elimination of trade-distorting measures. Thirdly, where State aid control is ultimately left to national authorities, there is a higher risk of regulatory capture, as national authorities are more likely to be hijacked by national interests than a supranational body. Finally, the idea of a single European internal market assumes a *certain* degree of uniformity in market-correcting intervention, as, even in the most open advanced market economies public intervention, intervention of this type will always be required. In other words, the need for supranational supervision and enforcement transcends the prohibition of State aid, and is reinforced by the need to formulate policy orientations and legal rules regarding the conditions under which State intervention should come into play.

As a state of affairs, not only does market integration provide the justification for such a regime, but it also emphasises the need for a strict enforcement of the rules, as the degree of interdependence among European economies in the single market exacerbates the negative effects of State aid. In fact, lacking a State aid regime, the free movement of economic factors would allow *subsidised* products to gain unfettered access across the single market, and to displace more expensive non-subsidised products; it would permit subsidised firms to place successful bids in public procurement procedures; it would encourage firms to relocate where governments operate selective tax exemptions. While cooperation suits an international regime with a smaller degree of interdependence and significantly greater regulatory autonomy, it does not seem to be sufficient to discourage Member States from pursuing their national self-interest in an integrated market where they are already constrained by the free movement provisions and, where this applies, by the existence of a single European currency.[62] Moreover, the existence of EU objectives which may justify State aid measures strengthens the case for a supranational common regime, as these are recognised at the same time as legitimate objectives but also as *common* objectives.

A. Direct Effect: Centralised and Decentralised Enforcement

Centralisation and decentralisation turn on the ability of individuals to rely on the direct effect of the relevant treaty provisions. A crucial difference between the free movement and antitrust provisions, on the one hand, and State aid, on the other, arises from the lack of direct effect of Article 107 TFEU.[63] Article 107(1) TFEU, which lays down a presumption of incompatibility of State aid measures, may not, as such, be invoked before national courts,[64] though the latter are able,

[62] Given the impossibility of competitive devaluations.

[63] Case 78/76 *Steinike und Weinlig v Federal Republic of Germany* [1977] ECR 595.

[64] Case 6/64 *Costa v ENEL* [1964] ECR 585. More precisely, rights arising from the provisions on State aid may only be enforced where the Commission has reached a final decision on the matter: Case 77/72 *Capolongo v Azienda Agricola Maya* [1973] ECR 611, para 6.

and required, to enforce the procedural obligations flowing from the last sentence of Article 108(3) TFEU.[65] The law of State aid is characterised by an apparent divide between the role of the Commission and the role of the (EU and national) judiciary; in the words of the Court of Justice, the courts and the Commission are called to 'fulfil complementary and separate roles'.[66] It is, in fact, the Commission's role to investigate an alleged State aid measure, to request information from the parties involved, and to conclude that there are (in)sufficient grounds for it to proceed towards a formal investigation. At this stage of analysis, national courts are involved in a prima facie assessment of the measure in the light of Article 107(1) TFEU; their examination, however, is instrumental to ensuring the respect of the notification and standstill obligations. National courts are to form a view on whether a measure constitutes aid in the first place, whether it is existing or new aid, in order to decide if there has been a violation of the standstill obligation. This two-tiered system allows for different conclusions to be reached at different ends; the Commission may in fact decide—contrary to the national court's assessment—that a measure does not constitute aid.

The second stage of analysis belongs to the exclusive domain of the Commission's competences, as national courts are ousted from this assessment. This division into two distinct stages of assessment is also reflected in the intensity of judicial review under Article 263 TFEU. While the judiciary plays a considerable part in the development of the legal notion of State aid, it has limited powers of review with regard to the determination of a measure's compatibility with the internal market. In relation to the latter, the Commission enjoys a wide discretion, 'the exercise of which involves complex economic and social assessments which must be made in an [EU] context'.[67] Where such discretion is involved, judicial review is confined to verifying whether the Commission has committed a manifest error of assessment, has provided an inadequate statement of reasons, or misused its powers.[68]

The centralised nature of State aid, associated with the lack of direct effect of Article 107 TFEU, is tempered by the recognition of the direct effect of the procedural obligations arising from Article 108(3) TFEU. The role of national courts undoubtedly constitutes a step forward in the protection of the interests of competitors. That step, however, rather than being an end in itself, is—arguably—a means to an end, the end being to ensure the effectiveness of the centralised administrative procedure. The instrumental nature of direct effect is not a peculiarity of the State aid provisions, as the very idea of 'direct effect' is itself the outcome of the Court's teleological interpretation. However, that characteristic

[65] The so-called 'standstill provision', which reads: 'the Member State shall not put its proposed measure into effect until this procedure has resulted in a final Decision'.

[66] Case C-39/94 *SFEI v La Poste* [1996] ECR I3547, para 41; Joined Cases C-261/01 and C-262/01 *van Calster and Others* [2003] ECR I-12249, para 74.

[67] Case 310/85 *Deufil v Commission* [1987] ECR 901, para 18; Case C-372/97 *Italy v Commission* [2004] ECR I-3679, para 83.

[68] Case C-372/97 *Italy v Commission* [2004] ECR I-3679, para 87; U Soltesz and H Bielesz, 'Judicial Review of State Aid Decisions' [2004] *European Competition Law Review* 133.

appears, in the field of State aid, to be even more pronounced than it is in free movement law. The direct effect of Article 108(3) TFEU is in fact triggered by a breach by a Member State of its procedural duties under the Treaty rules on State aid, duties which, rather than laying the ground for a substantive right not to be harmed by State aid, give rise to an interest vis-a-vis the prescribed administrative procedures.[69] By contrast, in the free movement area, individuals may invoke directly effective rights, which are the correlative of substantive, rather than procedural, obligations of the Member States;[70] free movement rights are frequently described by the Court as 'fundamental freedoms'.[71] Moreover, while State aid (and competition law) claims are limited by a 'de minimis' rule, free movement claims are not subject to such limits.[72]

Similarities emerge, instead, from the comparison between the rights protected under Article 108(3) TFEU and the hybrid legal tool created by the Court in relation to Directive 83/189.[73] The Directive was intended to permit the Commission to exercise preventive scrutiny over national regulation presenting potential obstacles to product market integration,[74] which was made possible by a set of

[69] Individuals may rely upon the breach of the procedural rules as a cause of action in damages against the State. In doing so they are to allege the existence of damage to their competitive sphere, a claim which is difficult to prove in practice. Case C-199/06 *CELF and Ministre de la Culture et de la Communication* [2008] ECR I-469, paras 53 and 55; Case C-368/04 *Transalpine Ölleitung in Österreich* [2006] ECR I-9957, para 56; and Case C-334/07 P *Commission v Freistaat Sachsen* [2008] ECR I-9465, para 54. A study in 2006 on the enforcement of State aid law in national courts commissioned by the European Commission found that 19% of all actions in national courts were actions by competitors against a Member State for damages, recovery and/or injunctive measures based on Article 108(3) TFEU, www.ec.europa.eu/comm/competition/state_aid/studies_reports/studies_reports.cfm. See also, www.ec.europa.eu/competition/state_aid/studies_reports/enforcement_study_2009.pdf. The Commission is keen to encourage private enforcement of the State aid rules before national courts. See generally, Commission notice on the enforcement of State aid law by national courts [2009] OJ C85/1.

[70] And, to a certain (now, considerable) extent, private entities. See Case C-281/98 *Roman Angonese v Cassa di Risparmio di Bolzano* [2000] ECR I-4139; Case C-438/05 *Viking Lines* [2007] ECR I-10779; Case C-341/05 *Laval un Partneri Ltd v Svenska Byggnadsarbetareförbundet and others* [2007] ECR I-11767. On the significance of these developments see D Wyatt, 'Horizontal Effect of Fundamental Freedoms and the Right to Equality after *Viking* and *Mangold*, and the Implications for Community Competence' (2008) 48 *Croatian Yearbook of European Law & Policy* 1; A Dashwood, '*Viking* and *Laval*: Issues of Horizontal Direct Effect' (2007–2008) 10 *Cambridge Yearbook of European Legal Studies* 525; S Prechal and S de Vries, 'Seamless Web of Judicial Protection in the Internal Market?' (2009) 34 *EL Rev* 5; H Schepel, 'Constitutionalising the Market, Marketising the Constitution, and to Tell the Difference: On the Horizontal Application of the Free Movement Provisions in EU Law' (2012) 18 *European Law Journal* 177.

[71] Eg Case C-262/09 *Meilike* (30 June 2011), para 41.

[72] Though, of course, other kinds of limits apply. On which see E Spaventa, 'The Outer Limit of the Treaty Free Movement Provisions: Some Reflections on the Significance of *Keck*, Remoteness and *Deliège*' in C Barnard and O Odudu (eds), *The Outer Limits of European Union Law* (Oxford, Hart Publishing, 2009).

[73] [1983] OJ L109 amended by Directive 98/34 [1998] OJ L204/37, itself amended by Directive 98/48 [1998] OJ L217/18.

[74] S Weatherill, 'A Case Study in Judicial Activism in the 1990s: The Status Before National Courts of Measures Wrongfully Un-notified to the Commission' in D O'Keefe (ed), *Liber Amicorum Slynn* (The Hague, Kluwer Law International, 2000); S Weatherill, 'Compulsory Notification of Draft Technical Regulations: The Contribution of Directive 83/189 to the Management of the Internal Market' [1996] *Yearbook of European Law* 129.

procedural constraints on national regulators. Under this system, the latter are required to notify draft technical regulations and to comply with a standstill obligation for a prescribed period. Similarly to Article 108(3), the Directive is silent regarding the consequences of a failure to comply with its requirements. In *CIA Security International v Signalson SA and Securitel SPRL*,[75] the Court held that 'the effectiveness of EU control will be much greater if the Directive is interpreted as meaning that breach of the obligation to notify constitutes a substantial procedural defect such as to render the technical regulations in question inapplicable to individuals'.[76] This ruling, as equivalent case law on State aid,[77] is designed to provide further incentives for Member States to cooperate with the Commission within the context of centralised supervisory regimes.[78] Of course, in both areas an individual interest in the compliance with the procedural rules may easily be found, as both systems allow traders and competitors to provide the Commission with useful information in order (eventually and indirectly) to influence the decision-making process.[79] However, the instrumental character of the involvement of individuals emerging from the two systems is in stark contrast with the Treaty free movement rules, characterised by ex post enforcement of substantive rights.

The correlative of this difference in content between the rights deriving from the Treaty rules on State aid and the rights enshrined in the free movement provisions is the basis upon which national courts exercise their power to review potential Treaty breaches in the two regimes. In the logic of a system of complementary functions, national courts are barred from assessing the policy justifications that might render a State aid compatible with the internal market.[80] Instead, in free movement law, the assessment of public interest justifications features as an integral part of domestic enforcement.

Competition law shares with State aid the central role of the European Commission both in the formulation of policy and in the enforcement process, but while the latter survives the modernisation process, the former has been significantly altered by the changes introduced by Regulation 1/2003.[81] Under the previous regime, governed by Regulation 17/62, a Commission authorisation was required to confer validity upon agreements that fell within the scope of Article 101 TFEU. As in State aid, the decision-making process was rigidly separated into two stages, dealing respectively with the prohibition and with the exemption. National courts could apply the treaty provision on restrictive agreements,

[75] Case C-194/94 *CIA Security International v Signalson SA and Securitel SPRL* [1996] ECR I-2201.

[76] Ibid para 48. Case C-443/98, *Unilever Italia* [2000] ECR I-7535. On the problem of incidental effect see M Dougan, 'When Worlds Collide! Competing Visions of the Relationship between Direct Effect and Supremacy' (2007) 44 *CML Rev* 931.

[77] Case 120/73 *Lorenz v Germany* [1973] ECR 1471.

[78] S Weatherill, 'A Case Study in Judicial Activism in the 1990s' (n 73) 484.

[79] There is a fundamental difference between the case law on Article 108(3) TFEU and the case law on Directive 83/189: while in the former the Court talks of direct effect, in the latter it does not.

[80] The Commission retains a monopoly over the compatibility stage, which examines the exceptions in Article 107(2) and 107(3) TFEU.

[81] Regulation 1/2003 [2003] OJ L1/1.

as Article 101(1) and (2) TFEU were endowed with direct effect, and could thus declare agreements to be void, but were barred from assessing individual exemptions under Article 101(3) TFEU. This monopoly over the exemption process allowed the Commission to shape the EU's policy in relation to different kinds of agreements.[82] After nearly four decades of development of this area of the law, as the number of notifications for individual exemptions had increased exponentially, thus dispersing the efforts of the Commission and reducing the effectiveness of its work, a process of reform was set in motion, which resulted in an important shift in the institutional balance between the EU and its Member States. On the one hand, the new regulation proceeded to decentralise decision-making within Article 101 TFEU *as a whole*, by attributing direct effect to Article 101(3) TFEU and setting aside the individual notification/exemption procedure, but, on the other hand, the new regime gave the EU fresh powers to formulate EU competition policy.[83]

Regardless of one's assessment of the degree of decentralisation arising from the Modernisation Regulation, a significant move has taken place from a system based on a centralised ex ante authorisation system to a system contemplating ex post national enforcement, which increases the isolation of State aid as a two-tiered ex ante centralised regime.[84]

B. Administrative Rule-Making

Administrative rule-making, that is, the Commission's power to develop guidelines in order to confer predictability and transparency to its decision-making, is a central feature of both the competition and the State aid regimes. These are rules, some of which may be labelled as 'soft law', for whose creation the Commission is chiefly (and sometimes solely) responsible, as the procedure for the production of such rules may be either a unilateral or a cooperative one.[85] Under unilateral rule-making, the Commission lays down block exemption regulations,[86] where it states which types of

[82] Whish and Bailey, *Competition Law* (n 12) 166.

[83] According to some, the agenda-setting powers of the Commission thus appear to have been strengthened by the Modernisation Regulation; see A Riley, 'EC Antitrust Modernisation: The Commission does very nicely—thank you!' [2004] *European Competition Law Review* 604.

[84] The extensive literature includes: C-D Ehlermann and I Atanasiu (eds), *European Competition Law Annual 2000: The Modernisation of EC Antitrust Policy* (Oxford, Hart Publishing, 2001); D Cahill (ed), *The Modernisation of EU Competition Law Enforcement in the EU* (Cambridge, Cambridge University Press, 2004); L McGowan, 'Europeanization Unleashed and Rebounding: Assessing the Modernization of EU Cartel Policy' (2005) 12 *Journal of European Public Policy* 986.

[85] The categorisation is used in H Hofmann, 'Negotiated and non-negotiated administrative rule-making: the example of EC competition policy' (2006) 43 *CML Rev* 153.

[86] In the field of competition law, the Commission's power to issue block exemption regulations derives from the Council, whose regulations granting such powers are based on Article 103(2)(b) TFEU. State aid block exemption regulations are also based on Council regulations, whose vires stem from Article 109 TFEU.

aid or agreements are automatically compatible with the single market, or it sets out criteria for the assessment of the issue of compatibility with the internal market. The function of these guidelines is to draw the boundaries of the Commission's discretion in these fields, and to 'reflect the Commission's desire to publish directions on the approach it intends to follow'.[87] The adoption of such guidelines is itself an instance of the exercise of the Commission's discretion and requires only a self-imposed limitation of that power.[88] Unlike competition law, State aid is also characterised by the presence of negotiated administrative rule-making, where the procedure involves a certain degree of cooperation between the Commission and the Member States. This procedure, occurring in the field of supervision and review of existing aid schemes, produces agreements which may only be modified with the consent of the parties involved, that is, the Commission and the Member State concerned.

As with all cases of rules enacted by the executive, questions of democratic legitimacy may be raised. Such questions do not simply concern the use of soft law instruments, but extend to the use of formal binding law rules. Article 107(2)(e) TFEU allows the Council, deliberating by qualified majority on a proposal from the Commission, to introduce through a decision new categories of aid that may be declared compatible with the Treaty. Article 109 TFEU on the other hand, allows the Council, again, voting by qualified majority on a proposal from the Commission, but only after having consulted the European Parliament, to make regulations for the application of Article 107 TFEU and 108 TFEU and to enact block exemption regulations. If the latter procedure may appear marginally more democratic, as the Parliament is involved (in a rather anodyne fashion), the exercise of the power to enact such legislative instruments has actually further distanced the Commission's exercise of its regulatory powers from the centre of democratic accountability within the European institutional system. The Enabling Regulation has delegated to the Commission the power to enact block exemption regulations, a power that is largely unchecked.[89] However, this sort of legislative exercise does not involve a complete autonomy on the Commission's part from the Member States or a departure from consensual law-making. The enabling regulation in fact provides that before publishing any draft regulation and before adopting any regulation, the Commission will consult an expert committee, the Advisory Committee on State Aid, which is composed of representatives of the Member States and chaired by a representative of the Commission. The supranational character, then, clearly prevails within this mode of law-making, though national interests are formally represented through the mechanism of the 'advisory procedure' set out in Article 4 of Regulation 182/2011.[90]

87 Case T-1107/99 *Agrana Zucker v Commission* [2001] ECR II-15107, para 56.

88 Case T-214/95 *Vlaamse Gewest v Commission* [1998] ECR II-717, paras 79–89.

89 Regulation 994/98 [1998] OJ L142/1. Recently the Commission has adopted a new block exemption regulation (the General Block Exemption Regulation), which covers SMEs, research, innovation, regional development, training, employment and risk capital: Commission Regulation (EC) No 800/2008 [2008] OJ L 214/3.

90 Article 4 Regulation 182/2011 of the European Parliament and of the Council laying down the rules and general principles concerning mechanisms for control by Member States of the Commission's

3. DISCRETION

A. Economic and Non-Economic Considerations

The use of technical discretion is common to all institutions involved in the monitoring and enforcement process within internal market law. In fact, the Commission, the courts, and competition authorities are all involved in evaluation of a technical nature; that discretion derives from the economic dimension of many of the issues arising in internal market law. However, the level of complexity of the issues involved varies across the three fields. State aid and competition law cases certainly involve institutions in the most complex economic assessments, whereas the Court employs looser economic criteria in the free movement cases. Whether or not the convergence between competition and free movement rules is being pursued, a debate that seems to have somewhat faded, it seems plain that the Court of Justice's approach to free movement has concentrated on legal concepts such as 'discrimination' or hybrid concepts such as 'market access' and 'double burden', rather than on economic concepts. Moreover, a major difference between free movement and competition and State aid law lies in the role of economic discretion in the assessment of the justifications applicable to otherwise incompatible measures. Although the three systems, broadly speaking, share the distinction between the scope of a measure and its justification, while State aid and competition law require economic assessments to be carried out, the case law on free movement expressly denies any role to economic reasons in justifying obstacles to free movement.[91]

The evaluation of non-economic interests against single market concerns involves a different form of discretion. This kind of discretion is not peculiar to free movement. Non-economic interests also feature in competition and State aid analysis, albeit to significantly different extents. Article 101(3) TFEU assessments have, from time to time, included references to non-economic criteria, although the Commission has often stressed that the *prevailing* criterion in the

exercise of implementing powers [2011] OJ L55/13. The European Parliament has expressed the view that it 'should at least be kept fully informed about the process of adoption of regulations exempting categories of aid from the obligation to notify and should be regularly informed about the opinions delivered by the Advisory Committee on State Aid and any deviating positions of Member States.' Report by the European Parliament's Committee on Economic and Monetary affairs on the seventh survey on state aid in the European Union in the manufacturing and certain other sectors COM(1999) 148 – C5-0107/1999 – 1999/2110(COS).

[91] Though economic arguments may become relevant in the assessment of non-economic justifications. On these issues see J Snell, 'Economic aims as justifications for restrictions on free movement' in A Schrauwen (ed), *The Rule of Reason: Rethinking another Classic of EC Legal Doctrine* (Groningen, Europa Law Publishing, 2004). See also N Nic Shuibhne, 'Annotation of Case C-76/05 *Schwarz and Gootjes-Schwarz v. Finanzamt Bergisch Gladbach*' (2008) 45 *CML Rev* 771.

assessment of agreements should always be efficiency.[92] The difference between competition and free movement in this regard would seem to reside in the fact that while non-economic interests may override single market concerns in free movement law, such an effect is not recognised under competition law unless the interest concerned can be translated into an enhancement in economic progress or efficiency.[93]

As in the case of the definition of restrictive agreements under Article 101(1) TFEU, there seems to have been a marked increase in the tendency for decision-making to be guided by economic analysis also in the application of Article 101(3) TFEU. In the past, employment policy and environmental protection have influenced decisions taken by the Commission and have often appeared in the reasoning of the Court and of the General Court. The process of modernisation and the decentralisation of the application of Article 101(3) TFEU entailed by it appear to have prompted the Commission to adopt a narrower reading of the balancing process. The Modernisation Regulation and the notice on the application of Article 101(3) TFEU implicitly eschew non-economic considerations. Moreover, there are a number of normative reasons why non-efficiency considerations should not figure in Article 101 TFEU. Odudu summarises them as follows:

> (a) considering non-efficiency goals confers rights and imposes obligations on those not properly entitled to those rights or subject to those obligations by eroding the public/private divide; (b) it is illegitimate to use Article [101 TFEU] as a Trojan horse to impose obligations or deny rights to private parties on the basis of Treaty provisions incapable of horizontal direct effect; (c) balancing competing goals within Article [101 TFEU] renders otiose Treaty provisions resolving conflicts of values; (d) a unitary goal provides greater legal certainty; and (e) a unitary goal is more justiciable than a norm pursuing multiple goals.[94]

These considerations clearly do not apply to State aid. The point of departure in Odudu's arguments for rejecting non-economic objectives in Article 101(3) TFEU analysis is the consideration that, on the one hand, entities governed and limited by the public interest should not be subject to private competition law, as the latter is exclusively concerned with the conduct of private actors; on the other hand,

[92] L Gyselen, 'The Substantive Legality Test Under Article 81(3) EC Treaty—Revisited in Light of the Commission's Modernization Initiative' in A von Bogdandy, PC Mavroidis and Y Mény (eds), *European Integration and International Co-ordination: Studies in Honour of Claus-Dieter Ehlermann* (The Hague, Kluwer Law International, 2002); G Monti, 'Article 81 and Public Policy' (2002) 39 *CML Rev* 1057; O Odudu, *The Boundaries of EC Competition Law* (Oxford, Oxford University Press, 2006).

[93] On the application of Article 101(3) TFEU see Commission guidelines on the application of Article 81(3) of the Treaty [2004] OJ C 101/08.

[94] Odudu, *The Boundaries of EC Competition Law* (n 92) 56. But see Monti, 'Article 81 and Public Policy' (n 92); for a very different perspective see C Townley, *Article 81EC and Public Policy* (Oxford, Hart Publishing, 2009). Recent case law has questioned the monopoly of consumer welfare as underlying rationale for EU antitrust law: Joined Cases C-501/06 P, C-513/06 P, C-515/06 P and C-519/06 P *GlaxoSmithKline Services Unlimited v Commission* [2009] ECR I-09291; Case C-8/08 *T-Mobile Netherlands BV, KPN Mobile NV, Orange Nederland NV and Vodafone Libertel NV v Raad van bestuur van de Nederlandse Mededingingsautoritei* [2009] ECR I-4529.

the balancing of internal market concerns against non-economic interests is an operation that can only be carried out in a public law setting, as these interests are the expression of the democratic process. In this light, it appears clear why both free movement law and the State aid system allow for a balancing of competing interests. Generally, free movement law applies to public entities or private entities endowed with regulatory powers, and often requires balancing public interest non-economic concerns against the interest of market integration.[95] Non-competition concerns are expressly recognised by the Treaty rules on State aid, as they are referred to in the headings of compatibility contained in Article 107(3) TFEU. Most Article 107(3) TFEU headings are of an economic nature, in that they can be ascribed to economic *policy* considerations, though—in contrast to competition policy—they are not based on economic efficiency or on consumer welfare.[96] The link between the efficiency considerations in Article 101(3) TFEU and the immediate benefit to consumers is a direct one, whereas the reasons that justify the authorisation of a State aid measure have only an indirect impact on consumer welfare. State aid measures declared to be compatible on grounds of regional cohesion, employment or environmental policy may benefit consumers in the long term, but they plainly cannot be ascribed to such an objective.

B. Discretion and the European Interest

It is clear from the treaty provisions, from secondary legislation and from the Court's case law that, to be regarded as justified, State aid should contribute towards the achievement of an *EU* objective. Thus, evaluating justifications for State aid involves economic and social assessments is an exercise which must be made in an EU context.[97] Moreover, in order to be considered for authorisation, the aid measure should promote 'a development which is in the interest of the EU as a whole', and the fact that a measure contributes to the national interest of a Member State does not warrant a finding of compatibility by the Commission.[98]

A brief overview of the various headings of justification reveals the existence of a European dimension as the common thread. Consider regional aid. Article 107(a) TFEU refers to 'areas where the standard of living is abnormally low or where there is serious underemployment': the Court has made clear that the underemployment and standards of living should be assessed in relation to the EU situation rather

[95] Of course, the Court now recognises the horizontal effect of most of the free movement provisions, even outside of the exercise of regulatory powers. On the intensely problematic nature of this issue, see the literature cited above (n 70).

[96] Some justifications are simply non-economic in nature: letter (d) of Article 107(3) TFEU ('aid to promote culture and heritage conservation') plainly falls outside the scope of economic policy.

[97] Case 730/79 *Philip Morris v Commission* [1980] ECR 2671.

[98] Twelfth Report on Competition Policy (1982) para 160.

than the national averages.[99] On the other hand, letter (c) derogations are based on the Commission's power 'to authorize aid intended to further the economic development of areas of a Member State which are disadvantaged in relation to the national average'.[100] However, the Commission's approach has been to view the matter from an EU perspective.[101] Both derogations are, according to the Court, 'based on the aim of Community solidarity', which is a fundamental objective of the Treaty.[102]

If the European dimension of an 'aid to promote the execution of an important project of common European interest' under Article 107(3)(b) TFEU is self-evident, aid to promote culture and heritage conservation permitted pursuant to Article 107(3)(d) TFEU would appear to be based on national interests, given the emphasis on cultural diversity and given the supplementary nature of EU legislative competence in the field (Article 167 TFEU).[103] However, there is a direct link between the ground for compatibility and the EU policy. Cultural justifications are indeed national interests, but they are also an expression of an EU policy which promotes cultural diversity on the one hand, and inter-State cooperation on the other. This stance appears to be substantiated in the Commission's approach to aid to film production. In order to classify for authorisation, such aid should allow the producer to spend at least 20 per cent of the film's budget in one or more *other* Member States without losing any aid.[104]

Different instances of the European interest also figure in competition law as values to be balanced against the objective of free competition, though Article 101(3) TFEU only allows for exemptions to be granted where the restriction (though not the elimination) of competition 'contributes to improving the production or distribution of goods or to promoting technical or economic progress'. Whilst market integration, as the paramount concern of EU law, is balanced against efficiency, other and more specific EU concerns feed into the assessment under Article 101(3) TFEU but are not formally part of the balancing exercise; they are taken into account but are not hierarchically equivalent to competition, market integration and efficiency.[105] Thus, whilst evidence shows that considerations such as employment policy and environmental protection have indeed

[99] Case 730/79 *Philip Morris v Commission* [1980] ECR 2671.

[100] Case 248/84 *Federal Republic of Germany v Commission* [1987] ECR 4013.

[101] For an assessment of the issue of area designation under Article 107(3)(c) see F Wishlade, *Regional State Aid and Competition Policy in the European Union* (The Hague, Kluwer, 2003).

[102] Case T-380/94 *AIUFFASS v Commission* [1996] ECR II-2265, para 54.

[103] Indeed that is the position taken by some authors with regard to cultural justifications under Article 101 TFEU. It is argued that the problem with cultural justifications is that Article 101(3) concerns *EU* and not national interests which means that cultural reasons should not be assessed within that context. C Schmid, 'Diagonal Competence Conflicts between European Competition Law and National Regulation—A Conflict of Laws Reconstruction of the Dispute on Book Price Fixing' 8 *European Review of Private Law* (2000) 155, 164.

[104] Commission 'Communication on certain legal aspects relating to cinematographic and other audiovisual works' [2002] OJ C 43/6.

[105] Monti, 'Article 81 and Public Policy' (n 92).

influenced the Commission's assessment under Article 101 TFEU as a whole, it is fairly plain that these concerns do not act as trumps.[106] Moreover, as argued above, positive and normative reasons militate against the introduction of non-efficiency based considerations within Article 101(3) TFEU.

A more nuanced consideration of the EU interest is involved in the scrutiny of the policy interests that may justify maintaining measures that restrict the four freedoms. Unlike the Treaty-based justifications, mandatory, or overriding requirements are the fruit of judicial creativity. The list of interests that could fit into this category is an open-ended one, as fresh concerns could be brought forward as legitimate justifications. Mandatory requirements arise within national contexts and are then recognised as legitimate by the EU judicature. In order to be justified by the mandatory requirements doctrine, national regulatory measures should be recognised as necessary to pursue a public interest. Although the interest might be a distinctly national one, mandatory requirements are scrutinised from the point of view of EU law, which involves an EU dimension of the public interest.[107] While the approach of the jurisprudence on mandatory requirements, especially in the field of consumer law, tends towards a certain degree of approximation between national regulatory patterns, domestic regulatory preferences do—on occasion—gain recognition.[108]

4. CONCLUSION

Despite the considerable injection of micro-economics into State aid policy fostered by the State Aid Action Plan, State aid remains a distant relative of antitrust law. While there are, as we shall see in the following chapter, areas in the definition of State aid in which economic notions are given crucial weight, the analysis of the impact of State aid on trade and competition remains largely confined to satisfying the Commission's duty to provide reasons for its decisions, and often relies on legal presumptions. Moreover, even if the more refined economic approach has some bite in the assessment of the compatibility of State aid measures with the internal market, economics plays a purely instrumental role which consists in containing the anti-competitive impact resulting from the pursuit of non-competition policy objectives.

[106] Ibid.

[107] The task of examining national measures for their compliance with the doctrine of mandatory requirements is a matter often carried out by the courts under the guidance of the CJEU, though the application of the law to the facts is a matter entirely for national courts to determine. This division of judicial competences has not always been observed by the CJEU.

[108] Eg Case C-220/98 *Estée Lauder Cosmetics GmbH & Co OHG v Lancaster Group GmbH* [2000] ECR I-117, para 29. See also S Weatherill, 'Recent Case Law Concerning the Free Movement of Goods: Mapping the Frontiers of Market Deregulation' (1999) 36 *CML Rev* 51.

The previous chapter referred to Maduro's taxonomy of models of economic constitution, according to which there are three models: a 'centralised' model, which favours market re-regulation at the European level to complement negative integration; a 'competitive model', which holds that the optimal level of market regulation should emerge spontaneously through mutual recognition and regulatory competition; and a 'decentralised model', which allows Member States to retain regulatory powers but requires them not to discriminate against foreign products/persons.

The overview carried out in this chapter seems to suggest that the State aid regime is light years away from an ordo/neo-liberal 'competitive' model of economic constitution. State aid, it has been argued, represents a significant constraint on the Member States' freedom to stimulate regulatory competition. The imposition of uniform standards, both through the prohibition of certain forms of regulation, and through the channeling of aid towards common objectives, reduces the opportunities that Member States have to rely on subsidies or on selective regulation as a means of attracting business to their location. The role of State aid control in preventing or curtailing the strategic use of regulation, and the degree of centralisation and discretion that it entails, is arguably what makes this policy stand out in the law of the internal market.

The questions that this chapter has considered have taken the existence of State aid within the meaning of Article 107(1) TFEU for granted. Yet, once we consider (as the following chapters will do) the detail of the legal problems surrounding the definition of State aid, and the circumstances in which public intervention falls outside of the scope of State aid, a more nuanced picture will emerge, which contemplates elements of decentralisation.

Part II

4

The State as Market Participant

State participation in economic activity has long been a common phenomenon in European economies. The founding fathers of the European Community took it for granted, but decided to regulate its various manifestations. This chapter investigates the role of State aid in constraining the freedom of Member States to participate in market transactions. The key notion in this respect is the principle of the market operator, a principle, which, from the 1980s onwards, has played a central role in setting the boundary line between legitimate transactions entered into by Member States and State aid. In setting a model of behaviour which the Member States' public authorities must follow in order to escape the prohibition of Article 107(1) TFEU, the principle grafts the 'rationality' of the market onto the State.

The chapter is structured as follows. It begins by considering the problem of State attribution, whether, in other words, the conduct of an undertaking controlled by the State may be imputed to the State, and by sketching out the legal principle of the market operator, which sets in where Member States intervene in commercial transactions. It then moves on to assess the normative significance of the principle, and to offer some conclusions on the limits of State intervention in light of the market operator principle.

1. STATE ATTRIBUTION

In order to fall within Article 107(1) TFEU, a measure should be attributable to a Member State and involve the use of public funds. The two criteria are connected but can be, and should be, treated separately.[1] State attribution is usually not in question where the measure emanates directly from a public authority, either at central or at local level. An exception is the *Deutsche Bahn* case, which concerned a German law that, in line with the Mineral Oil Directive, exempted commercial airliners from the mineral oil tax established under the Directive.[2] The General Court, upholding the Commission decision on the case, held that the measure

[1] Case T-351/02 *Deutsche Bahn v Commission* [2006] ECR II-1047, para 103.

[2] Council Directive 92/81/EEC [1992] OJ L316/2.

could not be attributed to the State as Germany had no discretion in implementing the Directive.

Most problems of attribution arise, instead, where public undertakings are involved, for not all forms of public *ownership* of, and/or public control over, undertakings *automatically* call the State aid provisions into play.[3] In *Stardust Marine*,[4] it was made clear that an undertaking may escape the constraints of State aid control where it is able to put some clear blue water between itself and the State, that is to say, where its conduct is not imputable to the State. The Commission had inferred the imputation to the State of financial assistance granted to Stardust Marine by two subsidiaries of the State-owned bank *Crédit Lyonnais* from the sheer fact that they were indirectly controlled by the State. The Court of Justice rejected this approach. According to the Court, even if an undertaking was under State control and even if the State was *able* to exercise a dominant influence over its operations, '*actual exercise* of that control in a particular case' could not be automatically presumed.[5] Instead, the real question was whether the public undertaking enjoyed a sufficient degree of autonomy from the State to allow it to act independently. It was also necessary to examine whether the public authorities had been involved, in one way or another, in the adoption of the measures taken by the public undertaking. The Court acknowledged, however, that State attribution could not involve requiring evidence that the public authorities had specifically incited the public undertaking to take the aid measures in question. Given the close nature of the relationship between States and public undertakings, there was a real risk that State aid could be channelled through the latter in a non-transparent way and in breach of the rules on State aid.[6] The nature of this relationship also made proving that aid measures taken by the public undertaking were in fact adopted on the instructions of the public authorities a particularly arduous exercise. For these reasons, the Court held that imputation to the State of an aid measure taken by a public undertaking could be *inferred from a set of indicators* arising from the circumstances of the case and the *context* in which that measure was taken.[7]

The Court went on to consider the indicators that could be taken into account for this purpose. Its past jurisprudence had given decisive weight to the consideration that the body in question could not take the contested decision without taking account of the requirements of the public authorities, or the fact that the undertaking had to take account of directives issued by a government body.[8] The

[3] Such problems have acquired greater topicality with the recent spate of nationalisations.

[4] Case C-482/99 *French Republic v Commission* ('Stardust Marine') [2002] ECR I-4397.

[5] Ibid para 52.

[6] Ibid para 53.

[7] Ibid para 54.

[8] Respectively, in: Cases C-67, 68 & 70/85 *Kwekerij Gebroeders van der Kooy BV and others v Commission of the European Communities* [1988] ECR 219; Case C-303/88 *Italy v Commission* [1991] ECR I-1433.

Court provided a long (and non-exhaustive) list of other indicators that could be relevant in drawing this inference. These were:

> [the undertaking's] integration into the structures of the public administration, the nature of its activities and the exercise of the latter on the market in normal conditions of competition with private operators, the legal status of the undertaking (in the sense of its being subject to public law or ordinary company law), the intensity of the supervision exercised by the public authorities over the management of the undertaking, or any other indicator showing, in the particular case, an involvement by the public authorities in the adoption of a measure or the unlikelihood of their not being involved, having regard also to the compass of the measure, its content or the conditions which it contains.[9]

The Court considered the issue of State attribution further in *Pearle*.[10] The reference concerned charges imposed by the Dutch 'Central Industry Board for Skilled Trades' on its members to fund a collective advertising campaign for the benefit of the undertakings in the optical services sector: the question was whether the charges amounted to State aid in favour of the latter. The Court found that even if the Board was a public body, the funds it raised through the levy were not made available to the national authorities, but were, instead, allocated by the Board to the advertising campaign which benefited its members. Moreover, the organisation and operation of that advertising campaign was due to a private association of opticians, and not to the Board, which, instead, served as a 'vehicle for the levying and allocating of resources collected for a purely commercial purpose previously determined by the trade and which had nothing to do with a policy determined by the Netherlands authorities'.[11]

Pearle was distinguished in *Salvat*,[12] a direct action against a Commission decision concerning certain para-fiscal measures introduced by a French professional body representing wine producers (CIVDN) in order to encourage producers to discontinue the use of a designation of origin which had proved to be particularly difficult to market, and to support their transition towards different productive strategies. In challenging the decision, the wine producers' body held, inter alia, that the measures were not attributable to the French State. Yet *Pearle*, the General Court found, was of no assistance to the applicants. First, while the funds used by CIVDN in order to pay for the measures, as in *Pearle*, had to be collected from its members, it was also clear that such measures were paid using a subsidy from a public authority and financed from funds which did not come solely from the collection of members' contributions, but were also, in part, debited from that body's general budget. In the second place, the applicants had not demonstrated

[9] Ibid para 57.
[10] Case C-345/02 *Pearle and Others* [2004] ECR I-7139.
[11] Ibid para 37.
[12] Case T-136/05 *EARL Salvat père & fils, Comité interprofessionnel des vins doux naturels et vins de liqueur à appellations contrôlées (CIVDN) and Comité national des interprofessions des vins à appellation d'origine (CNIV) v Commission* [2007] ECR II-4063.

that the beneficiaries of the aid were always those liable to pay the charges—on the contrary, it appeared that certain undertakings made substantial contributions without receiving any benefit in return. Thirdly, unlike in *Pearle*, there was no evidence that the initiative for the organisation and implementation of the measures in issue was attributable to some private association and not to the CIVDN; the latter had not acted as a conduit for any private association. Lastly, and again contrary to the situation in *Pearle*, where the sums had been collected for a purely commercial purpose and not in furtherance of a public policy, the applicants themselves had acknowledged that the establishment of the contributions which financed the initiatives formed part of a policy pursued by the State.

The question that may arise is whether the conduct of a public undertaking which acts in a commercially unsound manner should be regarded as being under the direction of the State. The *Stardust Marine* indicators suggest that the conduct of an undertaking should be taken into account in determining the degree of public interference. The fact that an undertaking takes commercial decisions that do not appear to conform to the logic of the market may indicate the existence of State influence on the undertaking's behaviour. Yet, other things being equal, that factor may not *in itself* be sufficient to prove the existence of State involvement: in other words, it seems that, in the absence of other indicators that support that inference, it is not possible to attribute unsound business judgements to the State.

One may find this interpretation objectionable, as situations that are substantially identical to a subsidy (in terms of their effects) may fall outside of the scope of Article 107(1) TFEU. Why, one may wonder, should an independent commercial decision taken by an undertaking which is financially dependent on the State be immune from State aid control when its actions may distort competition to the same extent and in the same manner as would be the case if those decisions were taken under specific instructions from the State? The answer calls into question the nature of the EU's economic constitution. Article 345 TFEU safeguards the Member States' freedom to maintain mixed economic systems, which includes the use of public undertakings to carry out government policy, but also the freedom for public undertakings to perform pure market activities alongside private undertakings. Plainly, if the conduct of public undertakings was automatically to be ascribed to the State, the independence of public undertakings would be undermined. To be meaningful, commercial autonomy should entail the freedom to take irrational business decisions.[13] Yet, from the EU's perspective, alongside strict monitoring of the undertakings' autonomy, which, admittedly is far from straightforward,[14] the internal market (and domestic taxpayers') interest

[13] Although the Commission often emphasises the effects of State aid on taxpayers, its role under the Treaty is not to champion the interests of taxpayers. The latter may, and often will, coincide with the interests pursued by EU State aid law, but it is not a necessary connection. See, however, L Coppi, 'The Role of Economics in State Aid Analysis and the Balancing Test' in E Szyszczak (ed), *Research Handbook on State Aid* (Cheltenham, Edward Elgar, 2011) 64–90.

[14] It has been remarked that the perception of an exceedingly narrow interpretation of commercial independence would lead undertakings to trade-off swift decision-making against the risks arising

is protected where poor commercial judgement leads the public undertaking to resort to the State for financial backing. In such cases, the market operator principle, to which we now turn, comes into its own.

2. THE MARKET OPERATOR PRINCIPLE AND ITS RAMIFICATIONS

The market operator principle is one of the key concepts of State aid. The question it addresses is whether the State confers an advantage that its recipient would not receive under normal market conditions.[15] The first formulation of the principle to have emerged from the Commission's practice is the so-called 'market economy *investor* principle', which assesses the significance of State shareholdings in undertakings in the light of the typical behaviour of the average private market investor.[16] If the State provides an undertaking with financial resources which, in principle, the latter could have obtained on the market, it enters into an investment which reflects 'normal market conditions' and, therefore, places itself outside the scope of EU State aid law. The difficulty lies in identifying the appropriate comparator for this exercise.[17] The comparator may be either hypothetical or actual, the latter being the most straightforward scenario. In fact, if private investors are also involved, the fact may help to establish whether the investment is a sound one. However, the Member State needs to prove that the private and public parties participate on *equal terms and conditions*.[18] Thus, in *Air France*, the Court rejected the argument that concomitant private investment was sufficient to exclude the presence of State aid, in that the value of the securities to which the private investors actually subscribed, and of those which they wished to subscribe to, were considerably below the total value of securities subscribed by the State.[19]

from a failure to notify (through their governments) a potentially unlawful measure. This emphasises the need for clear guidance from the Commission and the EU judicature. See T Lubbig and M von Merveldt, '*Stardust Marine*: Introducing Imputability into State Aid Rules—Plain Sailing into Calm Seas or Rowing Back into Shallow Waters?' (2003) 24 *European Competition Law Review* 629.

15 Case C-39/94 *SFEI and Others* [1996], para 60; Case C-342/96 *Spain v Commission* [1999] ECR I-2459, para 49.

16 Commission Communication on the application of Articles 92 and 93 of the EC Treaty to public authorities holdings, Bulletin EC 9 1984. See also the later Communication on the application of Articles 92 and 93 of the EC Treaty to public undertakings in the manufacturing sector, [1993] OJ C 307/3. The Court endorsed the principle in Case 40/85 *Belgium v Commission (Boch)* [1986] ECR 2321.

17 M Ross, 'State Aids and National Courts: Definitions and other Problems—a Case of Premature Emancipation?' (2000) 37 *CML Rev* 401.

18 Case T-296/97 *Alitalia v Commission* [2002] ECR II-3871, para 81.

19 T-358/94 *Air France v Commission* [1997] ECR II-2109, paras 148–49. On another occasion, Joined Cases C-328/99 and C-399/00 *Italian Republic and SIM 2 Multimedia SpA v Commission* [2003] ECR I-4035, the concomitance argument was dismissed by noting that, even if the private participation was significant, the (public and private) investors had behaved in a way that did not respond to the criteria of rationality that an average investor would follow. The Court thus implicitly accepted the Commission's strongly worded statement that public authorities 'should not become involved in senseless investments even if poorly advised private investors take that risk', para 29.

In the absence of a concomitant investment, the comparator is necessarily hypothetical. The attributes that define the conduct of the comparator are his (or her) being 'rational',[20] 'informed',[21] or 'prudent'.[22] Such standards of behaviour typically dictate that a commercial decision should be guided by prospects of profitability.[23] Profitability, however, does not necessarily require the adoption of a short-term outlook, as considerations such as the desire to maintain a group's image or to redirect its activities may come into play, provided that profitability is ensured at least on a long-term perspective.[24] However, social, political or other considerations that a private investor would not typically take into account are to be discarded by public authorities acting in their capacity as investors. In the *WestLB* judgment, the General Court has also made clear that the profitability requirement, whether in its short- or long-term version, means that the investor should seek to achieve the 'maximum reasonable return' as opposed to limited profits.[25] Whilst the 1993 Communication on the application of State aid to public undertakings in the manufacturing sector stated that an *existing* investor may accept a lower return when increasing an investment,[26] *WestLB* suggests that that approach might no longer hold sway.

The paradigm of the average market operator comes into play even where a public body does not invest but is *owed* money. Whenever the State is to decide whether to reschedule or to waive debts, the model of the private investor gives way to the private creditor test. Unlike the private investor, the private creditor does not pursue profit, but is concerned with finding the most effective means of recovering a debt.[27] This was first made clear in *Tubacex*.[28] The case concerned agreements between an insolvent undertaking and Fogasa, a Spanish body responsible for paying employees' salaries in the event of an employer's insolvency,[29] and the Social Security Fund, whereby Tubacex would repay the sums due and repayment of social security contributions at the statutory rate. The Commission considered these agreements as loans and found that the interest rate charged by Fogasa was below the market rate. The Court took a different line.

[20] Case T-98/00 *Linde v Commission* [2002] ECR II-396, para 149.

[21] Eg Joined cases T-228/99 and T-233/99 *Westdeutsche Landesbank Girozentrale v Commission* [2003] ECR II-435, para 255.

[22] Eg Case 482/99 *France v Commission* [2002] ECR I-4397.

[23] Ibid para 84; *WestLB* (n 21) para 255.

[24] Case C-305/89 *Italian Republic v Commission* [1991] ECR I-1603, para 20; Joined Cases T-126/96 and T-127/96 *BFM and EFIM v Commission* [1998] ECR II-3437, para 79; Case T-296/97 *Alitalia v Commission* [2000] ECR II-3871, para 96.

[25] *WestLB* (n 21) para 314.

[26] Commission Communication (n 16).

[27] Case C-256/97 *DMT* [1999] ECR I-3913, Opinion of Advocate General Jacobs, paras 35–36; Case 480/98 *Spain v Commission* [2000] ECR I-8717, Opinion of Advocate General Mischo; Case C-276/02 *Spain v Commission* [2004] ECR I-8091, Opinion of Advocate General Maduro.

[28] Case C-342/96 *Spain v Commission* [1999] ECR I-2459.

[29] Pursuant to Council Directive 80/987/EEC of 20 October 1980 on the approximation of the laws of the Member States relating to the protection of employees in the event of the insolvency of their employer [1980] OJ L283/23.

Such agreements could not be viewed as loans but as a renegotiation of existing debts by a creditor who, unlike a loan provider, was concerned not with pursuing a profit, but with recovering the sums it was owed.[30]

A crucial issue, in this context, is the cost-benefit analysis that the private creditor test is supposed to carry out with regard to the decision to cause the debtor undertaking to wind up or to waive recovery of debts and allow the undertaking to continue to operate. According to Advocate General Poiares Maduro, the latter choice must fulfil three conditions:

> First, it must be possible in principle to make the undertaking economically viable and to improve its financial position. Second, everything possible must be done in order to prevent further credit being obtained and new debts accumulated. Third, the State must be able to rely on the recovery of the debts owed to it within a reasonable period.[31]

The private operator principle may also apply to transactions involving the sale of assets. Again, the underlying rationale is that the price should reflect normal market conditions. Privatisations may give rise to a number of State aid problems concerning the price paid, the terms of sale, or previous State aid liabilities of the privatised undertaking.[32] The Commission's policy is to presume that no State aid is involved if the sale has occurred through flotation on the stock market,[33] or through an open and unconditional tender.[34] Moreover, the Commission accepts as a valid defence, and a reason for Member States legitimately to abstain from notification, the existence of independent expert reports commissioned *prior* to the sale. The Court of First Instance has stretched the Commission's policy in its *Valmont* judgment.[35] Publicly owned land had been sold to Valmont without a prior tender procedure or a prior expert report; that alone, according to the Commission, was sufficient to trigger the presumption that the measure contained State aid. The General Court, however, rejected the existence of such a presumption and held, instead, that the Commission should have examined the

30 For a critique see A Criscuolo, 'The State in a Liberal Market Economy: A Private Investor and Creditor or a Public Authority' (1999) 24 *EL Rev* 525.

31 Case C-276/02 *Spain v Commission* (n 27) para 25. See also Case T-1/08 *Buczek Automotive* (not yet reported) in which the General Court found that the Commission had not applied the private creditor test correctly.

32 On which see F Töpler and J Butler, 'Proceed with Care: Purchasing Companies with Potential State Aid Liabilities' (2004) 25 *European Competition Law Review* 421; I Simonsson, 'Privatisation and State Aid—Time for a New Policy' (2005) 26 *European Competition Law Review* 460.

33 Flotation is deemed not to involve State aid even if debt is written off or reduced prior to the sale, provided that the proceeds exceed the reduction in debt. See 23rd Report on Competition Policy (1993) 255.

34 The Commission will also accept that no aid is involved where the State follows a procedure similar to public procurement in which: a) a competitive tender is held that is open to all comers, transparent and not conditional on the performance of other acts; b) the company is sold at the highest bidder; c) bidders are given enough time and information to carry out a proper valuation of the assets as the basis for their bid. Specific guidelines, based on the same principle, apply to the sale of public land: Communication on State aid elements in sales of land and buildings by public authorities [1997] OJ C209/3.

35 Case T-274/01 *Valmont Nederland BV v Commission* [2004] ECR II-3145, para 45.

expert report even if carried out after the sale had taken place. The Commission was to compare the sale price to the price suggested in the export report, which could only result in a finding that State aid had been granted if there was a sufficient divergence between the two.

The State may also confer State aid when purchasing goods or services. One of the most controversial areas for the application of the market operator test is the compensation for the provision of Services of General Economic Interest (SGEIs). As we shall see in chapter seven, the difficulty in applying a market-orientated approach in this area resides in the awkwardness of attempting to relate to market-based criteria services that, in the absence of regulation, would not normally be delivered by the market. Jurisprudential oscillations in this area stem from this difficulty. As in the case of privatisations, however, the Commission and the EU Courts have favoured a solution that promotes the use of public procurement procedures, that is, the creation of a market through regulatory means. Outside the sphere of public services, the Commission and Courts have also added that, for public purchases to reflect normal market conditions, it is not sufficient that the price paid by the State reflect the market value of the goods/services in issue; the purchase must also originate from a genuine need for such goods/services.[36]

A. Questioning the Market Operator Principle

A key feature of the market operator principle is its flexible and open textured nature, plainly a consequence of the principle's origins as a compromise between competing visions of the role of the State as market participant, but also a consequence of the interface that it creates between legal and economic concepts. The principle seeks to achieve a delicate balance in reconciling the need to extend the application of the EU rules to the commercial activities of Member States with the need to avoid preventing any kind of State participation in the economy and suppressing diversity among domestic preferences regarding the role of the State in the economy. The reliance on economic concepts in the definition of the outer limits of State aid is similarly fraught: the risk in this respect is for the principle to fail to reflect the economic reality that it is supposed to capture, but also to be susceptible to criticism on legal grounds.

The market operator principle has rarely been subjected to critical scrutiny in the research literature. A notable exception is Parish.[37] His main argument is that the principle rests on conceptually frail ground and poses a serious threat to legal certainty. The principle, he argues, is conceptually flawed in that it relies

[36] Joined Cases T-116/01 and T-118/01 *P&O European Ferries (Vizcaya) SA and Diputación Foral de Vizcaya v Commission* [2003] ECR II-2957, para 117; the judgment was upheld on appeal in Case C-442/03 P *P&O European Ferries (Vizcaya) SA and Diputación Foral de Vizcaya v Commission* [2006] ECR I-4845.

[37] M Parish, 'On the private investor principle' (2003) 28 *EL Rev* 70.

on a comparator which is an 'idealisation' of the figure of the economic agent; in the real world, no private investor engages in decision-making in 'such a pure fashion' as the Commission (and the Court) would have it. In order to reach the definition of its ideal-type, the principle strips decision-making of all motives bar the maximisation of profit. Yet, Parish argues, there are two problems with this. First, although EU law purports to base the assessment of State intervention on its effects rather than its intention, it is immediately apparent that the market operator principle implies an investigation of the public authority's motives and aims; it does not ignore motives, instead, it *selects* them. Secondly, by promoting behaviour motivated by sheer self-interest, EU law appears to promote a neo-liberal view of the relationship between the State and the market which is plainly at odds with the Treaty of Rome's neutrality towards the way in which Member States choose to structure their economies.

B. From Neutrality to Substantive Equality

Parish's claim that the market operator principle threatens the idea of a mixed economy merits further scrutiny. It is indeed the case that in Article 345 TFEU the Treaty appears to commit the EU to a position of 'neutrality' or 'agnosticism' towards the national choices regarding property ownership.[38] Moreover, evidence of tolerance towards mixed economic systems is easily found throughout the Treaty. Article 37 TFEU, which governs the existence of State monopolies of a commercial character and Article 106 TFEU, which concerns public undertakings, or undertakings endowed by the State with special or exclusive rights, are provisions based on the idea that Member States may continue to play a role in economic life by acting as market participants, provided that, in doing so, they do not undermine the fulfilment of the EU's internal market objectives. This is hardly surprising. In the 1950s, the State's role as a direct participant in economic activity was a given. The Treaty did not seek to challenge that state of affairs, and Article 345 TFEU was, in fact, understood to safeguard State ownership.

It might seem surprising that, while seeking to liberalise trade between Member States, the Treaty legitimised the continued presence of public undertakings. Yet, one should not be oblivious to the fact that the reconstruction of European economies and the spectacular growth in the post-war period largely depended on various forms of State intervention.[39] Public ownership, in particular, has been, for a number of reasons, political and ideological, but also economic ones, a crucial feature of the European post-war economy, a feature which did not

[38] The term agnosticism is used in E Szyszczak, *The Regulation of the State in Competitive Markets in the EU* (Oxford, Hart Publishing, 2007). See also B Akkermans and E Ramaekers, 'Article 345 TFEU (ex Article 295 EC), Its Meanings and Interpretations' (2009) 15 *European Law Journal* 292.

[39] A Milward, *The European Rescue of the Nation State*, 2nd edn (London, Routledge, 2000).

solely derive from an ideological commitment to collective ownership or towards centralised economic planning, or from the desire to build and maintain political consensus, but from economic reasons too. Market failures, such as natural monopoly, lack of privately-supplied risk-capital, regional disparities, and widespread unemployment, played a significant part in justifying the creation and maintenance of public undertakings.[40]

With the economic downturn of the 1970s, and the 'degeneration' of State intervention,[41] the tide began to turn and the role of the State as market participant came to be surrounded by a negative aura.[42] In 1978, the Danish Presidency of the European Council requested the Commission to issue a statement on its policy on State aid in light of the economic problems in order to initiate an exchange of views on the matter. In its communication, the Commission drew some explicit links between the use of State aid and the (then) current economic situation.[43] 'The economic crisis, with the resultant high levels of unemployment and slow growth, could' it held 'lead to the danger of a drift towards protectionism ... through the growth in number and intensity of State aids'.[44] The increased focus on State aid brought with it a need to ensure that the Commission's efforts in scrutinising State aid measures would not be frustrated by the opacity of the arrangements between Member States and publicly-owned undertakings. A directive was enacted, which required governments to provide information on their relations with public undertakings thus allowing the Commission to exercise its powers under the State aid provisions.[45] The aim was to ensure that any public

[40] G Majone, 'The rise of the regulatory State in Europe' (1994) 17 *West European Politics* 77; C Lawson, 'The Theory of State-Owned Enterprises in Market Economies' (1994) 8 *Journal of Economic Surveys* 283.

[41] Aid was used to keep artificially alive those industries that had been hit the hardest by the forces of international competition.

[42] The case of Italy illustrates the parabola of State ownership/participation. While State-owned undertakings, and undertakings in which the State held a participation were at the very heart of post-war industrial reconstruction and at the root of the 'economic miracle' of the post-war era, by the 1980s, they came to be associated with inefficiency and political corruption. This perception, coupled with pressure from 'Brussels', increased the political acceptability of privatisations. See E Bertero and L Rondi, 'Hardening the soft budget constraint through "upward devolution" to a supranational institution: The case of the European Union and Italian State-owned firms' in L Sun (ed), *Ownership of Governance of Enterprises: Recent Innovative Developments* (London, Palgrave Macmillan, 2003) 124–58; see also F Barca and S Trento, 'State ownership and the evolution of Italian corporate governance' (1997) 6 *Industrial and Corporate Change* 533.

[43] Commission, 'Commission Policy on Sectoral Aid Schemes' COM (78) 221 final.

[44] Ibid para 2.

[45] Commission Directive 80/723/EEC on the transparency of financial relations between Member States and public undertakings [1980] OJ L195/35. The Directive was amended by the following: Commission Directive 85/413/EEC [1985] OJ L 229/20; Commission Directive 93/84/EEC [1993] OJ L 254/16; Commission Directive 2000/52/EC [2000] OJ L193/75; Commission Directive 2005/81/EC of 28 November 2005 amending Directive 80/723/EEC on the transparency of financial relations between Member States and public undertakings as well as on financial transparency within certain undertakings [2005] OJ L312/47. On the first version of the Directive see M Brothwood, 'The Commisssion Directive on Transparency of Financial Relations between Member States and Public Undertakings' (1981) *CML Rev* 207.

funds made available directly or indirectly to public undertakings, and the use to which public funds were actually put, would emerge clearly. This was a fundamental step in the enforcement of State aid—the 1980s saw an exponential increase in the detection of State aid, much of it directed towards the public sector.

Against this economic, political and ideological background,[46] the contours of Article 345 TFEU began to reveal a rather different content: the increase in the EU's attention towards the State's activities, in fact, led to the suggestion that such developments were undermining the very idea of 'neutrality' that Article 345 TFEU had grafted onto the European economic constitution.[47] However, when Member States voiced these concerns, these were consistently dismissed by the Court.[48] In the aftermath of the Transparency Directive, France, Italy and the UK brought a challenge claiming that the Directive placed on public undertakings burdens that their private competitors did not have to bear. The Court replied as follows:

> It should be borne in mind that the principle of equality, to which the governments refer in connection with the relationship between public and private undertakings in general, presupposes that the two are in comparable situations. Within the limits laid down by the applicable legislation, private undertakings determine their industrial and commercial strategy by taking into account in particular requirements of profitability. Decisions of public undertakings, on the other hand, may be affected by factors of a different kind within the framework of the pursuit of objectives of public interest by public authorities which may exercise an influence over those decisions. The economic and financial consequences of the impact of such factors lead to the establishment between those undertakings and public authorities of financial relations of a special kind which differ from those existing between public authorities and private undertakings.[49]

More recently, in *WestLB*, Article 345 TFEU was invoked (by the applicants) to argue that the Commission's application of the market operator principle resulted in unequal treatment between the public and the private sectors, to the public sector's detriment. While the behaviour of a public investor was to be assessed against the benchmark of a typical market investor, the applicants argued, the same was not true of the behaviour of private investors. The General Court held:

> The principle of equal treatment prohibits like cases from being treated differently, thereby subjecting some to disadvantages as opposed to others, without such differentiation being justified by the existence of substantial objective differences ... However, a

[46] The period coincided with the increasing appeal of neo-liberal economic ideologies to the European elites.

[47] W Devroe, 'Privatizations and Community Law: Neutrality versus Policy' (1997) 34 *CML Rev* 267; A Verhoeven, 'Privatisation and EC Law: is the European Commission "Neutral" with respect to Public versus Private ownership of Companies?' (1996) 45 *ICLQ* 861.

[48] For the Commission's position see Communication of the Commission to the Member States concerning public authorities' holdings in company capital, 17 September 1984, in Bulletin EC, 9-1984. For the Court, inter alia, Case C-303/88 *Italy v Commission* [1991] ECR I-1433, para 20; Case C-261/89 *Italy v Commission* [1991] ECR I-4437, para 15; and Case T-358/94 *Air France v Commission* [1996] ECR II-2109, para 70.

[49] Joined Cases 188 to 190/80 *French Republic, Italian Republic and United Kingdom of Great Britain and Northern Ireland v Commission of the European Communities* [1982] ECR-2545, para 21.

> public investor is not in the same situation as a private investor. The private investor can count only on his own resources in order to finance his investments and is liable, up to the limits of those resources, for the consequences of his decisions. The public investor, on the other hand, has access to resources flowing from the exercise of public power, in particular from taxation. Consequently, as the situations of those two types of investors are not the same, there is no discrimination against the public investor if the conduct of an informed private investor is taken into account in order to assess the conduct of the public investor.[50]

It seems clear from this interpretation of Article 345 TFEU that the recognition of the peculiar nature of the link between public authorities and public undertakings does not mean that Member States may shelter public undertakings from the impact of EU law. In fact, the Court holds that the nature of that relationship creates a competitive imbalance between the public and the private sector that EU law should seek to redress. The emphasis does not lie on safeguarding the role of the State as market participant but on preventing an abuse of economic power by the State, a reading of Article 345 TFEU which appears to eschew a deferential approach to State ownership.

This reading, however, also seems to be at odds with EU law's claim to neutrality vis-a-vis national choices concerning property ownership. Neutrality is associated with formal equality; the idea, that is, that the same rules apply to public and private market participants in the same fashion. Yet, a fundamental feature of State aid law is that its rules regulate the behaviour of States, not that of undertakings. Moreover, under the market operator principle, the point of view of the *private* market operator becomes the paradigm against which to assess the *public* market operator's behaviour. This apparent inequality finds its justification in a *substantive* notion of equality, which entails the formulation of special rules designed to redress the fundamental competitive imbalance created by the presence of the State on the market. Equality, it seems, lies not in the application of the market operator principle, which involves asymmetrical treatment, but in the outcome that the principle seeks to achieve, which is, the equality of competitive conditions.

While neutrality appears to throw scant light on the interpretation of the market operator principle, it is also true, however, that the EU's approach to State intervention is not *incompatible* with the principle of neutrality, if neutrality is understood purely as a negative commitment—a commitment, that is, to abstain from imposing changes to the legal *status* of property ownership within the Member States.[51] State aid does not formally *require* such changes to be made. Yet, any form of EU regulatory intervention which, in seeking to redress a fundamental inequality between public and private market participants, makes deep inroads into national economic choices, which fall short of imposing a change

[50] *WestLB* (n 21) para 272.

[51] This is also the Court's understanding of the legitimacy under Article 345 TFEU of EU intervention affecting intellectual property rights: whilst the Treaty does not affect those rights, their exercise may be restricted by Treaty prohibitions. See Case 119/75 *Terrapin v Terranova* [1976] ECR 1039, para 5.

in the legal nature of ownership, is deemed to be compatible with Article 345 TFEU. A teleological interpretation would have involved a commitment not to *undermine* the participation of the State in commercial operations, which would seriously have curtailed the application of the market operator principle. Instead, the Court's view of Article 345 TFEU is consistent with a state of affairs in which the effect of EU law is to induce a Member State to question, and reconfigure, its role as market participant.

The series of events surrounding the issue of the German regional banks illustrates this point. The network of regional public banks, the so-called Landesbanken, is considered to be a cornerstone of the German model of capitalism. During the post-war reconstruction of the country and the strong economic growth that followed, the banks acted as corporate lenders to regional businesses, provided financial services to the local governments, and acted as clearing banks to local savings banks (the 'Sparkassen'). The Landesbanken also played a crucial part in the implementation of industrial policy and regional economic development. All such activities were made possible by robust public support in the form of a liability guarantee ('Anstaltlast') and an institutional guarantee ('Gewärträgerhaftung').[52] This meant that the Landesbanken, which, because of this guarantee, commanded the highest ratings for their financial products among international credit rating agencies, were able to borrow at significantly lower cost and to expand their activities beyond their traditional remit and beyond the regional (and national) borders. In the 1990s, in fact, the Landesbanken began competing directly with large commercial banks in international financial markets.

The financing system of the Landesbanken came under attack when the German federation of commercial banks lodged a complaint with the Commission claiming that Westdeutsche Landesbank (WestLB) had received illegal State aid from its majority shareholder, the Land Nord-Rhein Westfalen. The aid stemmed from the decision of the latter State's parliament to transfer to WestLB the assets of its Housing Promotion Agency, a body that had existed as an independent public law institution. The increase in the bank's equity capital arising from the transfer, so the commercial banks claimed, had not been adequately remunerated. The Commission opened the formal investigation procedure on the case. Crucially, a few months later, during the Amsterdam intergovernmental conference, the German government (under pressure from the regional governments) sought a formal recognition at EU level that Article 345 TFEU prevented State aid rules from applying to guarantees to public banks. However, it failed to obtain the

52 The Anstaltlast was recognised as a general principle of law under German law. It consisted in an unlimited guarantee by the regional authorities which was not remunerated and ensured not only the financial viability of credit institutions, but also made it impossible for banks to become bankrupt. Gewärträgerhaftung, which was introduced by law, ensured the direct liability of regional governments towards the banks' creditors in the event of insolvency. See S Moser, N Pesaresi, K Soukup, 'State Guarantees to German Public Banks: A New Step in the Enforcement of State Aid Discipline to Financial Services in the Community' (2002) 2 *EC Competition Policy Newsletter* 1. For political background, see MP Smith, *States of Liberalization* (New York, State University of New York Press, 2005).

necessary support in Council, and had to accept a far weaker statement in a declaration annexed to the Amsterdam Treaty, which simply recognised the public service role performed by the public banks, and stated that, while the financial arrangements between the banks and regional governments were a matter for Germany, such facilities should not affect the conditions of competition beyond what was required in order to perform these particular tasks and which was contrary to the interests of the Community.[53]

In 1999 the Commission decided that WestLB had received illegal State aid that it would have to pay back to the Land of Nord-Rhein Westafalen. The decision was based, inter alia, on the finding that the Land had not acted as a normal market investor, as such an investor would have demanded a higher rate of return in exchange for transferring the Housing Development Funds to WestLB. All attempts by the German authorities and WestLB to deploy Article 345 TFEU were firmly rebuffed by the Commission. In particular, the argument was made that because of the statutory constraints imposed by the special purpose assigned to the Housing Development Fund, the only possible use of these resources was to transfer them to a similar public law body. As the transfer represented the most commercially sensible option, any remuneration for the transfer would be justified under the market investor principle. The Commission recognised the Member States' autonomy in deciding to use 'public funds for public sovereign purposes', and their freedom not to demand any profits in return. It also recognised 'the right of the Member States to create special-purpose funds in order to fulfil tasks of general interest'. However, it added, 'as soon as the State decides to assign public-purpose assets to a commercial use, normal market-economy rules have to be applied'.[54]

In the meantime, the liability guarantee and the institutional guarantee, the very core of the public assistance to Landesbanken, had also attracted the Commission's scrutiny. The impulse for the investigation came from a complaint lodged by private banks through the European Banking Federation.[55] After a failed attempt to convince the parties to find a national solution, and a long process of confrontation and mediation, involving a number of different actors and interests at Commission, national, and sub-national level, the German authorities reached

[53] Declaration 37 annexed to the Amsterdam Treaty: 'The Conference notes the Commission's opinion to the effect that the EU's existing competition rules allow services of general economic interest provided by public credit institutions existing in Germany and the facilities granted to them to compensate for the costs connected with such services to be taken into account in full. In this context, the way in which Germany enables local authorities to carry out their task of making available in their regions a comprehensive and efficient financial infrastructure is a matter for the organisation of that Member State. Such facilities may not adversely affect the conditions of competition to an extent beyond that required in order to perform these particular tasks and which is contrary to the interests of the EU. The Conference recalls that the European Council has invited the Commission to examine whether similar cases exist in the other Member States, to apply as appropriate the same standards on similar cases and to inform the Council in its ECOFIN formation.'

[54] Commission Decision *Westdeutsche Landesbank—Gsirozentrale* [2006] OJ L30/3.

[55] The complaint was backed by a threat by the European Baking Federation to take an Article 232 action against the Commission.

an agreement with the Commission on the gradual phasing out of guarantees. The understanding provided for a four-year transitional period (from 2001 to 2005) after which the guarantees would have to be replaced by 'a commercial owner relationship governed by market economy principles',[56] with the implication that the obligation to support the banks would disappear.

To claim that these developments mark the twilight of the very idea of a mixed economy is to draw an unwarranted conclusion. Yet, there is no doubt that the application of the market operator principle has caused a radical re-orientation in the role of the State as market participant. The idea that the State can exploit its extraordinary economic might to finance *any* economic operation seems destined to become obsolete. The use of the State's power to engage in commercial activities for non-commercial purposes, which is a recurrent phenomenon in many of the European States where a public sector and a private sector co-exist in various areas, is greatly reduced. But so is the use of the State's financial and regulatory might to the benefit of the public undertakings' *commercial* operations.

The constellation of events surrounding the German Landesbanken does not necessarily signify the end of the German model of capitalism.[57] Neither the Commission nor the Court required the public authorities to relinquish ownership of the Landesbanken; but the effect of their determinations is that a system conceived to be intrinsically immune from risk would be obliged to share the typical risks that private banks are exposed to. Many of these banks have resorted to debt to raise capital in anticipation of the end of the system of public guarantees,[58] and many were affected by the recent liquidity crisis on the financial markets.[59] This extension of risk to areas previously sheltered from it is the ostensible effect of the market operator test and is exactly the purpose served by the subjection of State-owned undertakings to the State aid rules. The difficulties that have affected the German Landesbanken in the recent market turmoil provide an eloquent illustration of the dramatic restructuring of economic activities that the pursuit of equality in competitive conditions involves. Where State-backed undertakings would have previously enjoyed the confidence deriving from generous public backing, they now share the same uncertainties and risks as private banks.[60]

56 Moser, Pesaresi and Soukup, 'State Guarantees to German Public Banks' (n 52).

57 MP Smith, 'Who Are the Agents of Europeanisation? EC Competition Policy and German Public Law Banks' (2001) EUI Working Paper 2001/39; E Grossman, 'Europeanization as an Interactive Process: German Public Banks Meet EU State Aid Policy' (2006) 44 *Journal of Common Market Studies* 325.

58 See I Simensen, 'Real test for Landesbanken still lies ahead' *Financial Times*, 28 August 2007.

59 The Commission cleared rescue aid for WestLB in relation to a risk shield granted by the Land Nord-Rhein Westphalen to protect the bank against the volatility of its structured investments portfolio caused by the repercussions of the crisis in financial markets. See *WestLB riskshield* NN 25/2008 (ex CP 15/08) [2008] OJ C189/1.

60 And, as a result of recent events, share the same level of attention from governments as private banks.

i. *The 'Split Personality' of States*

The market operator principle, it has been argued so far, pursues substantive equality. It seeks to achieve a situation in which undertakings, regardless of their relationship with the State, compete on an equal footing. In order to achieve that objective, State aid law seeks to neutralise the effects of State intervention by subjecting it to preventative scrutiny based on market-drawn criteria. At the root of this exercise, however, there is a fundamental distinction in internal market law, which turns on the nature of a Member State's activities, between *imperium* and *dominium*, between State sovereignty and the market, and, arguably, between the State's role as regulator and as market participant.[61]

The distinction appears in the so-called 'transparency directive', introduced to allow the Commission to acquire information concerning transactions between public authorities and public undertakings, which would 'enable a clear distinction to be made between the role of the State *as public authority* and its role *as proprietor*'.[62] According to the Court's interpretation of the directive, that distinction flowed 'from the recognition of the fact that the State may act either by exercising public powers or by carrying on economic activities of an industrial or commercial nature by offering goods and services on the market'.[63] The two roles could be performed by the same body, as, in the words of Advocate General Mischo, 'States frequently have such "split personality"'.[64] Not only is it possible to distinguish between the two dimensions, but, according to the Court, it is also necessary to do so, as undertakings that benefit from public assistance should not be placed in such a position as to benefit from a blending of the commercial and the prerogative sphere.

In *Spain v Commission*,[65] Spain sought the annulment of a Commission decision in which it had found the Spanish authorities (the 'Patrimonio del Estado') to have acted in a manner which was at odds with the market investor test. In the lead-up to privatisation, the Spanish authorities had made a contribution of capital which was costlier than selling the assets of the undertakings, and which clearly had no prospects of profit, given that the undertakings were being sold. Spain attempted to reject this claim by arguing that from a public authority's perspective, accepting a low share price was preferable to liquidating the companies' assets, an operation which would have entailed significant costs to the Patrimonio del Estado. The Court replied to this contention:

> A distinction must be drawn between the obligations which the State must assume as owner for the share capital of a company and its obligations as a public authority. Since the three companies in question were constituted as limited companies, the Patrimonio

[61] T Daintith, 'The Techniques of Government' in J Jowell and D Oliver (eds), *The Changing Constitution* (Oxford, Clarendon Press, 1994); G Majone, *Dilemmas of European Integration* (Oxford, Oxford University Press, 2005) 31.

[62] Commission Directive 80/723/EEC (n 45).

[63] Case 118/85 *Commission v Italy* [1987] ECR-2599, para 7.

[64] Ibid Opinion of Advocate General Mischo, 2612.

[65] Joined Cases C-278–280/92 *Spain v Commission* [1994] ECR I-4103.

> del Estado, as owner of the share capital, would have been liable for their debts up to the liquidation value of their assets. That means in the present case that the obligations arising from the cost of redundancies, payment of unemployment benefits and aid for the restructuring of the industrial infrastructure must not be taken into account for the purpose of applying the private investor test.[66]

A similar approach emerged in a case concerning the privatisation of a steel firm in the former GDR.[67] The Court, as in the previous case, was asked to evaluate the costs and benefits of privatisation and liquidation from a private investor's point of view. One of the arguments that the German government used to defend its decision to privatise was that the alternative, that is, the decision to wind up the undertaking, would have entailed costs associated with the obligation to clear the site. The Court was unconvinced: even if the undertaking was under an obligation to clear the site, a private investor would not have provided it with additional funds when it was to be wound up.

The potential clash between the regulatory and the commercial spheres is a central preoccupation of a number of Treaty provisions, which are designed to resolve possible *conflicts of interest* between the two. Article 106 TFEU provides that, when adopting regulatory measures in regard to undertakings that they endow with exclusive rights or place in an otherwise privileged position, Member States are to exercise their powers in a manner that would not involve a breach of the internal market rules by such undertakings. That provision has been read as preventing Member States from creating a situation where a commercial activity and a regulatory activity are bundled in the same entity, thus creating a conflict of interest. In *France v Commission* (Terminals Equipment),[68] the Court was asked to rule on a directive based on Article 106(1) and (3) TFEU, which obliged Member States to ensure that responsibility for regulatory and supervisory matters regarding telecommunications terminal equipment was entrusted to a body independent of the undertaking operating the public network. The Court held:

> [A] system of undistorted competition, as laid down in the Treaty, can be guaranteed only if equality of opportunity is secured as between the various economic operators. To entrust an undertaking which markets terminal equipment with the task of drawing up the specifications for such equipment, monitoring their application and granting type-approval in respect thereof is tantamount to conferring upon it the power to determine at will which terminal equipment may be connected to the public network, and thereby placing that undertaking at an obvious advantage over its competitors.[69]

In *GB-INNO-BM*,[70] the Court added that the maintenance of effective competition and the guaranteeing of transparency require that the body adopting regulatory

66 Ibid para 22.
67 Case C-334/99 *Germany v Commission* [2003] ECR I-1139.
68 Case C-202/88 *French Republic v Commission (Terminal Equipment)* [1991] ECR I-1277.
69 Ibid para 54.
70 Case 362/88 *GB-INNO-BM v Confédération du commerce luxermbourgeois* [1990] ECR I-667.

measures and granting type-approval is independent of any undertaking acting on the market for terminal equipment.[71]

EU law's treatment of services of general economic interest under Article 106(2) TFEU, the legislation emanating from Article 106(3) TFEU, and the case law on the treatment of potential State aid measures arising from the provision of such services are also instances in which the tension between public interest and market concerns is played out. A central tenet of such regulation is the avoidance of cross-subsidisation from public interest activities to market activities. As we shall see, however, the attempt to sever market participation from the public dimension does not result in a complete separation of the two dimensions, but takes stock of the hybrid nature of this type of public intervention.

ii. The Transformative Role of State Aid Law

The assumption that public, regulatory functions should be kept separate from market activities raises, however, the question whether classifying an activity as pertaining to the State's role as market participant and applying the market operator principle has a bearing on considerations that are typically associated with the exercise of public powers. The existence of public values that are inevitably linked with State intervention, even where such intervention takes the form of participation on the market, makes this a salient question. More precisely, the very fact that public money is involved calls for democratic accountability in national settings. Yet, through the application of the market operator principle, EU law appears to foster a parallel form of accountability. Accountability may be defined as a process through which a body is required to justify its actions towards a forum on the basis of a set of standards and values.[72] The crucial variables in this process are the direction of accountability (who is accountable to whom) and the basis of accountability (the standards against which the body in question needs to justify its actions).

The areas of public intervention to which the market operator principle applies have, traditionally, been subject to different systems of accountability. Attempting to provide an even remotely accurate picture of the dynamics of accountability

[71] In a high-profile line of jurisprudence, the Court held that (then) Article 10 EC required Member States to abstain from introducing or maintaining in force legislation that allowed undertakings to infringe competition law thus depriving the latter provisions of their *effet utile*. Despite the attention that this case law received it became clear that the Court was not prepared to stretch this approach to its full extent. See Case 13/77 *GB-INNO-BM v ATAB* [1977] ECR 2115; Case 311/85 *Vereniging van Vlaamse Reisbureaus v ASBL* [1987] ECR 3801; Case 267/86 *Pascal Van Eycke v ASPA NV* [1988] ECR 4769; Case 2/91 *Criminal Proceedings against Meng* [1993] ECR I-5751; Case C-185/91 *Reiff* [1993] ECR I-5801; Case C-35/96 *Commission v Italy* [1998] ECR I-3851; Case C-198/01 *CFI v AGCM* [2003] ECR I-8055. There is a rich academic commentary on these cases: eg H Schepel 'Delegation of Regulatory Powers to Private Parties Under EC Competition Law' (2002) 39 *CML Rev* 31.

[72] For a discussion of the many meanings of the term in national settings and the conceptual and practical implications of its application to the EU, see generally C Harlow, *Accountability in the European Union* (Oxford, Oxford University Press, 2002).

in relation to public intervention within the different Member States would be, given the variety of such systems across Europe, a pointless exercise to engage in; yet it is possible to capture the essential features. Public undertakings are typically accountable towards government. Governments may, for instance, appoint members of the undertaking's board, provide broad policy directives, and give their consent to strategic decisions. Governments may in turn be accountable for the undertakings' actions before Parliament; administrative courts may, in certain settings, be capable of reviewing decisions taken by the undertakings and the accounts of public undertakings may be audited by independent experts.[73]

Broadly, these forms of accountability are united by two fundamental features: they are confined within national borders; they serve a public purpose and are, in principle,[74] grounded on values that may be described as being 'other-regarding'. The market operator principle has a significant impact on both fronts. First of all, the obvious effect of the principle is that accountability of the State as market participant from a purely national question becomes an issue of EU relevance. The other, equally striking, point is that the new standards, which rest on the primacy of 'self-regarding behaviour', become the touchstone of market participation. The 'new' regulatory standards that State aid law introduces nudge public bodies towards actions that are justified on the grounds of their *commercial self-interest*. Member States are to act upon reasons that satisfy a particular conception of self-interest that models itself upon values that *may* hitherto have been foreign to the public body. Thus defined, the self-interest of Member States as market participants may be in conflict with their role as public authorities or with policy objectives that embody the authority of the public mandate.[75]

Moreover, the national forms of accountability, where in place, were predominantly political rather than legal: the effect of EU law is to inject an element of legal accountability and to (re)-regulate the activities of Member States within the commercial sphere. What is striking about the market operator principle is that the *market* itself becomes an essential component in the process of accountability and an essential element of regulation. Not only do *market-drawn* standards provide the *basis* for accountability, but, arguably, the market itself becomes a *forum* of accountability. Naturally, one should distinguish between accountability in its

[73] See T Prosser, *Nationalised Industries and Public Control* (Oxford, Blackwell, 1986); L Hancher, 'The Public Sector as Object and Instrument of Economic Policy' in T Daintith (ed), *Law as an Instrument of Economic Policy* (Berlin, De Gruyter, 1988) 165. The channelling of public funds to private undertakings *may* also be subject to forms of political/legal accountability. But that is by no means necessarily the case. Subsidies may completely escape any form of political or legal accountability.

[74] Ie, discounting any form of capture that may affect the Member States' authorities' decision to grant State aid.

[75] Indeed, State aid control may be in conflict with domestic political accountability and State aid control may be regarded as making local public authorities less politically accountable. In granting State aid, national politicians pursue local collective interests (for instance, by deciding to bail out a major employer in a locality) and may be rewarded by the electorate for doing so. For an exploration of this dimension see M Dewatripont and P Seabright, '"Wasteful" Public Spending and State Aid Control' (2006) 4 *Journal of the European Economic Association* 513.

looser meaning, as an actor's responsiveness to certain values assessed by a forum, and as a legal mechanism, which entails scrutiny of a body for its conformity with certain standards departure from which involves legal consequences.[76] Market accountability, it seems, is a useful label to describe the *consequences* of applying the market operator principle, but also to describe the *legal* standards which determine the existence of an advantage for the purpose of Article 107(1) TFEU.

The first question to ask, when examining the market operator principle through the prism of accountability, is *who* is accountable. The machinery of State aid control does not directly involve the *beneficiaries* of aid in the mechanism of accountability that it introduces—as a matter of EU law they are not answerable to the Commission.[77] However, it is a *consequence* of the market operator principle that those who benefit from State assistance are to become accountable to other market participants. Accountable, that is, in the looser meaning: they become responsive towards the market. There is thus an inextricable link between the direction of accountability (who is accountable to whom?) and its basis (for what?). Undertakings that benefit from public assistance become accountable to the market for the very reason that they become subject to market-drawn criteria.

Consider, to illustrate the point, the example of the *France Telécom* decision.[78] France Telécom, a company in which the majority shareholder was the French government, suffered from 'severe structural problems' and 'an unbalanced balance sheet'. As its debt problems increased, the rating agencies downgraded the company's credit ratings, therefore making it harder for it to finance its operations on the open market. Subsequently, the French Minister for Economic Affairs and Finance made a series of declarations promising support for the ailing undertaking in the form of a shareholder loan and a commitment to subscribe to the recapitalisation of the company. A direct result of these statements was the immediate updating, by rating agencies, of France Telécom's credit rating to reflect the company's increased financial strength resulting from public intervention. Interestingly, the Commission considered the mere announcement of such measures to fall, in principle, within the scope of Article 107(1) TFEU, but conceded that, given the novelty of such an interpretation, the recovery of the aid would infringe legitimate expectations. As the Commission held, the market's reaction to the government's intervention could not be regarded as providing the benchmark for the State's conduct, as the effect of the minister's declarations was to '*contaminate* the

[76] M Bovens, 'New Forms of Accountability and EU Governance' (2007) 5 *Comparative European Politics* 104.

[77] Although, of course, a Member State's obligation to recover aid implies that beneficiaries are, as a matter of national law, required to pay back the money that they have received from the State.

[78] Commission Decision 2006/621/EC on the State Aid implemented by France for France Télecom, [2006] OJ L257/11. The General Court has annulled the Decision on the basis that the Commission had not demonstrated that the advantage was conferred through State resources, Joined Cases T-425/04, T-444/04, T-450/04 and T-456/04 *French Republic, France Télécom SA, Bouygues SA and Bouygues Télécom SA and Association française des opérateurs de réseaux et services de télécommunications (AFORS Télécom) v European Commission* [2010] ECR II-2099.

market's perception and to influence the conduct of market operators'.[79] Thus, once the 'contaminant' was removed, the markets would be able to evaluate the company for its true worth. The effect of applying the market operator test was therefore to make France Telécom responsive to market mechanisms and cause its standing to become more transparent to market participants.[80]

Accountability of such a kind may also be seen at work in the case of the German Landesbanken. As seen before, a consequence of the Commission decision on the public guarantee system was the radical change in the market's perception of these banks' standing and the official downgrading by the international ratings agencies of many of these institutions. The fact that such banks were forced to rethink their business models as a result of these developments is also indicative of the normative significance of market accountability, that is, the capacity of the market operator principle to shape the behaviour of certain market participants.

Accountability's etymology is in itself evocative, for the term shares common roots with 'accounting'.[81] The market operator principle requires that economic activities that are carried out through public funds be amenable to scrutiny on the basis of conventional accounting criteria. The requirement that undertakings charged with public interest tasks keep separate accounts for public service and commercial activities stems from this rationale. But the etymology is also evocative in highlighting another crucial effect of applying the market operator principle, which concerns the change in the undertakings' evaluation of their own role and conduct. This effect is known as the 'hardening' of a previously 'soft' budget constraint. The terminology belongs to a theory developed to describe a syndrome that affected undertakings that benefited from consistent State support.[82] The crux of the theory is that the expectation that a 'supporting organisation' (typically, the State and its emanations) will regularly intervene to cover losses and/or prevent insolvency affects an undertaking's behaviour.[83] The decisions of an undertaking under a 'soft budget constraint' will not be strictly influenced by the difference between revenue and expenditure in its accounts; instead, such an undertaking will either pursue a quiet life, without engaging in strategies aimed

79 P Nicolaides 'Markets and Words: the Distortive Effect of Government Pronouncements' (2005) 26 *European Competition Law Review* 119.

80 The General Court, however, has annulled the decision insofar as the aid was not granted through State resources. Cases T-425/04, T-444/04, T-450/04, and T-456/04 *France and others v European Commission* [2010] ECR II-2099.

81 In fact, as Harlow points out, the term was originally used exclusively in accountancy and management.

82 J Kornai, 'The Soft Budget Constraint' (1986) 39 *Kyklos* 3. The theory has been hugely influential and has given rise to a number of different applications. While its original formulation pertained to socialist economies, the theory has been regarded as capturing market economies as well. For a more recent re-formulation of the theory and references to its manifold applications, see J Kornai, E Maskin and G Roland, 'Understanding the Soft Budget Constraint' (2003) 41 *Journal of Economic Literature* 1095. For an application of the theory to State aid, see I Atanasiu, 'State Aid in Central and Eastern Europe' (2001) 24 *World Competition* 257.

83 The body that is responsible for the undertaking's soft budget constraint is the State, whereas in a capitalist system, it could be a parent company that covers the losses of its subsidiaries.

at increasing its market share, or, on the contrary, it will take excessive risks, in the knowledge that, in any event, State assistance will always be forthcoming.

Market accountability and hard budget constraints do not solely serve to illustrate the effects of the market operator principle on the beneficiaries of State intervention; these concepts are also capable of throwing light on the *prescriptions* that the market operator principle imposes upon the behaviour of those who are legally bound by the State aid rules—the Member States themselves. Member States, despite not being legally accountable to markets, are accountable to the Commission and the courts on the basis of market standards, by which we mean the requirement for Member States to justify their choices and actions on the basis of reasons that are expected to be amenable to the 'rationality' of a typical market participant. The *effect* of applying the market operator test is to make the behaviour of Member States *transparent* to the market.

Consider the Commission decision concerning the privatisation of the Austrian Bank, Bank Burgenland.[84] After a tender procedure, the Austrian regional government of Land Burgenland decided to accept the offer of the second highest bidder, the Austrian insurance group Grazer Wechselseitige (GRAWE). In doing so, it disregarded a higher bid by an Austro-Ukranian consortium. That decision was justified by the existence of 'Ausfallhaftung', a legal guarantee given by Austria that covered at the time of the sale large part of Bank Burgenland's liabilities, which had been the object of a Commission decision to allow the system to remain in place after the privatisation for existing liabilities and to be phased out by 2017. Austria claimed that the sale to GRAWE at a lower price was justified by the reduced risk of drawing on its guarantee obligation. The Commission decision confirmed that a public vendor needs to clearly distinguish its role as a seller of an asset on an open market, and its role as a public authority that had granted State aid in the form of a guarantee to Bank Burgenland. A private seller would not have taken existing guarantee liabilities into consideration but would have taken the highest bid. By not doing so, Land Burgenland provided an undue competitive advantage to GRAWE that constituted incompatible State aid. Thus, the application of the private seller test exposed the non-conformity of the Austrian government's decision to market rationality. As an effect of the decision, Austria would have to justify its choice in a manner that ensured transparency towards the market.

The idea of hardening the budget constraint is also relevant to the Member States both in describing the normative content of the market operator principle, but also as a means of accounting for the effects of the principle. Not only are Member States induced, as an effect of the principle, to operate on the basis of a budget constraint, but they are effectively required to do so by the State aid rules. In both cases, however, the budget constraint that applies to Member States is a *hypothetical* one. Lacking a supporting organisation to back them, Member States

[84] Commission Decision of 30 April 2008 on State aid C 56/06 [2008] OJ L 239/32.

do not operate under a budget constraint.[85] However, the significance of the market operator principle is that Member States operate *as if* they were bound by a budget constraint comparable to the one that private market participants typically operate under. The example of *WestLB* serves to illustrate the point. On that occasion, the Court of First Instance based its assessment of the existence of State aid on the assumption that the return on the contribution of an asset to the bank's capital by the regional government was to be benchmarked on the average return on such investments. Thus, the absence of a negative return was not sufficient to rule out the existence of State aid. Of course, given the fundamental difference in the availability of resources between a public authority and the average investor, the reality is that the former does not operate under a budget constraint comparable to the constraint that the latter is harnessed by. Yet, the effect of the General Court's approach was for the public authority to operate *as if* it had such a budget constraint, which *in effect* amounted to introducing such a constraint on the public budget.

C. The Limits of the Market Paradigm

The contention that EU State aid law seems to commit Member States to a form of economic neo-liberalism, may, from what has been said so far, appear to stand on solid ground. Not only does this branch of internal market law rely on the principle, characteristic of economic liberalism, of the separation between State and market, but it also imposes the logic of economic efficiency on the commercial activities of Member States in an attempt to ensure that the advantages deriving from the co-existence of commercial and regulatory powers are neutralised and that public and private bodies compete on an equal footing. In all of this, the victim is, one might argue, the autonomy of Member States to pursue public interest goals through market participation. There is, therefore, from the viewpoint of national public interest, inevitably something to be lost in harnessing market intervention to the internal market objective and the contention that negative integration may stifle the diversity intrinsic in mixed economic systems does appear to be a valid one.

There are some important qualifications to be made, however. It should be borne in mind that the pursuit of national policy objectives does not necessarily result in a negative outcome from the point of view of State aid, even where the public authority is unable to satisfy the market operator test. The State aid question consists of two distinct stages, the latter of which may in effect lead to a finding of compatibility of the national measure with the internal market. Moreover, the fact that the market operator principle excludes, as a matter of law, the existence

85 Although, of course, there are budget constraints arising from the rules on monetary union.

of an advantage within the meaning of Article 107(1) TFEU ('favouring') does not necessarily mean that in reality such advantage is non-existent.

The essential rationale of the principle is that the efficiency considerations that are fed into the test are designed to ensure that the advantage which may derive from State support is deemed to have a limited impact on competition. This exercise may be described as a very rough cost-benefit analysis carried out *in limine*, rather than at the exemption stage. The cost of allowing the flow of funds from public authorities to undertakings is mitigated by the efficiency of the investment. A prima facie efficient investment is unlikely to harm competition; yet, an investment, or a State guarantee, in favour of an undertaking is in itself an advantage, though not necessarily an advantage within the meaning of Article 107(1) TFEU.

According to its notice on State guarantees,[86] the Commission follows the principle of the market operator in stating that a public guarantee does not amount to State aid where a market premium is paid. Yet, while the Commission requires the guarantee to reflect market conditions, and requires the borrower not to be in financial difficulties, there is, nonetheless, little doubt that a public guarantee carries greater weight in the eyes of the lender than a private one and is therefore an intrinsic benefit to the borrower.

Moreover, it is doubtful whether the private operator test may be characterised as an embodiment of economic neo-liberalism, or monetarism, as Parish puts it. It would appear that EU law rejects the most extreme forms of economic neo-liberalism, not only in allowing for certain kinds of State intervention to be exempted in accordance with Article 107(3) TFEU, but also because it rejects an efficiency test to the areas that it regards as being within the concept of *imperium*. As we shall see in the next chapter, where *imperium* is involved, the market operator test gives way to a non discrimination test—clearly an approach that economic neo-liberalism would eschew. Economic neo-liberalism would have it that regulation should be amenable to efficiency considerations.

Furthermore, the application of the market operator principle may not always be as rigid as it may seem. In *ENI Lanerossi*, the Court drew a distinction between an investor, whose sole motive is profit, and private entrepreneurs, such as an industrial holding whose decisions may be governed not merely by short-term profitability but also by the intention to protect its reputation. The State's behaviour, however, was to be compared with the behaviour of a normal private investor whose intention was always to realise at least a long-term profit.

There is further evidence of flexibility in the application of the market operator principle in the *Chronopost* line of cases, which confirms that neither the Commission nor the Court appear to be prepared to take the comparison with the private benchmark to the extreme. At the root of the *Chronopost* controversy was a Commission decision on a set of transactions between La Poste (the French

[86] Commission Notice on the application of Article 87 and 88 of the EC Treaty to State aid in the form of guarantees [2008] OJ C155/10.

post office) and one of its subsidiaries, SFMI-Chronopost, which operated an express parcels delivery services.[87] The complainants had alleged that the commercial and logistical assistance provided by the parent company to its subsidiary had not been adequately remunerated and therefore amounted to State aid. In approaching the question, the Commission had examined whether the terms of the transaction between parent and subsidiary were comparable to those of an equivalent transaction between a private company, which may well be a monopoly (for instance, because of the ownership of exclusive rights), and its subsidiary. It found that, on the basis of this approach, Chronopost derived no financial benefit from the transaction, as the internal prices at which products and services were provided between the two companies were 'full-cost prices'.[88] The General Court annulled this decision, finding that it had wrongly applied the market economy investor principle by referring to the costs incurred by La Poste itself rather than using as a benchmark a private undertaking *not operating in a reserved sector*.[89] It added:

> To require that the remuneration which a public undertaking with a monopoly receives in return for the provision of commercial and logistical assistance to its subsidiary should correspond to the payment which would have been demanded under normal market conditions, does not prohibit such a public undertaking from entering an open market but subjects it to the rules of competition, as the fundamental principles of Community law require. Such a requirement does not adversely affect the system of public ownership and merely ensures that public and private ownership are treated equally.[90]

On appeal, the Court of Justice took an altogether different view of the appropriate comparator:

> In the absence of any possibility of comparing the situation of La Poste with that of a private group of undertakings not operating in a reserved sector, normal market conditions, which are *necessarily hypothetical*, must be assessed by reference to the objective and verifiable elements which are available.[91]

The General Court had erred *in law* in using a test based on comparisons with normal market conditions, because La Poste's network, built to meet non-commercial public service requirements and on the basis of a reserved sector, was too dissimilar to a commercial network to allow the comparisons that the

[87] Commission Decision 98/365/EC [1998] OJ L 164/37.

[88] More precisely, the Commission found the payments made by Chronopost did not cover total costs over the first two years of operation, but it considered that, in the first place, it was normal for payments made by a new undertaking to cover only variable costs in the start-up period, and, in the second place, after this period the remuneration paid by Chronopost covered all the costs incurred by La Poste plus a return on the equity capital invested by the latter.

[89] Case T-613/97 *UFEX and Others v Commission* [2000] ECR II-1531.

[90] Ibid para 77.

[91] Joined Cases C-83/01P, C-93/01P and C-94P *Chronopost and Others v UFEX and Others* [2003] ECR I-6993, para 38.

General Court had proposed. The Court set aside the General Court's judgment and referred the case back to the General Court.[92]

One may regard *Chronopost* as evidence of the Commission and the Court's departure from the more 'aggressive' use of the market operator principle displayed in earlier decisions and case law—it may, in fact, be seen as a recognition of the limitations of the principle. Unlike the Court of First Instance, the European Court of Justice did not believe that State aid should contribute to redressing the competitive imbalance between the public undertaking and private competitors, even at the cost of basing State aid analysis on an entirely hypothetical analysis. At the heart of these two views regarding the scope of the market operator principle lies a different conception of the role of State aid in shaping the respective spheres of the State and of the market. In other words, the two approaches conceal an ideological divide among the two courts *in this particular instance*.[93]

The General Court's approach in *Chronopost* seems to ascribe a transformative role to the law of State aid. Its ideological matrix is the idea of substantive equality outlined above, which requires the comparison to be drawn in such a manner as to redress the imbalance suffered by the competitors of the undertaking benefiting from State support. Market and State, on this view, are to be conceived of as entirely separate, and the role of State aid control is to ensure that this separateness is enforced. The transformative role of State aid, therefore, is to aim to create an open market where such a market does not exist. Thus, even though no market equivalent existed to a relationship between a parent and a subsidiary in a reserved market, that market equivalent had to be construed in order to place public and private undertakings on an equal playing field. On the other hand, the Commission and the Court of Justice's view is consistent with an interpretation of the principle which takes a stricter approach to the limits deriving from Article 345 TFEU. On this view, the application of the State aid rules may not prejudice public ownership by imposing upon it conditions that ignore the regulatory constraints that the public undertaking has to bear. No transformative role is therefore accorded to the market operator principle or to State aid in general. Instead, the Court seems keen to ensure that any inevitable distortion to the normal functioning of the market is kept to the minimum, by requiring the transaction to be transparent in accounting terms.[94]

[92] In its new judgment, the General Court annulled, once again, the Commission decision: Case T-613/97 *UFEX and Others v Commission* [2006] ECR II-1531. On appeal, the Court set aside the General Court's judgment: Joined Cases C-341/06 P and C-342/06 P *Chronopost* [2008] ECR I-4777.

[93] The qualification is due to the fact that there is no evidence to corroborate the claim that such divide is as deep-seated as to emerge in a consistent line of jurisprudence.

[94] However, the Court's ruling in *Chronopost* should be examined in light of the particular factual and regulatory context to which it belongs—that of a monopolist operating a universal postal service network.

D. Legal Certainty

Apart from being an illustration of a more nuanced approach to State participation in economic life, the *Chronopost* case law may be taken as an indication of the underlying challenge involved in applying the principle, which is to turn *economic* rationality into *legal* rationality; in other words, to accommodate extra-legal concepts into the categories and values ascribable to the rule of law, such as predictability and legal certainty. The importance of the problem may only be appreciated if one considers its potentially capillary reverberations at domestic level. The role that the principle plays in defining the notion of State aid is such that, in national settings, courts, public authorities and undertakings take their decisions and plan their conduct in accordance with the interpretation of the principle provided by the Union Courts.

In the past, the Court is said to have taken a deferential approach towards the Commission with regard to the application of the market operator principle.[95] According to the Court, in cases involving 'complex economic appraisal', its role would be confined to verifying whether the Commission complied with the relevant rules governing procedure and the statement of reasons, the accuracy of the statement of the facts, and whether there has been any manifest error of assessment or a misuse of powers.[96] Today, it remains true that the EU judiciary accords a considerable degree of discretion to that institution as far as economic matters are concerned. However, taking the cue from the *Tetra Laval* developments in judicial review,[97] the Court has stated that acknowledgement of such discretion 'does not mean that the EU judicature must refrain from reviewing the Commission's interpretation of information of an economic nature'.[98] It made clear that the EU judicature should not only 'establish whether the evidence relied on is factually accurate, reliable and consistent', but also 'whether that evidence contains all the information which must be taken into account in order to assess a complex situation and whether it is capable of substantiating the conclusions drawn from it'.[99] However, it added, such review was to be carried out on the stipulation that the Court would not substitute its own economic judgement for that of the Commission.

Another step towards safeguarding legal certainty is to crystallise the criteria that guide the Commission's discretion in matters involving the application

[95] L Hancher, 'State Aids and Judicial Control in the European Community' (1994) 4 *European Competition Law Review* 134.

[96] Case C-56/93 *Belgium v Commission* [1996] ECR I-723, paras 10–11; Joined Cases C-328/99 and C-399/00 *Italy and SIM v Commission* [2003] ECR I-4035, para 39; Case T-358/94 *Air France* [1996] ECR II- 2109, paras 71–72; Case T-296/97 *Alitalia* [2000] ECR II-3871, para 105; Joined Cases T-126/96 and T-127/96 *BFM* [1998] ECR II-3437, para 81; Case T-36/99 *Lenzing* [2004] ECR II-3597, para 150.

[97] Case C-12/03 P *Commission v Tetra Laval* [2005] ECR I-987.

[98] Case C-525/04 P *Spain v Lenzing* [2007] ECR I-9947, para 56.

[99] Ibid para 57.

of the market operator principle in soft-law instruments. Instances of this are the guidelines on rescue and restructuring aid,[100] or the notice on guarantees. Consolidation in these areas, however, is often viewed as fettering discretion, and adding complexity to an area that could be dealt with flexibly and correctly through the private operator test.[101]

Both the increase in intensity of judicial review and consolidation of Commission practice and of jurisprudential principles into guidelines undoubtedly make a contribution to the formalisation of the market operator principle. However, the point of both endeavours may be lost where the guidelines are implicitly side-stepped. Take as an illustration the demise of the so-called 'owner effect'. Until the General Court's judgment in *WestLB*,[102] the assumption, based on the 1993 Communication and the Court's case law, was that a distinction was to be drawn between majority and minority shareholders for their different attitudes towards profitability: majority shareholders would not necessarily pursue short-term profit but would take a longer-term approach to profitability.[103]

In *WestLB*, the General Court narrowed down the 'owner effect' considerably: 'normally a private investor is not content to avoid losses or to obtain a limited return on his investment, but attempts to maximise the return on his assets in accordance with the circumstances and his interests, even in the case of an investment in an undertaking in which he already has a shareholding'.[104] The General Court held that even if this represented a departure from the 1993 Communication and from the related case law, the case law on the concept of State aid adopted a material test which implied that it was possible to use an average return when applying the private investor principle.[105]

3. CONCLUSION

The story that has unfolded in this chapter has two aspects. On the one hand, it is an account of a legal system that attempts to reconcile the existence of State participation on the market, and the existence of mixed economic systems, with

[100] Community Guidelines on State aid for rescuing and restructuring firms in difficulty [2004] OJ C244/2.

[101] This is the kind of argument that runs through some of the criticism of the old 'Commission Notice on the Application of the EC Treaty to State Aid in the Form of Guarantees' [2000] OJ C71. eg M Friend, 'State Guarantees as State Aid: Some Practical Difficulties' in A Biondi, P Eeckhout and J Flynn (eds), *The Law of State Aid in the European Union* (Oxford, Oxford University Press, 2003); L Prete, 'State Aid Reform: Some Reflection on the Need to Revise the Notice on Guarantees' (2006) 29 *World Competition* 421. The Commission has since issued a new Notice [2008] OJ C155.

[102] *WestLB* (n 21).

[103] Commission Communication and Case 40/85 *Belgium v Commission* (n 16).

[104] *WestLB* (n 21) para 134.

[105] Ibid para 262. Interestingly, however, the case law cited by the General Court simply contains the general principle that an aid represents a departure from 'normal market conditions', which, plainly, adds nothing to support or to contradict the owner effect.

the imperatives of the internal market. On the other hand, it is an account of the progressive colonisation by market principles of domestic areas that, more or less directly, belong to the public domain. Keeping both perspectives in mind helps to avoid simplistic conclusions. There is little doubt that the application of the market operator principle has had a remarkable impact on the way in which Member States are able to structure their participation in commercial activities; it is no longer possible for Member States to pursue *generic* domestic policy objectives through market participation without taking into account the efficiency of their operations. For instance, funding ailing undertakings for the sake of keeping their workers in employment is no longer in itself a legitimate course of action. This does not mean, however, that State resources may not be deployed to fund public interest activities; it means, instead, that Member States are significantly restricted in the routes that they may follow in doing so. Clearly, the effect of the market operator test is both de-regulatory and re-regulatory in nature. It is de-regulatory in that it allows Member States to escape the strictures of State aid control if they conduct themselves in a manner that reflects normal market behaviour. It is re-regulatory, however, in that it imposes standards that did not necessarily apply beforehand. To use Maduro's taxonomy of models of economic constitutions, as far as State participation in economic activity is concerned, State aid law contains elements of both a centralised and a decentralised model.

The extent to which centralisation or decentralisation are at play is also relevant to the discussion over the possibility of variety in the organisation of capitalism in Europe, which was touched upon in chapter two. It may be argued that the market operator principle is capable of causing a reconfiguration of the role of the State in the economy and of engendering a greater degree of uniformity among European models of capitalism. The example of the German Landesbanken could be used to this effect. At the same time, however, while the Commission has eliminated the competitive advantage enjoyed by the Landesbanken (epitomised by the triple A rating that hinged on the State guarantee), it seems clear that the application of State aid does not prevent the use of public banks to continue to provide lending to small and medium-sized businesses and to pursue long-term investment strategies. In other words, the survival of variety among European capitalist economies remains—to a certain degree—possible.

5

The State as Regulator

In developing the notion of the market operator, EU law seeks to disentangle commercial transactions entered into by Member States from the non–commercial elements that accompany them. However, where States act in their capacity as regulators, different analytical tools come into play: the market operator principle (generally) gives way to other criteria that act as boundary markers for Article 107(1) TFEU. The question 'does the State act according to the rationality of a market operator?' is replaced with the questions 'does regulation benefit a specific undertaking or group of undertakings?', and 'does the measure involve public resources?'. Clearly both questions have an impact on sensitive matters of national competence, as areas such as fiscal policy, regional autonomy, environmental and social policy may or may not be encroached upon depending on answers given to them.

The chapter begins by attempting to make sense of the distinction between market participation and regulation. This is, to date, a fluid area, as, in two recent judgments, the General Court seems to have extended the scope of the market operator principle to include measures that are prima facie regulatory in nature. The chapter then goes on to address the interpretative challenges associated with the search for boundary markers between State aid and the legitimate exercise of national regulatory competence. The final section examines the significance of a further limitation on the scope of Article 107(1) TFEU consisting in the requirement, introduced two decades ago, that aid be funded through State resources.

1. THE MARKET PARTICIPANT–REGULATOR BOUNDARY

The idea that regulation may be subject to EU scrutiny under the State aid rules finds its roots in the early jurisprudence of the Court of Justice,[1] which made clear

[1] The term 'regulation' as used here excludes direct grants and other subsidies. The term 'regulation' may indeed include subsidies, as these are a means to influence behaviour. However, for the purpose of this book, the term refers to a set of commands emanating from a public authority. Any State–imposed rule falls under this category, including tax measures, which, although undoubtedly a form of incentive, are also, primarily, a form of command. The reason why we follow this approach, as will become clear, is that command-type regulation entails costs that undertakings have to internalise. This is a crucial point to State aid law. On these distinctions see A Ogus, *Regulation: Legal Form and Economic Theory* (Oxford, Oxford University Press, 1994); R Baldwin, C Scott and C Hood, *A Reader on*

that the purview of Articles 107 to 109 TFEU did not exhaust itself in the notion of subsidy, but encompassed 'interventions which, in various forms, mitigate the charges which are normally included in the budget of an undertaking and which, without, therefore, being subsidies in the strict meaning of the word, are similar in character and have the same effect'.[2] The Court has since rejected attempts by domestic governments to fence off their fiscal or social policies by reiterating that 'Article [107] does not distinguish between the measures of State intervention concerned by reference to their causes or aims but defines them in relation to their effects', and, as a consequence, 'the alleged fiscal or social aim of the measure in issue cannot suffice to shield it from the application of Article [107]'.[3]

Since the development of the market operator principle and corresponding array of tests,[4] the law of State aid has proceeded along two distinct tracks: situations in which Member States engage in commercial transactions follow the market operator principle/tests; situations in which Member States regulate the market follow the selectivity test. However, two recent General Court rulings have raised some doubts as to the precise scope of the market operator principle, and have led to questioning the validity of this dichotomy.

In *Ryanair*, the General Court annulled the Commission decision concerning aid granted by the Walloon regional government to Ryanair.[5] In 2001, the Irish carrier Ryanair and the Walloon regional government had reached an agreement the terms of which required the former to commit towards operating a number of its flights from Charleroi airport, the airport owned by the latter, in return for which it would receive a 50 per cent reduction in the amount of landing charges. As a result, Ryanair would decrease its operating costs and gain an advantage vis–a–vis its competitors, while the airport and its owner would benefit directly and indirectly from the effects of an increase in passenger traffic. According to the Walloon Region, the agreement was a commercially sound transaction which it had entered into as owner of the airport and was therefore compliant with the market investor principle.

In its decision, the Commission flatly rejected this view: it held that the act of fixing airport fees fell within the legislative and regulatory competence of the Walloon Region; since the Walloon Region was acting as a regulator, not as a company, the principle of the private investor was not available to it as a justification

Regulation (Oxford, Oxford University Press, 1998); M Moran, 'Understanding the Regulatory State' (2002) 32 *British Journal of Political Science* 391; C Scott (ed), *Regulation* (Aldershot, Ashgate, 2002).

[2] Case 30/59 *Steenkolenmijnen v High Authority* [1961] ECR 1, para 19; Case T-55/99 *Spain v Commission* [2000] ECR II-3207, para 82; Case C-143/99 *Adria-Wien Pipeline and Wietersdorfer & Peggauer Zementwerke* [2001] ECR I-8365, para 38; Case C-501/00 *Spain v Commission* [2004] ECR I-6717, para 90; Joined Cases C-78/08 to C-80/08 *Paint Graphos and Others* (8 September 2011), para 45.

[3] Case 173/73 *Italy v Commission* [1974] ECR 709, para 13. See also Case C-241/94 *France v Commission ('Kimberly Clark')* [1996] ECR I-4551.

[4] Charted in the previous chapter.

[5] Commission Decision 2004/393/EC [2004] OJ L137/1. See F Gröteke and W Kerber, 'The Case of Ryanair—EU State Aid Policy in the Wrong Runway?' (2004) 55 *ORDO* 313.

for its actions.[6] The Commission relied on a number of arguments to support this conclusion. The level of fees was fixed in a decree of the Walloon Regional government, which also provided for a system of reductions in landing charges available to every user on the basis of objective criteria. Moreover, the airport charges allowed the financing of a transfer of resources to the airport concession holder and to an environment fund.[7] By granting a reduction to Ryanair, the Commission held, the Walloon Region had infringed the relevant national regulations and placed itself in a situation of 'confusion of powers'.[8]

Four years later,[9] the General Court quashed the decision on the ground of error of law resulting from the Commission's misinterpretation of the scope of the market operator principle, which consisted in holding that the setting of landing charges was not amenable to that principle. The General Court set out the broad terms of the question very clearly: the domain of the principle turned on whether or not the activities concerned were economic activities. If the State acted 'as an undertaking operating as a private investor' the market operator principle would apply; if, instead, the State acted as a public authority, its conduct could never be compared to that of a market participant. It was clear from the case law that the dividing line turned on whether the activity consisted in 'offering goods and services on a given market'.[10] The management of airport infrastructure fell within that definition and so did the fixing of landing charges, as the latter was directly connected with the former. The charges fixed by the Walloon Region had to be regarded as remuneration for the provision of services, notwithstanding the fact that 'a clear and direct link' between the charges and the services rendered to users was 'weak'.[11] What is more, the Commission itself had classified these charges as fees rather than taxes; moreover, the Commission should have differentiated between the economic activities and those activities which fell strictly under public authority powers.[12] The Commission's reliance on the fact that the Walloon Region had not complied with the law was irrelevant to the question whether that authority had granted State aid. In any event, the mere fact that the Walloon Region had regulatory powers in relation to fixing airport charges did not mean that a scheme reducing those charges could not be examined by reference to the private investor principle, 'since such a scheme could have been put in place by a private operator'.[13]

A year after *Ryanair*, in *EDF*,[14] the General Court annulled a Commission Decision that had found certain measures implemented by France in favour of

[6] Commission Decision 2004/393/EC (n 5) para 145.

[7] Ibid para 146.

[8] Ibid para 153.

[9] Case T-196/04 *Ryanair* [2009] ECR II-3643.

[10] Ibid para 87.

[11] Ibid para 89.

[12] Ibid para 98.

[13] Ibid para 101.

[14] Case T-156/04 *Electricité de France* [2009] ECR II-4503. For commentary, see A Bartosch, *Case Note on EDF* (2010) 9 *European State Aid Law Quarterly* 679; and M Köhler, 'New Trends Concerning the Application of the Private Investor Test' (2011) 10 *European State Aid Law Quarterly* 21; P

the state-owned energy company Electricité de France (EDF) amounted to State aid. According to the Commission, the aid resulted, among other things, from a restructuring of the company's balance sheet, the result of which was to convert a tax debt into capital.[15] In challenging the decision, EDF claimed that the Commission had erred in law in refusing to apply the private investor test, as the restructuring of the company's balance sheet effectively amounted to a capital injection which was comparable to the rational decision of a private investor. In its reasoning, the General Court maintained the distinction that it had traced in *Ryanair*, between economic activities and activities connected with the exercise of public power. However, it added, the distinction could not be traced on the basis of the legal form used by the State, but should instead be based on the nature, aim and the rules to which the State's activities were subject, and, crucially, of the *objectives* that they pursued.[16] If the conclusion to be reached after this examination was that the activity pursued an objective that was amenable to a private investor, rather than a public interest objective, the State's actions would be assessed under the market investor test. The General Court noted that, as the law in question sought to restructure EDF's accounts and to increase its capital, it did not have a fiscal nature, but was an accounting measure with fiscal consequences. In light of these considerations, the General Court concluded that the measure at issue could not be regarded as the exercise of public powers, but had to be examined through the lens of the private investor test. The appropriate comparison, it held, was between the State's decision to forego a tax credit in order to increase the capital of an undertaking of which it is the sole shareholder, and the decision of a private investor who opts to forego a credit in order to achieve the same aim.

In his Opinion for the appeal judgment, Advocate General Mazák advised that the General Court's judgment should be set aside.[17] In addition to finding that the General Court had distorted the facts of the case, he argued that the General Court had based its assessment of the question whether the State had acted as shareholder or as public authority on the *objectives* pursued by the State. In particular, to buttress its claim that the objective pursued by the State was relevant to the definition of State aid, the General Court had wrongly relied on the *SAT* case, which concerned the question whether an organisation was an undertaking, not whether a certain operation carried out by the State was State aid.[18] According to the Advocate General, the General Court's approach of focusing on the objectives pursued by the State was to be discarded for four reasons. First,

Nicolaides and IE Rusu, 'Private Investor Principle: What Benchmark and Whose Money?' (2011) 10 *European State Aid Law Quarterly* 237.

15 Commission Decision 2005/145/EC [2005] OJ L49/9.

16 Case T-156/04 *Electricité de France* (n 14) para 229.

17 Case C-124/10 P *European Commission v Électricité de France and Others*, Opinion of Advocate General Mazák (20 October 2011).

18 Case C-364/92 *SAT* [1994] ECR I-43.

such an approach was 'subjective and open to interpretation'.[19] Secondly, it would be open to manipulation, as there was a real risk that Member States would 'feel encouraged merely to plead (*ex post*) profit-making preoccupations' in order to evade the application of State aid law.[20] Thirdly, the reliance on objectives was difficult to reconcile with the objective nature of the concept of aid. Finally, the presence of aid had to be 'assessed with reference solely to available objective and verifiable elements'.[21] The Advocate General was also unconvinced by the General Court's attempt to rely on its judgment in *Ryanair*. The two cases, he argued, could easily be distinguished. While, in *Ryanair*, the General Court considered the act of fixing landing charges as an activity that could be carried out by a private operator, the same could not be said of the fiscal activities of the State, such as imposing taxes, but also waiving tax debts, which were activities undertaken in the exercise of public authority and could not 'by definition' be undertaken by a private investor.[22]

In June 2012, the Court of Justice (Grand Chamber) handed down its ruling in *EDF*.[23] Contrary to the Advocate General, the Court approved of the approach followed by the General Court. It did not deny that it was for the Member State, in the first place, to demonstrate, on the basis of objective and verifiable elements, that the measure it had implemented was to be ascribed to the State acting as shareholder.[24] However, it added, the Commission was to carry out a 'global assessment', based on the evidence provided by the Member State and on 'all other relevant evidence', *including the objective pursued* and the rules to which the measure was subject, so as to determine if the Member State had acted as a shareholder or as a public authority.[25] If, as a conclusion of this 'global assessment', it appeared that, 'notwithstanding the fact that the means used were instruments of State power', the State had acted as a shareholder, the Commission would have to apply the market investor test.[26]

The new line of case law inaugurated by *Ryanair* is not entirely transparent in its reasoning. The assumption in the General Court's reasoning in *Ryanair* is that there is a global definition of economic activity which straddles disparate fields of internal market law. This view is clear from the range of case law that the General Court cites, which concern the interpretation of the notion of public authority under the original Transparency Directive,[27] the notion of undertaking for the

[19] Case C-124/10 (n 17) (Opinion of Advocate General Mazák) para 71.
[20] Ibid.
[21] Ibid para 72.
[22] Ibid para 79.
[23] Case C-124/10 P *European Commission v Électricité de France and Others* (5 June 2012).
[24] Ibid, para 82.
[25] Ibid, para 86.
[26] Ibid, para 92.
[27] Case 118/85 *Commission v Italy* [1987] ECR 2599, para 7, on the interpretation of Commission Directive 80/723/EEC of 25 June 1980 on the transparency of financial relations between Member States and public undertakings [1980] OJ L 195/35.

purpose of Articles 101 and 102 TFEU,[28] and the definition of 'services' under Article 56 TFEU.[29] This case law, according to the General Court, yields a notion of economic activity that is also applicable to the scope of the market operator test.

There are undoubtedly a number of advantages to a global definition of economic activity. Among these, legal certainty, and the fact that both competition and free movement are a means to the same end—the internal market.[30] Yet, such an approach is also questionable, as it ignores the fundamental difference in legal scope and purpose among the different areas in which the concept of economic activity plays a role. The reasons that allow for an out-of-State patient in a public hospital to be treated as a service recipient for the purpose of Article 56 TFEU in the host State, and therefore to classify the service as an economic activity for the purpose of that provision, are different to the reasons that justify regarding the same hospital as *not* being involved in an economic activity and, therefore, as *not* counting as an undertaking for the purposes of Articles 101 and 102 TFEU.[31]

The difficulties that this global approach encounters are evident in the General Court's application of the notion of economic activity to the scope of the market operator principle. Admittedly, the State aid case law relies on the same notion of economic activity as the one adopted under Articles 101 and 102 TFEU in order to determine whether the body that receives State aid is an undertaking.[32] However, that question is logically distinct from determining the scope of the market operator principle and, consequently, the outcomes may be different. If the aid *recipient* does not carry out an economic activity the measure does not fall within the scope of Article 107(1) TFEU; whereas, excluding a measure from the scope of the market operator test does not imply that Article 107(1) TFEU is not engaged.

One might argue that the General Court's approach to the question is a functional one: it applies economic principles to economic activities and excludes their application where prerogative powers come into play. Yet, it is submitted,

[28] Case T-128/98 *Aéroports de Paris v Commission* [2000] ECR II-3929, para 107.

[29] Case C-355/00 *Freskot* [2003] ECR I-5263.

[30] On the theme of convergence within internal market law: K Mortelmans, 'Towards convergence in the application of the rules on free movement and competition?' (2001) 28 *CML Rev* 613; J Baquero Cruz, *Between Competition and Free Movement* (Oxford, Hart Publishing, 2002); P Oliver, 'Competition and Free Movement: Their Place in the Treaty' in P Nebbia and T Tridimas (eds), *Competition Law for the 21st Century* (Oxford, Hart Publishing, 2004).

[31] J Baquero Cruz, 'Beyond Competition: Services of General Interest and European Community Law' in de Búrca (ed), *EU Law and the Welfare State—In Search of Solidarity* (Oxford, Oxford University Press, 2005) 169–212, 183, and Opinion of Advocate General Poiares Maduro in Case C-205/03P *FENIN* [2006] ECR I-6295, para 50. The case law indicates that the notion of economic activity for the purpose of free movement law and for the purpose of competition law do not coincide. See Case C-519/04 P *David Meca-Medina and Igor Majcen v Commission* [2006] ECR I-6991, paras 30–33; Case C-350/07 *Kattner Stahlbau* [2009] ECR I-1513, paras 66, 72, 74 and 75. But see generally O Odudu, 'Economic Activity as a Limit to Community Law' in C Barnard and O Odudu (eds), *The Outer Limits of European Union Law* (Oxford, Hart Publishing, 2009) and specifically, O Odudu, 'Are State-Owned Health-Care Providers Subject to Competition Law?' (2011) 32 *European Competition Law Review* 231.

[32] Case C-172/03 *Heiser* [2005] ECR I-1627; Case C-222/04 *Cassa di Risparmio di Firenze* [2006] ECR I-289 paras 107–08; for a different analysis see A Bartosch, 'Aid to Social Housing and European State Aid Control' [2007] *European Competition Law Review* 563, 566.

the flaw in this approach lies in looking exclusively at the problem from the point of view of the grantor of State aid, rather than considering the effect of the State's activity on the economic circumstances of undertakings. A change in regulatory environment undoubtedly impacts on the undertakings' cost structure, as regulation entails costs that undertakings internalise. According to a long-established principle in State aid law, measures which alter undertakings' cost structure are, other things being equal, State aid, regardless of the nature of the power that caused that change.[33] According to this case law, aid derives from the fact that undertakings are relieved of 'charges that they would normally have to bear'. And, it seems, these charges do not need to be linked to the exercise of public authority; what matters is that they are charges normally borne by undertakings.

In *Ryanair*, the Walloon government's conduct effectively altered a regulatory framework which undertakings were normally subject to, and it did so to the exclusive benefit of Ryanair. Both the power to set landing charges and the level of those charges were laid down in advance through public law instruments. Undertakings therefore had internalised this regulation and the derogation from it clearly alleviated a burden that an undertaking in Ryanair's position would normally have borne. It is true that the earlier *ADP* judgment ruled that the provision of services by a publicly-owned airport in return for a fee was an economic activity; yet, it is worth noting that in that case the fee was freely fixed by the airport itself, not by the public authority.[34] The crucial point is not whether or not the activity is economic in nature. What matters, it is submitted, is whether or not there is a departure from normal market conditions, including a departure from the normal application of a regulatory framework. In *EDF*, that departure was blatant, as the French government effectively exempted EDF from tax that the undertaking, under normal circumstances, would have been expected to pay. Normal market conditions, as far as the facts in *Ryanair* were concerned, were the conditions set in the regulatory framework, as in a regulated market, normal market conditions are shaped by regulation. Naturally, the authorities could have decided to scrap the regulatory framework and replace it with a contractual arrangement with the various airlines. Instead, they entered into an agreement with Ryanair while at the same time maintaining the regulatory framework in place.

This is not to suggest that the distinction between market participation and market regulation is to be applied in a formalistic fashion. The nature of the power to which the conduct under scrutiny pertains should not automatically exclude market comparisons. The relevant question should be, instead, how regulation interacts with the economic structure and with the expectations of the undertakings that are subject to it. Cases involving the so–called market creditor test illustrate this point. In *DMT*,[35] for instance, the granting of periods of grace in

[33] See (n 2) above.

[34] Case T-128/98 *Aéroports de Paris v Commission of the European Communities* [2000] II-3929; and on appeal C-82/01 P *Aéroports de Paris v Commission* [2002] ECR I- 9297.

[35] Case C-256/97 *DM Transport* [1999] ECR I-3913.

the payment of social security contributions to certain employers by a public body responsible for collecting employers' and workers' social security contributions was deemed to fall within the scope of the market creditor principle. In applying the test on that occasion, the Court did not consider whether the activity was economic in nature. Instead, it held that the public creditor's actions were to be compared to those of a private creditor who seeks to recover sums owed to it by a debtor in financial difficulties.[36] Crucially, the regulatory framework permitted the body to exercise discretion regarding, inter alia, extending repayment periods. The Court therefore found that the decision at issue fell within that discretion and went on to apply the market analogy. However, the determining factor in this ruling was not the presence or absence of a regulatory framework, but the precise scope of that framework and the resulting assumptions that undertakings could reasonably be expected to entertain in relation to it. Given that the body collecting social security payments was able to exercise discretion, undertakings could expect this discretion to be exercised in line with economic rationality.[37]

It is not a coincidence that the Court of Justice had never before *Ryanair* applied the market economy *investor* test to regulatory measures.[38] The market operator principle yields a test which is based on a direct, and individual, correlation between the investment by, and a benefit for, the public authority; and that correlation should be amenable to *quantification*. Normally, regulatory measures, by their very nature, are unlikely candidates for such a test. That is so, not only because the benefits to the undertaking stemming from a relaxation of regulatory requirements may be hard to quantify; but also because the benefits that a public authority receives from such measures are equally hard to pin down. The selective relaxation of regulatory standards therefore looks inherently suspicious from the point of view of State aid, as there is no clear reason why a public authority should choose regulatory tools rather than ordinary commercial tools to effect a commercial transaction. The suspicion that naturally arises in such cases is that the use of regulatory measures is a means of avoiding transparency. For the market operator principle to play a meaningful role as an effective boundary marker, it is essential, as Advocate General Mazák has pointed out, that it applies to commercially transparent measures.

2. SELECTIVITY

Cases concerning regulation and, more frequently, taxation often turn on whether the scope of a measure is general or selective: a measure falls, other things being

36 Ibid para 24.

37 See also Advocate General Maduro in Case C-276/02 *Spain v Commission* [2004] ECR I-8091, para 23.

38 As opposed to the market creditor test which was applied in *DMT* (n 35).

equal, within the definition of State aid if it is selective. The existence of this distinction, while controversial among international economic lawyers and economists, seems all but natural under EU law, as far as its textual foundations are concerned.[39] The focus of State aid on selective measures derives not only from the wording of Article 107(1) TFEU, which requires aid to favour '*certain* undertakings or the production of *certain* goods', but also from the fact that the other provisions in the Treaty that address distortions of competition stemming from legislative or regulatory measures have as their object distortions arising from differences in the legislation and regulations of *different* Member States (Articles 116 and 117 TFEU, in particular), rather than regulatory and legislative differences within Member States.[40] The Treaty points to a clear division of roles between Article 107 TFEU, and the provisions on harmonisation/approximation of laws.[41]

The clear logic behind this distinction, however, is overshadowed by its practical application. Many of the complexities that arise here stem from the tension, from which the case law on the definition of State aid generally suffers, between the competing commitments to a functional approach, on the one hand, and to legal certainty, on the other. A functional approach requires a wide net to be cast in order to safeguard the Commission's control over potentially distortive public intervention, and to underpin its monopoly over the evaluation of the costs and benefits of individual State measures. At the same time, however, the commitment by public authorities across borders to play by the same rules across time, which is essential to the effectiveness of State aid, requires stability in the definition of State aid.

This tension is also seen when considering the desirability or otherwise of a rule of reason in State aid law.[42] The Court insists that the definition of State aid is an *objective* exercise.[43] A measure may not escape the prohibition of State aid on the basis of policy considerations, as these come into play once the question as to the existence of a State aid is answered affirmatively. It is then for the Commission, and for the Commission alone, to evaluate a State measure in light of the policy that it pursues. There is, on the Court's view, no room for a rule of reason, no open mechanism to attenuate the expansive force of the prohibition

[39] For an account of the controversies surrounding this issue in international trade law see L Rubini, *The Definition of Subsidy and State Aid* (Oxford, Oxford University Press, 2009) 359–77.

[40] The exclusive reference in Article 107(1) TFEU to manufacturing is an anachronism. Undertakings carrying out services are regularly treated as aid recipients.

[41] The State aid rules belong to Chapter 1 ('rules on competition') of Title VII TFEU ('Common rules on competition, taxation and approximation of laws'); the rules on harmonisation are contained in Chapter 3 (entitled 'Approximation of Laws') of Title VII, which is comprised of Articles 114 to 118 TFEU.

[42] Eg K Bacon, 'The Concept of State Aid: The Developing Jurisprudence in the European and UK Courts' (2003) 24 *European Competition Law Review* 54; A Bartosch, 'Is there a Need for a Rule of Reason In European State Aid Law?' (2010) 47 *CML Rev* 729.

[43] Case C-241/94 *France v Commission* [1996] ECR I-4551, paras 19 and 20; Case T-52/94 *Ladbroke Racing Ltd v Commission* [1998] ECR II-1, para 52.

by recognising legitimate policy concerns. Yet this approach runs into difficulty as soon as it is realised that its application would potentially involve questioning, as one Advocate General put it, 'the entire social and economic life of a member state'.[44] The Court, as a result, is cornered by its own commitments: it is forced to open up new pathways to prevent crossing the State aid threshold, but, at the same time, is compelled to dress up its constructs in objective garb, so as to maintain the distinction between prohibition and justification.

The principle of selectivity is of particular relevance, and is in fact mostly employed, in cases concerning fiscal measures.[45] The fundamental question in these cases is whether a measure favours, as the wording of Article 107(1) TFEU requires, 'certain undertakings or the production of certain goods',[46] or whether it is a measure of general economic policy. Clearly, the effect of this criterion is to define the parameters of national regulatory autonomy in relation to the use of fiscal tools either as a form of regulatory competition or as a form of incentive towards the promotion of public interest goals (such as environmental protection).

A. Competitors and Comparators

Much of the controversy on the definition of State aid turns on identifying the features that make up the distinction between general and selective measures.[47] Part of the difficulty with this distinction derives from the fact that, given that regulation is asymmetrical in its effects, it is hard to determine whether the difference in the impact on market participants is to be treated as a normal application of national regulation, or as a manifestation of an advantage conferred on certain undertakings. Some authors ascribe selectivity to the category of discrimination; unlike discrimination in its most common form, which implies pejorative treatment, selectivity implies more favourable treatment: measures that treat certain undertakings more favourably than other undertakings fall under Article 107(1) TFEU.[48] The focus on the economic impact of State aid requires the Court to look beyond direct discrimination and to regard as selective those measures that

[44] Advocate General Jacobs, Opinion in Cases C-52–54/97 *Viscido and others v Ente Poste Italiane* [1998] ECR I-2629, para16; on similar lines, S Weatherill, *Law and Integration in the European Union* (Oxford, Oxford University Press, 1995) 272.

[45] For reasons that will become apparent from the analysis of the State resources condition.

[46] The exclusive reference to manufacturing is, of course, an anachronism. Undertakings carrying out services are regularly treated as aid recipients under Article 107(1) TFEU.

[47] R Plender, 'Definition of Aid' in A Biondi, P Eeckhout and J Flynn (eds), *The Law of State Aid in the European Union* (Oxford, Oxford University Press, 2003); M Schütte, 'The Definition of State Aid' in M Sánchez Rydelski (ed), *The EC State Aid Régime: Distortive Effects of State Aid on Competition and Trade* (London, Cameron May, 2006).

[48] For instance, K Bacon, 'State Aids and General Measures' (1997) 17 *Yearbook of European Law* 269; P Werner, 'Fiscal State Aid' [2006–2007] *Cambridge Yearbook of European Legal Studies* 481.

appear to be general in scope, but, in their application, potentially favour certain undertakings/sectors. In *CETM*, the Court held that:

> [t]he fact that the aid is not aimed at one or more specific recipients defined in advance, but that it is subject to a series of objective criteria pursuant to which it may be granted, within the framework of a predetermined overall budget allocation, to an indefinite number of beneficiaries who are not initially individually identified, cannot suffice to call in question the selective nature of the measure and, accordingly, its classification as State aid within the meaning of Article [107(1)] of the Treaty. At the very most, that circumstance means that the measure in question is not an individual aid. It does not, however, preclude that public measure from having to be regarded as a system of aid constituting a selective, and therefore specific, measure if, owing to the criteria governing its application, it procures an advantage for certain undertakings or the production of certain goods, to the exclusion of others.[49]

In *GEMO*,[50] the Court found that a free carcass disposal service, which was open to any user, benefited slaughterhouses and farmers. While slaughterhouses were expressly mentioned in the French provision in issue, which thus constituted a form of de jure selectivity, or direct discrimination, the Court found de facto selectivity, or indirect discrimination, to arise in favour of farmers. De facto selectivity may also arise where *discretion* is involved in the application of a prima facie general measure. In *Kimberley Clark*,[51] the Court held that a system under which a public body, the 'French National Employment Fund', contributed to measures accompanying the social plans of undertakings in difficulties was liable to place certain undertakings in a more favourable situation than others as the fund in question enjoyed under the applicable regulations a degree of latitude with regard to a number of considerations such as, in particular, the choice of beneficiaries, the amount of the financial assistance and the conditions under which it is provided. The mere existence of discretionary power in administering a financial benefit was as sufficient to trigger the application of the State aid machinery.

As in other areas where a discrimination test is applied, the real source of difficulty lies in identifying the relevant comparator. It may seem surprising, given the emphasis on promoting undistorted competition, that the Court does not actually require discrimination to be understood as unequal treatment of *competing* undertakings, but, instead, as different treatment of undertakings that fall within a common reference framework. Selectivity includes, in fact, not only measures that favour certain undertakings, but also measures that favour certain sectors over others, regardless of the competitive relationship between them.[52] For instance, in *Adria-Wien Pipeline*, the Court found that a rebate on energy taxes in favour of

[49] Case T-55/99 *CETM v Commission* [2000] ECR II-3207, para 40.

[50] Case C-126/01 *Ministère de l'Économie, des Finances et de l'Industrie v GEMO SA* [2003] ECR I-13769.

[51] Case C-241/94 *France v Commission (Kimberley Clark)* [1996] ECR I-4551, paras 23–24; Case C-295/97 *Piaggio* [1999] ECR I-3735, para 39.

[52] Case 173/73 *Italy v Commission* (n 3) para 33; Case 248/84 *Germany v Commission* [1987] ECR 4013, para 18; Case C-75/97 *Belgium v Commission* [1999] ECR I-3671, para 32.

undertakings in the manufacturing sector to the exclusion of undertakings in the services sector was a selective measure.[53]

The reason why the existence of a competitive relationship is not a necessary condition for selectivity is that the presence of a competitor at the *national* level is not a necessary condition for establishing a competitive imbalance between the beneficiary of aid and its EU competitors; in other words, favouring one sector over another may not translate in relative competitive advantage, but that advantage may manifest itself in the competition with an equivalent sector in other Member States.[54] However, the Court does not actually require an analysis of the relative positions of the beneficiary of aid and of its competitors in *other* Member States. Instead, aid which is selective at a national level is presumed to alter the competitive balance across the internal market. The Court does not require the actual position of competitors across the internal market to fall into this analysis.

The reasons behind this approach are apparent in *Italian Textiles*.[55] The Italian government defended a reduction in the social charges for Italian textiles, which were higher than those occurring elsewhere in the EU, by arguing that the measure sought to realign the domestic textile industry with the position of undertakings in the same sector across the common market. The Court's answer was that Article 107(1) TFEU required the competitive position occurring within the common market before the introduction of the measure in question to be set as the relevant 'point of departure'.[56] That position was determined by *various factors* affecting production costs differently in different Member States. These differences, however, the Court added, could only be targeted by relying on Articles 114 to 117 TFEU, which enabled the EU to take action against distortions of competition arising from general measures. Unilateral action taken by a Member State to reduce a production cost in a particular sector of its economy would, instead, have the effect of 'disturbing the existing equilibrium' (the situation that pre-dated intervention by a Member State).[57]

These considerations are particularly important as a means of making sense of the Court's interpretation of selectivity. A selective advantage does not derive from a comparison between competitors, because the result of such a comparison would not fully capture the effects of regulatory intervention on the undertakings that benefit from it. Undertakings, as the Court made clear, operate against a set of assumptions, which form the backdrop to their decisions, concerning, among other things, the costs deriving from regulation. Any intervention that alters an undertaking's regulatory environment alters its competitive standing. Thus, a

[53] Case C-43/99 *Adria-Wien Pipeline* (n 2).

[54] B Kurcz and D Vallindas, 'Can General Measures be...Selective? Some Thoughts on the Interpretation of a State Aid Definition' (2008) 45 *CML Rev* 158.

[55] Case 173/73 *Italy v Commission* (n 3).

[56] Ibid para 17.

[57] Ibid.

reduction in social security charges creates an advantage in favour of a given set of undertakings, even if there are no competitors in the same Member State, and even if the beneficiaries were previously subject to charges that placed them at a competitive disadvantage vis-a-vis their competitors elsewhere in the EU. What matters is that the alteration of those undertakings' costs enables them to exploit the artificially induced change in their competitive position. If selectivity covered only situations in which Member States discriminate among competing undertakings, State aid law would fail to take account of this effect. It is equally plain why the Court does not engage in comparative analysis of the respective positions of the aid beneficiaries and their competitors in the internal market. If national regulatory intervention were considered to be State aid to the extent that it lowered the standards below the standards applicable in other Member States, State aid law would represent a form of harmonisation and would wipe out regulatory diversity.

All of this may lead to the suggestion that the real significance of selectivity resides in attempting to establish whether the result of public assistance is to cause an undertaking to be better off than before. That suggestion was flatly rejected by the Court in *Adria-Wien Pipeline*: 'for the application of Article [107] of the Treaty' it held 'it is irrelevant that the situation of the presumed beneficiary of the measure is better or worse in comparison with the situation under the law as it previously stood, or has not altered over time'.[58] What is, instead, relevant is that certain undertakings are favoured over 'other undertakings which are in a legal and factual situation that is comparable in the light of the objective pursued by the measure in question'.[59] In other words, there is a presumption that selective measures create an advantage for the beneficiary undertakings, even where the advantage simply consists in an asymmetric modification of the reference framework, which does not effectively improve the beneficiary undertaking's competitive position. For instance, Member State A may decide to increase the corporation tax rate for all sectors except one, sector *x*. Even if undertakings in sector *x* do not have competitors in A, and even if they are subject to the same rate of taxation as undertakings in sector *x* in Member State B, they are nonetheless regarded as recipients of State aid. This is one of the most puzzling aspects of selectivity, which may, arguably, only be explained in light of the absence of detailed microeconomic analysis where regulatory measures are concerned. It may well be that an increase in tax for other sectors may have indirect benefits for *x*, which derive from the fact that, while *x* does not have direct competitors in the output market, it may gain a competitive edge on the input market, which may in turn produce an advantage over its competitors in Member State B.[60] In practice,

[58] Case 143/99 *Adria-Wien Pipeline* (n 2) para 41.

[59] Ibid.

[60] For instance, sector *x* may compete with sector *y* over specialised labour. The fact that sector *y* is subject to an increased rate of tax may have an impact on its decisions on pay or recruitment. As a result, sector *x* may be able to pay its employees less than before, or may find it easier to hire specialised labour. All of this may give *x* a competitive edge on the output market.

however, the competitive advantage may not actually verify itself, as other factors, such as the increase in the costs of certain other inputs of sector *x*, come into play. Yet, as chapter three has argued, the preventative character of State aid is especially pronounced in relation to regulatory measures: the idea is that Member States should not introduce selective measures, as these are *likely* to distort competition, even if they are not certain to do so.

B. The Relevance of Objectives

Some have argued that the way to tell whether a measure is selective is through an 'objective-based analysis'.[61] Drawing on the *Adria-Wien Pipeline* judgment, Kurcz and Vallindas argue that the identification of the *objective* of a measure is essential to understanding the relevant system, or reference framework, on which the answer to the selectivity question is to be based.[62] For instance, if the objective is to promote Research and Development (R&D), the reference point should be the taxation of corporate R&D and not corporate taxation generally. Once the objective is established, they go on to argue, the measure in question should not actually differentiate between undertakings. In order to ensure that the objective is not set in such a way as to allow sectors to become the reference framework for the analysis of selectivity, they introduce a distinction between 'objectives of general policy/general interest' (such as promoting reductions in harmful emissions) and 'specific objectives' (such as promoting reductions in emissions only for cars).

The Union Courts have not always been at one on the matter. This was particularly evident in *British Aggregates*, which concerned a UK levy on materials used in the construction industry as aggregates.[63] The rationale behind the tax was to deter the extraction of 'virgin' aggregates and favour the use of 'recycled' materials or materials whose environmental impact is reduced. The Act of Parliament that introduced the aggregates levy, therefore, exempted certain materials from the scope of the levy.[64] The General Court was seized of the matter after the British Aggregates Association brought an action against the Commission decision which had found the levy not to constitute State aid. The applicants contended, inter alia, that the Commission had failed to recognise that the levy contained certain exemptions that

61 Kurcz and Vallindas, 'Can General Measures be...Selective? Some Thoughts on the Interpretation of a State Aid Definition' (n 54) 159.

62 In Case C-143/99 *Adria-Wien Pipeline* (n 2) para 41, the Court held: '[t]he only question to be determined is whether, under a particular statutory scheme, a State measure is such as to favour "certain undertakings or the production of certain goods" within the meaning of Article 92(1) of the Treaty in comparison with other undertakings which are in a legal and factual situation that is comparable in the light of the objective pursued by the measure in question'.

63 Case T-210/02 *British Aggregates Association v Commission* [2006] ECR II-2789.

64 There was an exemption for spoils resulting from the extraction of certain materials, such as slate, shale, ball clay and china clay, and an exemption for aggregates which were exported or removed from the UK before being processed.

could not be ascribed to the environmental impact rationale. In its judgment, the General Court held that an environmental levy was 'an *autonomous* fiscal measure ... characterised by its *environmental objective* and its *specific tax base*' which sought to tax certain goods or services in order to cause undertakings to internalise their environmental costs, and to increase the competitiveness of, and reorient demand towards, alternative—less environmentally damaging products.[65]

The General Court went on to add that the fact that the environmental levy did not apply to activities similar to those which were taxed and which had a *comparable* impact on the environment could not be viewed in the same way as a tax exemption which derogated from the system of burdens ordinarily imposed on undertakings. It was open to the Member States, who had retained their powers in the field of environmental policy, to introduce sectoral environmental levies in order to attain environmental objectives. In particular, Member States were free, 'in balancing the various interests involved, to set their priorities as regards the protection of the environment and ... to determine which goods or services they are to decide to subject to an environmental levy'.[66] The General Court held that, in assessing the environmental levy against the State aid rules, the Commission was to take account of the environmental protection requirements of Article 6 TFEU.

In his opinion for the *British Aggregates* appeal case,[67] Advocate General Mengozzi described the General Court's judgment as being 'highly innovative' in relation to the established case law on selectivity and on the concept of aid, according to which the aims of a State measure, including environmental protection objectives, are not sufficient to shield it from the application of the State aid provisions. That case law made clear that '[t]he objectives pursued by a measure ... fall to be considered only at a point subsequent to its classification as State aid, that is to say, in the course of assessing whether it is compatible with the common market'.[68] The conclusion reached by the General Court that the disparity in treatment of *comparable* situations was justified by the levy's environmental objectives signalled the General Court's intention 'to move beyond that case law'. That seemed to the Advocate General to be an unwarranted approach:

> Neither the competence enjoyed by the Member States in matters relating to taxation or the environment, nor the principle laid down by Article [11 TFEU] of the integration of environmental protection requirements into the definition and implementation of Community policies, justifies the wholesale removal of public measures that could distort competition from the ambit of the supervisory power conferred on the Commission by the Treaty rules on State aid. In particular, it seems to me that compliance with Article [11 TFEU] does not require the environmental objectives of a measure to be taken into account for the purposes of its classification on the basis of Article [107(1) TFEU], since the requirement that those

[65] Case T-210/02 *British Aggregates Association v Commission* (n 63) para 114.

[66] Ibid para 117.

[67] Case C-487/06P *British Aggregates v Commission* [2008] ECR I-10515, Opinion of Advocate General Mengozzi.

[68] Ibid para 97.

> objectives be integrated into the Community monitoring of State aid can easily be satisfied by taking them properly into consideration when it comes to assessing the measure's compatibility with the common market on the basis of Article 107(3) TFEU.[69]

The Advocate General's Opinion points to a conspicuous circularity in the General Court's reasoning, which runs as follows: selectivity is unequal treatment in light of the objective of a measure; it is for the Member State to define the objective and to carve out the scope of a measure accordingly; once that scope is determined, the treatment of situations falling outside it compared to situations that fall within it is irrelevant from the perspective of EU State aid law. If a Member State may choose which undertaking, among undertakings that are comparable in terms of environmental impact, to subject to a regulatory burden without having to justify that choice, the focus of selectivity is narrowed down to verifying equal or unequal treatment of *what the Member State defines* as situations that should be treated equally. Yet, arguably, the point of selectivity is to verify how the Member State has drawn up the scope of a measure.

The Court of Justice followed its Advocate General in pointedly rebuffing the General Court's approach.[70] The General Court, it stated, had 'disregarded Article 107(1) TFEU, as interpreted by the Court of Justice'.[71] However, the Court of Justice did not reject the proposition that Member States are free to draw the scope of their fiscal measures in accordance with environmental objectives. Yet, the scope of fiscal or regulatory measures has to be consistent with the broad environmental objectives of the measure.

The issue also arose in *Netherlands v Commission* ('Emissions Trading'),[72] concerning a Dutch scheme which capped nitrogen oxide emissions for the most highly polluting industries and allowed undertakings to reach that objective by introducing a system of tradable credits. Ruling on a direct action against the Commission decision which had found the measure to amount to State aid, the General Court held that whilst, in allowing undertakings to trade in emission credits, the scheme created an advantage in their favour, the measure was not selective, as it was aimed at those undertakings which, being the biggest polluters, were subject to an obligatory cap on emissions, and therefore it distinguished undertakings according to an objective criterion, which was in conformity with its environmental aim.

In the *Emissions Trading* case, the General Court simply used the objective of environmental protection to define the regulatory context of the measure and to delimit the 'parameters of the system':[73] only those undertakings that were obliged to comply with the ceiling on emissions were in a comparable situation with regard to the possible advantages stemming from the emission credits. The other

69 Ibid para 102.
70 Case C-487/06P *British Aggregates Association* (n 63).
71 Ibid para 86.
72 Case T-233/04 *Netherlands v Commission (Emission Trading)* [2008] ECR II-591.
73 The expression is borrowed from Bacon, 'State Aid and General Measures' (n 48).

undertakings could not benefit from the trading scheme as they were not required to reduce their emissions below the ceiling set for the most polluting industries. The fact that those undertakings that fell outside the scope of a measure were treated differently was not simply accepted as a given but subject to scrutiny on the basis of the regulatory objective pursued by the system. The objective difference in terms of environmental impact of the undertakings that were subject to that system allowed the conclusion to be reached that those undertakings that benefited from the trading scheme (the 250 most polluting undertakings) were not in a comparable position to those that fell outside the scheme.

On appeal, however, the Court of Justice found that the General Court had erred in law in reviewing the application of the selectivity criterion.[74] The fact that every undertaking the operations of which produced nitrogen oxide emissions was to comply with obligations regarding the limitation or reduction of those emissions meant that the undertakings that benefited from the Dutch scheme were singled out for preferential treatment. Contrary to the General Court, the Court of Justice regarded all undertakings that produced nitrogen oxide emissions as relevant comparators, as all undertakings were subject to an obligation to limit or reduce their emissions. In other words, the Commission had correctly found that there was an unjustified difference in treatment of comparable situations.

The two EU courts have also recently been at odds in the *Gibraltar* case, concerning the reform of Gibraltar's corporate tax system, which included the introduction of a payroll tax and a business property occupation tax (BPOT). In its decision, the Commission had found the reform to confer an advantage on offshore companies, companies that did not have premises or employees in Gibraltar, since these would effectively be exempt from corporate tax.[75] In annulling the decision, the General Court held that the Commission had failed to show that the taxes in question derogated from the normal tax regime, rather than being, as they were, integral to that regime.[76] The Court of Justicetook a significantly different approach. The Court held that, even though the two taxes were founded on general criteria, in practice, they discriminated between companies which were 'in a comparable situation with regard to the objective of the proposed tax reform, namely to introduce a general system of taxation for all companies established in Gibraltar'.[77]

The difference in approach between the two courts is significant. While the General Court seems to endorse a wide interpretation of national autonomy in relation to the pursuit of regulatory objectives, the Court of Justice is prepared to look beyond the Member States' choices in that respect. The Court of Justice takes a more global approach to the regulatory system: it does not confine its analysis to the objectives of the measure in question, but considers the system as

[74] Case C-279/08 P *Commission v Kingdom of the Netherlands (Emission Trading)*(8 September 2011).

[75] Commission Decision 2005/261/EC [2005] OJ L85/1.

[76] Case T-211/04 *Government of Gibraltar v Commission* [2008] II-03745.

[77] Joined cases C-106/09 P and C-107/09 P *Commission and Spain v Government of Gibraltar and UK* (11 November 2011), para 101.

a whole, and, on the basis of the guiding principles of such system, it scrutinises the national measure's treatment of comparable situations.

C. Regulatory Justifications for Unequal Treatment

When unequal treatment is established, such that there are effectively two different regulatory regimes within a system, it remains possible for a Member State to argue that such difference in treatment is justified on the basis of the 'nature or general scheme' of the regulatory system. Despite the use of the term 'justification', the concept relates to the classification stage of State aid analysis. The concept, which emerged for the first time from an obiter dictum in *Italian Textiles,* is particularly (albeit not exclusively) relevant to fiscal State aid.[78] In its 1998 'Notice on State Aid and Business Taxation',[79] the Commission states that the concept denotes 'measures whose economic rationale makes them necessary to the functioning and effectiveness of the tax system'.[80] This leaves out those so–called 'external' considerations that lie behind individual tax measures but do not stem from the tax system as a whole.[81] A significant difference between this justification and selectivity analysis is that the burden of proving the existence of an inherent justification lies with the Member States.[82]

Defences based on the nature and general scheme of the regulatory system have, in the past, rarely been crowned with success.[83] *Tiercé Ladbroke* is one such occasion.[84] The case turned on the question whether the fact that a different tax regime applied to totalisator betting on horse racing according to whether the races took place in France or in Belgium. The Court took the view that the difference in treatment was justified by the fact that the fiscal regime applying to races taking place in France was organised according to the specific economic and regulatory conditions prevailing with regard to totalisator betting on horse races in France, and that, given the different economic and regulatory conditions prevailing in different countries, that regime could not be transposed to totalisator betting on Belgian races.[85]

[78] Case 173/73 *Italy v Commission* (n 3) para 15.

[79] Commission (EC) 'Notice on the application of the State aid rules to measures relating to direct business taxation' [1998] OJ C 384/3.

[80] Ibid [23].

[81] Examples of 'internal' justifications are the redistributive goal inherent in most tax systems, or a particular method for calculating asset depreciation and stock valuation peculiar to a Member State's tax system; whereas, the social or regional objectives pursued through taxation are external justifications, which have no bearing on the question regarding the selective nature of a tax measure.

[82] Case C-159/01 *Netherlands v Commission* [2004] ECR I-4461, para 43.

[83] Examples of failed defences include: Case C-390/98 *Banks* [2001] ECR I-6117, para 33; Case C-351/98 *Spain v Commission* [2002] ECR I-08031, para 41; Case C-43/99 *Adria-Wien Pipeline* (n 2) paras 47–53; Case C-88/03 *Portugal v Commission* [2006] I-07115, paras 81–83.

[84] Case C-353/95P *Tiercé Ladbroke v Commission* [1997] ECR I-7007.

[85] Ibid para 35.

Another example of successful reliance on this justification was *GIL Insurance*.[86] The Court was asked to pronounce on the question whether a higher rate insurance premium tax (IPT) on insurance sold alongside certain goods and services conferred an advantage on those activities that remained subject to the standard rate of insurance premium tax. The higher rate had been introduced by the UK to counter the practice of value shifting, that is, of manipulating the price of insurance sold with goods and services in order to take advantage of the fact that insurance was not subject to VAT but to a lower tax. The Court accepted that, in view of its purpose and effect, the higher rate of IPT was 'intended specifically as a deterrent to the conclusion of connected insurance contracts' and was therefore justified as being integral to the tax system as a whole.[87]

In *AEM*, the Court dealt with the question whether a measure which imposed a higher charge for a certain period of time for access to and use of the national electricity transmission system on undertakings that generated and distributed electricity from hydroelectric or geothermal installations amounted to State aid.[88] The Court held that the different treatment of undertakings was attributable to the nature and general scheme of the system of charges in question, which was to offset the advantages that those undertakings subject to the charge benefited from as a result of the liberalisation of the electricity market.

In *Emissions Trading*, the General Court considered the justification in an obiter dictum. It held that even if, ex hypothesi, the view were to be taken that the measure in question differentiated between comparable undertakings, that differentiation arose from the nature or overall structure of the scheme of which it was part. The beneficiary undertakings were determined in accordance with the nature and general scheme of the system, on the basis of their significant emissions and of the specific reduction standard to which they were subject, as ecological considerations justified distinguishing undertakings which emitted large quantities of nitrogen oxides from other undertakings.[89] On appeal, the Court of Justice found that there was a prima facie unjustified difference in treatment, but went on to add that the considerations entertained by the General Court could not be regarded as being inherent to the system. In particular, a differentiation between undertakings based on a quantitative criterion (thermal installation capacity), could not be justified by reference to a system which was intended to reduce industrial pollution.[90]

Both courts, however, found a justification stemming from (EU) secondary legislation to be a convincing explanation for the difference in treatment of prima facie similar situations. The *Bouygues* case concerned the award of licences for

[86] Case C-308/01 *GIL Insurance* [2004] ECR I-4777.

[87] Ibid para 75.

[88] Joined Cases C-128 and 129/03 *AEM v AEEG* [2005] ECR I-2861. See M Maier and P Werner, 'Review of *AEM Spa v Autorità per l'Energia Elettrica e per il Gas*' (2005) 4 *European State Aid Quarterly* 657.

[89] Case T-233/04 *Netherlands v Commission* (n 72) paras 97–99.

[90] Case C-279/08 P *Commission v Netherlands* (n 74) paras 77–78.

the operation of 3G mobile phones in France: the French authorities had initially awarded licences to two operators, SFR and Orange, for the same fee; subsequently, another licence was awarded to a third operator, Bouygues Télécom, for a smaller sum; in order to respect the principle of equality between operators, the authorities reduced the fees due by SFR and Orange to bring them in line with the sum paid by Bouygues Télécom. Both courts found that the realignment of the fees payable by the different operators was justified by the nature of system in that EU telecommunications law required the award of licences to be based on non-discrimination.[91]

The justification on the nature and logic of the tax system is undoubtedly evocative of other concepts within internal market law. A parallel may in fact be drawn with the ground of justification for national tax rules restricting the exercise of fundamental freedoms, first introduced in *Bachmann*,[92] based on the need to ensure the cohesion of the tax system. *Bachmann* concerned the non-deductibility under Belgian tax law of payments made in respect of sickness, invalidity and life insurance contracts made in another Member State. The Court found that there was a risk that the provisions in question could operate to the detriment of workers who were nationals of other Member States. However, it then went on to hold that the restriction could be justified, given the connection between the deductibility of contributions and liability to tax of sums payable by insurers under pension and life assurance contracts, as the loss of revenue deriving from the deduction of contributions was offset by the taxation of the sums paid by insurers. The cohesion of this tax system, which was a matter to be left to each Member State, presupposed that, if a Member State was to allow the deduction of life assurance contributions paid in another Member State, it would also have to be able to tax the sums payable by insurers in another Member State, something that it could not ensure.[93]

The Court has subsequently taken a very restrictive view of what falls under the tax cohesion heading, stating that such a justification could only be accepted if a direct link between a tax advantage and the offsetting of that advantage by a particular deduction was established, and only if the advantage and the deduction related to the same tax and taxpayer. In *Verkooijen*,[94] the Court rejected the justification based on the cohesion of the tax system, finding there to be no direct link between the grant to shareholders residing in the Netherlands of an income tax exemption in respect of dividends received and taxation of the profits of companies with their seat in another Member State as it considered these as two separate taxes levied on different taxpayers. In *Manninen*,[95] a Finnish provision

[91] Case T-475/04 *Bouygues v Commission* [2007] ECR II-2097; Case C-431/07 P *Bouygues SA and Bouygues Télécom SA v Commission of the European Communities* [2009] ECR I-2665.

[92] Case C-204/90 *Bachmann v Belgium* [1992] ECR I-249.

[93] Ibid para 23.

[94] Case C-35/98 *Staatssecretaris van Fiananciën v B.G.M. Verkooijen* [2000] ECR I-4071.

[95] Case C-19/02 *Manninen* [2004] ECR I-7477.

granted shareholders of a company a tax credit in respect of dividends, only on condition that the company had paid tax on the profits for which the credit was granted; the aim was to avoid double taxation of company profits (at company and at shareholder level). The Court held that even if a direct link between the tax advantage and the offsetting tax levy existed in the case at hand, the legislation did not appear necessary to preserve the cohesion of the tax system in question. Since then, the justification has almost always failed.[96]

The Court's treatment of the justification on the nature and logic of the tax system under State aid law, however, differs from this latter strand of internal market case law in two important respects. While under free movement the fiscal cohesion justification is limited to a specific, and narrowly defined principle inherent in domestic fiscal systems, there is some degree of ambiguity in the State aid case law as to the reference framework on which the assessment of specific measures should be based; it is unclear whether the system should be the tax, or the regulatory system, as a whole, or whether it should be the individual measure. Arguably, the preferable approach, and the one which avoids depriving the justification of any meaning, should be that the aid measure itself should not be regarded as the relevant benchmark; instead reference should be made to a broader benchmark encompassing the generality of undertakings.[97] A similar level of ambiguity affects the nature of the justifications that may come to the rescue of national measures. Under free movement law, fiscal cohesion justifications exclude considerations that do not pertain to narrowly-drawn fiscal principles. Under State aid law, environmental considerations now seem to be firmly located within the province of acceptable justifications. Above all, the fundamental question is whether the existence of a justification amounts to a recognition that, where regulatory measures come into play, the law of State aid also contemplates a rule of reason, a question to which we now turn.

D. Towards 'a Rule of Reason' in State Aid Law?

One the most recent attempts to lend support to the recognition of a rule of reason in State aid law is made by Bartosch.[98] He argues that the question of selectivity should hinge on 'whether any different treatment of at least two groups of undertakings is justified by an objective that the Member State may legitimately

[96] Eg C-169/08 *Presidente del Consiglio dei Ministri v Regione Sardegna* [2009] ECR I-10821. However, it was accepted in Case C-157/07 *Krankenheim Ruhesitz am Wannsee-Seniorenheimstatt* [2008] ECR I-8061.

[97] K Bacon, 'The Concept of State Aid: The Developing Jurisprudence in the European and UK Courts' (2003) 24 *European Competition Law Review* 54.

[98] A Bartosch, 'Is there a Need for a Rule of Reason In European State Aid Law?' (2010) 47 *CML Rev* 729; see also L Hancher, 'Towards a New Definition of a State Aid under European Law' (2003) 2 *European State Aid Law Review* 365; H López, 'General Thought on Selectivity and Consequences of a Broad Concept of State Aid in Tax Matters' (2010) 9 *European State Aid Law Quarterly* 807.

pursue without risking the effectiveness of State aid control and the competition concerns that the latter intends to address'.[99] Bartosch proposes to extend the range of policy justifications beyond the narrow fiscal principles (such as progressivity, ability to pay) that characterise the inherent justification, to include not only environmental concerns, but also 'other political motives, based on considerations of a social, cultural or educative kind'.[100] This would, however, require distinguishing 'permissible goals from impermissible ones' on the basis of the objectives of State aid control, which means that 'all considerations related to improving the competitiveness of certain undertakings, industries, sectors or regions are from the very outset impermissible and consequently give rise to selectivity'.[101] Once the measure is identified as pursuing a permissible objective, the question would then be to verify if the implementation of this measure is justified by the nature or general scheme of the reference framework of which it forms part.

Undoubtedly, a rule of reason offers greater flexibility than traditional approaches do, provides greater scope for national regulatory autonomy, and, moreover, is attractive in its simplicity. However, this simplicity may turn out to be deceptive, as what appear to be measures that pursue a permissible objective may be covertly protectionist. In free movement law, the doctrine of mandatory/overriding/imperative requirements excludes economic justifications so as to avoid protectionist motives from seeping through. Yet, the dividing line between economic and non-economic justifications, which is not entirely straightforward in free movement, seems entirely artificial as far as State aid is concerned.

The Court's approach to the definition of State aid revolves around two fundamental interpretative principles: first, that the existence of State aid is not determined by reference to the causes and aims of a measure, but to its effects;[102] and, second, that the notion of State aid 'is a legal concept which must be interpreted on the basis of objective factors'.[103] True, as Bartosch has remarked, the Court, in principle, accepts that certain measures may be justified on the basis of the nature or general scheme of a *regulatory* system rather than solely on the basis of the 'technical' features of a fiscal system.[104] If that is so, then, the implication seems to be that some sort of evaluation of the policy considerations that justify differences in treatment may be necessary and that the Court has effectively qualified its two interpretative principles.

Yet, as was argued earlier, since the definition of State aid involves considering the regulatory environment in which undertakings operate, what the justification on the basis of the regulatory system does is to take a wider view of the regulatory

99 Bartosch, 'Is there a Need for a Rule of Reason In European State Aid Law?' (n 8) 742.
100 Ibid 747.
101 Ibid.
102 Case 173/73 *Italy v Commission* (n 3) para 13.
103 Case C-83/98 P *France v Ladbroke Racing and Commission* [2000] ECR I-3271, para 25.
104 This emerges from a string of cases: Case 173/73 *Italy v Commission* (n 3); Case T-55/99 *CETM v Commission* [2000] ECR II-3207; Joined Cases C-128 and 129/03 *AEM v AEEG* [2005] ECR I-2861; Case T-233/04 *Netherlands v Commission* [2008] ECR II-591.

environment, or reference framework. This does not involve sorting policy objectives into good and bad ones. Instead, it involves considering objective factors which form the fundamental features of a regulatory system *as a whole*. Thus, the polluter pays principle or the prevention of tax avoidance are fundamental features of regulatory and tax systems and differences in treatment may be justified on these bases. Moreover, the fact that Member States are charged with the burden of proving that the difference in treatment stems from the system does not detract from the objective nature of the definition of State aid. That is because the difference in treatment which requires justification arises from the measure at issue taken in isolation from its regulatory context, and it is for the Member State in question to offer the wider picture, in other words, to demonstrate that the difference in treatment contained in an individual measure stems from, and is justified by, the regulatory system as a whole. For instance, the insurance premium tax at issue in *GIL Insurance*, taken in isolation, seemed to treat similar situations differently—it was only when viewed in its regulatory context that its actual impact could be appreciated.

3. THE USE OF PUBLIC RESOURCES

The expansive potential of State aid scrutiny over regulatory measures has caused the Court to reconsider another aspect of the definition of State aid—whether the involvement of State resources is a necessary condition. The debate over the nature of this criterion stems from an ambiguity in the Treaty, as Article 107(1) TFEU refers to aid 'granted by a Member State or through State resources'. After decades of oscillations in the case law,[105] the matter came to a head in a string of judgments, *Sloman Neptun*, *Kirsammer Hack*, and *Viscido*,[106] all of which concerned derogations from generally applicable employment law. In the first case, ships registered in Germany were able to employ non-EU workers under less generous conditions than those applicable to EU seafarers. In the second, a provision exempted small and medium-sized undertakings from unfair dismissal legislation. In the third, legislation concerning fixed-term employment contracts contemplated an exemption in favour of the Italian Post Office. In all three cases, the Court confirmed that Article 107(1) TFEU is engaged only if State resources are involved, and found there to be no transfer of resources from the State to the undertakings in question.

[105] Case 82/77 *Van Tiggele* [1978] ECR 25; Joined Cases 213/81 to 215/81 *Norddeutsches Vieh- und Fleischkontor Will and Others v BALM* [1982] ECR 3583; Joined Cases C-67/85, C-68/85 and C-70/85 *Van der Kooy* [1988] ECR 219.

[106] Joined Cases C-72/91 and C-73/91 *Sloman Neptun* [1993] ECR I-887; Joined Cases C-189/91 *Petra Kirsammer-Hack v Nurhan Sidal* [1993] ECR I-6185; Joined Cases C-52/97, C-53/97 and C-54/97 *Epifanio Viscido, Mauro Scandella and Others and Massimiliano Terragnolo and Others v Ente Poste Italiane* [1998] I-02629.

This line of approach was further consolidated and extended in *Preussen Elektra*.[107] The question submitted to the Court was whether a German law, which compelled electricity suppliers to purchase energy from renewable sources *at a fixed minimum price*, amounted to State aid. While the Court acknowledged that the statutory purchase obligation worked to the benefit of certain undertakings, that is, producers of renewable energy, it concluded that the law in question did not involve any direct or indirect transfer of resources from the State to those undertakings. The Court added that the fact that the financial burden arising from the obligation to purchase at minimum prices was likely to have negative repercussions on the economic results of the undertakings subject to that obligation, and therefore to entail a diminution in tax receipts for the State, this was 'an inherent feature of such a legislative provision' and could not be regarded as a means of granting producers of electricity from renewable energy sources a particular advantage at the Member State's expense.[108]

Views on this line of cases were broadly divided into two camps: those who believed that the use of State resources is necessary for pragmatic reasons in order to contain the expansionist nature of Article 107(1) TFEU in relation to the exercise of national regulatory competences;[109] and, on the other camp, those who regarded this as a formalistic approach which leaves open the possibility that measures with anti-competitive effects remain undetected.[110] In his Opinion in *Enirisorse v Sotacarbo*, Advocate General Maduro put his weight behind the latter camp.[111] The reference concerned an Italian law which derogated from general company law in providing that members of a State-controlled undertaking, Sotacarbo, could withdraw from that undertaking on condition that they relinquished all claims over its assets, a situation that gave rise to an advantage for Sotacarbo. Advocate General Maduro acknowledged that the situation would fall outside Article 107(1) TFEU, if the Court were to rely on the State resources test. That approach, he also acknowledged, addressed a genuine preoccupation of the Court, which was to prevent broadening the scope of the EU rules to such an extent as to cover distortions of competition that were simply the result of differences in legislative policy

[107] Case C-379/98 *PreussenElektra* [2001] ECR I-2099.

[108] Ibid para 62.

[109] Alongside Advocate General Jacobs, Weatherill, *Law and Integration in the European Union* (n 40); P Davies, 'Market Integration and Social Policy in the Court of Justice' (1995) 24 *International Law Journal* 49; A Biondi, 'Some Reflections on the Notion of "State Resources" in European Community State Aid Law' (2007) 30 *Fordham International Law Journal* 1426.

[110] M Ross, 'State Aids: Maturing into a Constitutional Problem' (1995) 15 *Yearbook of European Law* 79; M Slotboom, 'State Aid in Community Law: A Broad or Narrow Definition?' (1995) 20 *EL Rev* 289; B Rodger, 'State Aid—A Fully Level Playing Field?' [1999] *European Competition Law Review* 251; M Ross, 'State Aids and National Court: Definitions and Other Problems—A Case of Premature Emancipation?' (2000) 37 *CML Rev* 401; L Rubini, 'The Elusive Frontier: Regulation under State Aid Rules' (2009) 8 *European State Aid Law Quarterly* 277–98; the Commission has also endorsed this view, eg in *Preussen Elektra*.

[111] Case C-237/04 *Enirisorse v Sotacarbo*, Opinion of Advocate General Poiares Maduro [2006] ECR I-2843.

between the Member States.[112] Nonetheless, he went on to say, the test was in many ways unsatisfactory.

The Advocate General's argument turned on three key points. First, the resource transfer test was not always relevant, as a regulatory measure may entail an indirect charge on the State budget greater than that arising from a measure involving a transfer of public resources.[113] He gave two examples to illustrate the point: legislation that facilitated the dismissal of workers in a particular sector and a measure authorising an undertaking to build in a zone that required major infrastructure to be put in place. The second point was that the selectivity criterion provided 'a better rationale for the restrictions set by the Court' in order to distinguish between economic advantages that undertakings derived purely as a result of differences in economic and fiscal policies across the Member States, and those advantages stemming from preferential treatment given by Member States to certain undertakings. Finally, 'with the growing interpenetration of the public and private sectors of the economy', there was a danger that Member States may be tempted to use their regulatory powers to encourage or compel private sector enterprises to alleviate the costs of certain undertakings. If such situations were to fall outside the scope of Article 107(1) TFEU, 'a significant portion of State measures having all the *effects* of State aid would escape the scrutiny of the Community authorities', an outcome which would be 'manifestly at variance with the objectives pursued by the Treaty and the principles laid down by the Court in its case-law.'[114]

Advocate General Maduro's solution to concentrate on selectivity is, however, not without its difficulties; the pitfalls of this approach become apparent when one considers some of the views expressed by another Advocate General who also believed that the real question should be whether the measure is selective. Advocate General Darmon argued, in *Sloman Neptun*, that defining the scope of State aid is an exercise that calls into question 'political and philosophical conceptions regarding the role of the State and the limits of its intervention in the economic sphere'.[115] That, he added, was unsurprising, since the *ratio legis* of Article 107 TFEU was to scrutinise intervention by the State which transcended 'the general legislative framework of economic activities', in particular in fiscal and social matters.[116] The flaws in Advocate General Darmon's approach became apparent in *Kirsammer Hack*, in which he took the view that the special employment rules for small undertakings were justified on the basis of the EU objective of favouring the creation and development of small and medium-sized undertakings, and were based on the consideration that the relationship between employer and employee in small undertakings was a highly personal one which was based on

[112] Ibid para 44.
[113] Ibid para 48.
[114] Ibid para 50. When the judgment was handed down, the Court did not dwell on the State resources condition, as it found that the Italian law in question did not confer an advantage on Sotacarbo.
[115] Opinion of Advocate General Darmon in *Sloman Neptun* (n 106) para 88.
[116] Ibid para 16.

trust and confidence. Yet, as Davies has pointed out, this view rests on an erroneous assumption: contrary to what the Advocate General argued, employees of smaller undertakings have the greatest need for the protection of the law, given the lack of alternative mechanisms provided by trade unions or internal grievance or disciplinary procedures.[117] What this demonstrates is that an exercise, such as the one proposed by both Advocate Generals, which involves an assessment based on the rationale of national regulation or legislation, would risk shifting the definition of State aid into subjective and contestable territory. This is not to say that the definition of State aid exhibits a hard-edged logic which national authorities/courts can follow in a mechanical fashion. But there are good reasons for the interpretation of Article 107(1) TFEU to be guided by simple rule of law concerns, such as legal certainty and equality.

Proponents of the State resources test are, nonetheless, confronted with some powerful objections. The use of State resources seems to be too wide a filter to prevent anti-competitive measures from seeping through. There is no doubt that regulatory measures not directly funded by the State may be equally damaging to competition as subsidies or fiscal exemptions. While there are other provisions in the Treaty, such as the free movement provisions, that could fill in the potential gap left by *Sloman Neptun* and subsequent case law, it is doubtful whether these may always be appropriate. In *Preussen Elektra*, the Court found that the legislation in issue was a measure having equivalent effect to a quantitative restriction as the obligation on electricity suppliers to purchase all of the renewable electricity produced in their area limited the supplies from energy producers in other Member States. Yet, the Court did not have to consider whether setting a minimum purchase price was also an infringement of Article 34 TFEU, an issue which was at the heart of the State aid assessment. In fact, it is doubtful whether, in the absence of a discriminatory element, similar measures would be caught by the free movement provisions.[118] A measure may be selective and discriminatory for the purpose of Article 107 TFEU, and yet be immune from Article 34 TFEU.

Moreover, one of the difficulties in the *Preussen Elektra* line of jurisprudence, as Advocate General Mengozzi has noted,[119] arises in recently liberalised markets in dealing with the non-recoverable (so-called 'stranded') costs arising from liberalisation. In that area, the Advocate General has argued, 'the Commission's powers to monitor national support measures for companies affected by such costs have been significantly reduced' by the 'rigid application' of the State resources condition, 'particularly bearing in mind that such measures are often designed in such a way that the economic burden of recovering those costs falls on final consumers, not infrequently as a result of the introduction of parafiscal charges'.[120] He

117 Above n 109.

118 A minimum purchase price bears all the hallmarks of a selling arrangement.

119 In Case C-206/06 *Essent v Netherlands* [2008] ECR I-5497.

120 Ibid para 97.

therefore suggested that the scope of the judgment in *Preussen Elektra* should be limited to 'circumstances in which a subsidy granted by the public authorities to specific undertakings is exclusively financed through the imposition of charges affecting *private operators* and is paid to the beneficiaries by those operators *directly*'.[121] It should be noted, however, that the Advocate General did not propose to overrule *Preussen Elektra*, but to delimit its scope.

The other difficulty with the State resources test is that it may be hard to calibrate. The Court has taken a middle ground between two approaches. At one end of the spectrum, the application of State aid may be confined to measures that consist in a *direct transfer* of State resources. This approach, however, would be contrary to established case law, which clarifies that the notion of State aid includes not only direct transfers, but also measures that mitigate the charges *normally borne* by undertakings. At the other end of the spectrum is an approach that embraces any measure that *has an impact* on State finances. This would include a reduction in the social charges paid by undertakings, but would potentially include derogations from *any* regulatory requirements that undertakings are normally subject to which may have an impact on the State's finances; plainly, such an approach would defeat the purpose of having a State resources test. The Court's solution in *Sloman Neptun* draws on the idea of *normal* regulatory impact, which, as has seen before, plays a fundamental role in defining selectivity. Advocate General Darmon had advised the Court on that occasion to focus on the question whether national regulation departed from a wider regulatory framework or flowed from it, rather than considering the involvement of State resources. While the Court declined to follow this advice, it appeared to retain the idea of a departure from the normal regulatory framework. The Court found that the legislation in issue was not aimed at providing an advantage in favour of the shipping undertakings, but to alter the regulatory framework of employment between the undertakings and the Third Country National sailors; in doing so, the Court held, such legislation had an impact on State resources, but that impact, far from being a means of creating an advantage for the undertakings, was inherent in the Member State's (de)regulatory intervention. The Court's assumption, therefore, seemed to be that it was only through an analysis of the aim of the relevant regulatory framework that the question regarding the existence of aid could be addressed. Awareness of the purpose of the legislation appeared, in the Court's view, to be necessary in order to distinguish between financial effects inherent in a regulatory system and the wider financial impact of State regulation. In other words, in order to distinguish relevant and irrelevant financial implications one needs to be aware of the link between the intention of legislation and its consequences in terms of State resources.

It is possible to rationalise this case law, without having to rely on regulatory intent, under what may be described as a *remoteness* test. One may argue that

[121] Ibid para 100. The Court has followed the Advocate General in distinguishing *Preussen Elektra*.

a State resources test should capture measures that display a *direct causal link* between the advantage and the commitment of public resources, and discard measures in which such link is too uncertain and indirect. Thus, in *Sloman Neptun*, the diminution of the wage of the TCN seafarers and the advantage received by the shipping undertakings were not the result of a commitment of public funds; the loss of tax receipts was only an indirect consequence of the undertaking's choice to pay its employees less that their colleagues from the EU, an event which was uncertain. This interpretation is also consistent with *Germany v Commission*,[122] in which the Court found that German legislation, which allowed investors to offset up to 100 per cent of any capital gain resulting from the sale of assets or shares in companies against acquisition or production costs, provided that the gain was used to acquire shares in companies that had their head office in one of the new *Länder*, involved State resources to the advantage of the latter companies. The Court held that the advantage indirectly conferred on the undertakings in the new *Länder* originated from the renunciation by the Member State of tax revenue which it would normally have received, as it was this renunciation which had enabled investors to take up holdings in undertakings on conditions which were fiscally more advantageous. The fact that investors then took independent decisions did not mean that the connection between the tax concession and the advantage given to the undertakings in question had been eliminated since, in economic terms, the alteration of the market conditions which gave rise to the advantage was the consequence of the public authorities' loss of tax revenue. More recently, in *Emission Trading*,[123] both the General Court and the Court of Justice took the view that the case, in which the involvement of public resources arose from the State's choice to allocate emission allowances free of charge rather than selling or auctioning them, was to be distinguished from *Preussen Elektra*.[124] In particular, the Court of Justice held that there was a '*sufficiently direct connection* between the measure in question and the loss of revenue', a link which did not exist in *Preussen Elektra*.[125]

4. CONCLUSION

There are a number of areas in which State aid intercepts national regulatory autonomy. These encounters are often problematic, not only for the challenges they pose to Member States that wish to pursue legitimate regulatory policies, but also for the difficulties that State aid law runs into in attempting to delimit its

[122] Case C-156/98 *Germany v Commission* [2000] ECR I-6857.

[123] Case T-233/04 *Netherlands v Commission (Emission Trading)* (n 72); Case C-279/08 P *Commission v Kingdom of the Netherlands (Emission Trading)* (n 74).

[124] Case C-379/98 *Preussen Elektra* (n 107).

[125] Case C-279/08 P *Commission v Kingdom of the Netherlands (Emission Trading)* (n 74) para 111.

scope so as not to encroach upon the legitimate exercise of domestic regulatory competence while remaining true to its key interpretative tenets. These difficulties arise from the fact that regulation requires considerably different analytical tools to the ones employed in reviewing direct participation in market transactions. Moreover, such analytical tools, or boundary markers, are relied on to reconcile rigorous scrutiny of the effects of regulation with the pursuit of a constitutional balance between EU, national and sub-national levels of competence. The development of the inherent justification and the recognition of the involvement of State resources as a necessary element in the definition of State aid may both be seen as attempts to acknowledge the need to offer greater space to national regulatory autonomy. Yet, both give rise to considerable objections. This chapter has argued against the recognition of a rule of reason in State aid law, if it means that policy objectives become an integral part of the definition of State aid, as this would subvert the fundamental structure of State aid control. Instead, the inherent justification should give Member States an opportunity to explain the apparent asymmetry contained in one of their measures on the basis of fundamental features of their regulatory or tax systems. Such a restrictive approach to the inherent justification can be combined with the recognition of the involvement of public resources as a necessary condition for State aid. While the two may appear difficult to reconcile, the advantage of this combination is that it avoids entertaining policy considerations at the wrong stage of State aid control, and, at the same time, it offers Member States a safeguard against the unnecessary intrusion in national legislation and regulatory policy. Bright lines such as this one, however, are not always satisfactory in their application. Yet, recent case law has shown that a remoteness test may be the right way to avoid abuse of this element in the definition of State aid.

Part III

6

State Aid and Self-Government

The power to tax is an essential feature of political autonomy, and claims to self-government that revolve around it are a recurring theme in history. A number of reasons explain why political communities should wish to set, impose and collect taxes from their own members. Not only are such communities attracted by the outcome of the exercise of fiscal power, the revenue that allows them to shape their own collective destinies; they are also drawn to the power to distribute the tax burden and redistribute wealth as they desire; and, crucially, they aspire to control the power to restrict the enjoyment of their own property rights, for, as the term suggests, this is the mark of autonomy.[1]

In Europe, self-government and fiscal decentralisation feature prominently in a number of constitutional systems and in national political discourses. Until recently, however, these matters were believed to lie outside the domain of EU law. A recent development in the State aid case law has prompted a reversal of this belief: the upshot of this case law is that an autonomous region should be able, under certain conditions, to introduce separate corporate tax measures without, in doing so, triggering the prohibition of State aid. However, this chapter argues that the internal logic of State aid law is, taken in isolation, unable to capture the full significance of this development, and that the normative justification for the Court's approach lies outside the domain of State aid law. Moreover, the new emphasis on regional autonomy may cause a shift in the space where tax competition occurs from the inter-State to the infra-State level, while the Court's approach frames the scope of the Commission's action in relation to harmful tax competition.

The chapter begins by introducing some concepts that are central to the definition of State aid in relation to fiscal measures; it then moves on to evaluate the recent case law on regional tax autonomy and to explore alternative normative justifications. The final part evaluates the significance of this case law in relation to tax competition.

[1] Autonomy, as the etymology (from the Greek *autós*, self, and *nómos*, law) suggests, implies the power by a community to make its own laws, which includes tax laws—hence the motto 'no taxation without representation'.

1. THE GEOGRAPHIC DIMENSION OF SELECTIVITY

In addition to material selectivity, which was explored in the previous chapter, the concept of selectivity also captures those measures that favour undertakings in a certain geographic area. Until recently, however, the full meaning of geographic selectivity was not readily determined: it was clear that the concept captured a Member State's decision to limit certain advantages to part of its territory; but what if those measures were, instead, an emanation of a regional authority—would they count as selective? This was the central question in the *Azores* case.[2] Under the Portuguese Constitution, the Azores islands are an autonomous region with their own government, and with fiscal competence and the power to adapt national fiscal provisions to regional specificities. The Azores introduced a scheme aimed at adapting the Portuguese tax system to the special needs and characteristics of those islands, by calibrating the corporate tax rate to a level that was markedly lower than the one in force in mainland Portugal. The Commission was in no doubt that the lower tax rate amounted to State aid. On its view, since undertakings established in the Azores operated in the same political and economic environment as those established in mainland Portugal, selectivity arose from the comparison between the former and the latter. Portugal challenged that decision. Amongst its pleas was the contention that the decision to lower the tax rate resulted from the exercise of the regional legislature's competences and was addressed to all undertakings established in the region. Moreover, the tax reduction stemmed from the exercise of constitutional sovereignty as it was intended to rectify the inequalities in economic development from which the islands suffered, in line with the constitutional principle of solidarity.

In what was to be one of his most influential Opinions on State aid, Advocate General Geelhoed argued that the issue of selectivity in relation to fiscal measures introduced by devolved authorities turned on the degree of autonomy that the taxing authority enjoyed from central government. In cases involving *genuine* autonomy, he submitted, it was appropriate to locate the benchmark at the devolved rather than at the national level. That would certainly be the case where symmetrical devolution was involved.[3] Asymmetrical devolution required, instead, a more complex analysis to determine whether the decision was taken by a truly autonomous entity; and true autonomy, according to the Advocate General, was to be found where, in taking the specific decision regarding its tax rates, the region enjoyed *institutional*, *procedural* and *economic autonomy*. By which, he meant that the region had a 'constitutional, political and administrative status separate from that of the central government' (institutional autonomy);[4]

[2] Case C-88/03 *Portugal v Commission (Azores)* [2006] ECR I-7115. See R Greaves, 'Autonomous Regions, Taxation and EC State Aids Rules' (2009) 34 *EL Rev* 779.

[3] Where symmetrical devolution occurs, each region enjoys the same powers; conversely, devolution is asymmetrical where autonomy is not equally distributed among regions.

[4] *Azores* (n 2) para 54.

that the central government did not have any power to intervene directly in the devolved authority's procedure in setting the tax rate, and that the local authority was not obliged to take the interest of the central State into account in setting the tax rate (procedural autonomy); and, finally, that the economic consequences of setting a lower tax rate would be borne by the devolved entity without there being a cross-subsidisation or other form of funding from central government (economic autonomy). In the case at issue, the Azores were undoubtedly autonomous from an institutional point of view, but their decision on corporate taxation lacked both procedural and economic autonomy, as it was taken on the basis of the principle of national solidarity, which entailed cooperation between the autonomous region and central government, and also entailed a direct transfer from the Portuguese State to the autonomous region so as to compensate for the reduction in the corporate tax rate.

The Grand Chamber followed the Advocate General. The starting point for a selectivity analysis was, it held, to find the 'reference framework' on which the question whether certain undertakings received more favourable treatment than others would have to hinge. That reference framework did not necessarily have to coincide with the national territory of a Member State—it could be made up by part of it. An 'infra-State body' could in fact enjoy a legal and factual status that would make it 'sufficiently autonomous in relation to the central government of a Member State' and, as a result, that body and not the central government would 'play a fundamental role in the definition of the political and economic environment in which undertakings operate'.[5] The Court then went on to apply the three criteria that the Advocate General had outlined. It found that while the Azores region could be regarded as institutionally *and* procedurally autonomous from the Portuguese State, it did not enjoy the same degree of autonomy in the economic and financial sense. The existence of budgetary transfers from the central government, which compensated for the reduced revenue resulting from the reductions in tax rates, meant that the region could not be regarded as being sufficiently autonomous to constitute the reference framework for the selectivity test.

Later, the question of regional tax autonomy resurfaced in *UGT-Rioja*,[6] and in the General Court's ruling in *Gibraltar v Commission*.[7] The *UGT-Rioja* case displayed some important analogies with the *Azores* case. The context was crucially different though. As Advocate General Kokott pointed out,[8] whilst, in *Azores*, the Court itself was to decide on whether the Commission had demonstrated the existence of State aid, in the latter case, the Court's task was to interpret Article 107(1) TFEU, leaving the referring court to decide on the selective or general

[5] Ibid para 34.

[6] Joined Cases C-428/06 to C-434/06 *Unión General de Trabajadores de La Rioja (UGT-Rioja) v Juntas Generales del Territorio Histórico de Vizcaya* [2008] ECR I-6747.

[7] Cases T-211/04 and T-215/04 *Gibraltar v Commission* [2008] ECR II-3745; the appeal ruling did not deal with geographic selectivity as it found the measures at issue to be materially selective, Joined Cases C-106/09 P and C-107/09 P *Commission and Spain v Gibraltar and UK* (11 November 2011).

[8] *UGT-Rioja* (n 6), Opinion of Advocate General Kokott, paras 59–60.

nature of the measure. The questions referred concerned measures adopted by the three independent provincial authorities (the 'Diputaciones Forales' of Vizcaya, Álava, and Guipúzcoa) that form the Autonomous Community of the Basque Country, which have the power to introduce tax legislation, such as the legislation at issue, that set the corporation tax rate at 32.5 per cent, below the 35 per cent rate generally applicable in Spain.

Regional autonomy is at the heart of the constitutional arrangements in contemporary Spain, and Advocate General Kokott identified the heightened constitutional sensitivity of the issues at stake. Article 4(2) TEU, she pointed out, requires the EU to respect the 'national identities of its Member States', a duty reinforced in the Lisbon Treaty, which expressly mentions respect for the 'constitutional structures' of the Member States.[9] On the other hand, the Advocate General recalled that the Court has consistently held that internal situations resulting from constitutional provisions are not immune from the application of EU law. On her view, the Court in *Azores* 'struck a reasonable balance between these two principles': '[o]n the one hand, it respects the autonomy which the Constitution of the Member State in question grants to its local and regional authorities', while, on the other hand, 'the requirements relating to the autonomy of the local legislator ensure that the Member States cannot hide behind their constitutional order and circumvent the prohibition on aid under Article 107 TFEU through a purely formal transfer of legislative powers'.[10]

The Advocate General rejected the Commission's suggestion that the assessment of the degree of autonomy enjoyed by a sub-national authority was to be based on its *general* freedom to determine its economic policy. She focused instead on its autonomy in adopting the *specific* measures in question. The Court's response was along similar lines: the fact that an authority played a fundamental role in the definition of the political and economic environment in which undertakings operated was not a precondition for autonomy, but a consequence of the autonomy that the region enjoyed from the institutional, procedural and economic point of view. The Court went on to offer some additional guidance on the second and third criteria. Procedural autonomy occurred, on the Court's view, even where a process of consultation and conciliation between the national and sub-national levels was in place, and where national authorities were required to take the State interest into account in order to respect the limits of their powers.[11]

On the economic and financial autonomy front, the Court dealt with the question about whether the existence of transfers from the centre to the regions was an indication of their lack of autonomy. The Court, along with the Advocate General,

[9] The first sentence of Article 4 TEU as amended by the Treaty of Lisbon states:
The Union shall respect the equality of Member States before the Treaties as well as their national identities, inherent in their fundamental structures, political and constitutional, inclusive of *regional and local self-government.*

[10] *UGT-Rioja* (n 6) para 56.

[11] Ibid paras 102–08.

held that the existence of financial transfers was not sufficient to demonstrate the absence of sufficient autonomy for the regions, given that those transfers could take place for 'reasons unconnected with the tax measures'.[12] It added, however, that the question whether the correct reference framework was to be the Spanish State or, instead, the Historical Territories was to be decided not only on the basis of the three criteria outlined in *Azores*, but also, as a preliminary matter, on the basis of a review of whether the regions had overstepped their competences—given that financial transfers had been drawn up on the basis of a precise division of competences and on the basis of limits to the exercise of devolved powers.

The General Court's *Gibraltar* ruling has added a further piece to this mosaic.[13] Gibraltar, an independent overseas territory of the UK, had planned to introduce a reform of its tax system consisting of a general abolition of taxation of company profits, with the exception of top-up taxes on utilities and financial services activities. The general tax system introduced would consist of a payroll tax, a business property occupation tax (BPOT) and an annual company registration fee. Liability for payroll tax together with BPOT would be capped at a maximum of 15 per cent of profits—the maximum UK corporate tax rate in place at the time was 30 per cent. The Commission found, therefore, that the reform was regionally selective since it provided for a system under which companies established in Gibraltar would be taxed, in general, at a lower rate than those in the UK.

That decision was challenged, but the General Court held that the three *Azores* criteria were satisfied. The competent Gibraltar authorities that had devised the tax reform enjoyed, from a constitutional point of view, a political and administrative status separate from that of the central government of the UK. The UK's residual power to legislate for Gibraltar and the various powers granted to the Governor of Gibraltar were to be interpreted as means of enabling the UK to assume its responsibilities towards the population of Gibraltar and to perform its obligations under international law, and not as allowing the UK to intervene directly on the content of individual tax measures adopted by the Gibraltar authorities, in particular since those residual powers had never been exercised in matters of taxation.

As to financial autonomy, the General Court found that none of the financing measures referred to by the Commission served to offset any financial consequences that the tax reform would entail for Gibraltar. As the Court of Justice had done in *Rioja*, the General Court made clear that the absence of offsetting mechanisms should be interpreted narrowly. The verb 'offset' used by the *Azores* ruling implied a causal link between the tax measure adopted by the infra-State body and the financial support from other regions or the central government.[14]

12 Ibid para 135.

13 Joined Cases T-211/04 and T-215/04 *Government of Gibraltar and United Kingdom v Commission* [2008] ECR II-3745.

14 Cases T-211/04 and T-215/04 *Gibraltar v Commission* (n 7) para 106. For criticism of the General Court's *Gibraltar* ruling, see PP Rossi-Maccanico, 'Gibraltar and the Unsettled Limits of Selectivity in Fiscal Aids' (2009) *European State Aid Law Quarterly* 63.

A. The Relevant Economic Space

The *Azores* jurisprudence is not without its critics, who claim that the Court may have sacrificed the objectivity of the definition of State aid and the effectiveness of State aid control on the altar of regional autonomy.[15] The focus, they argue, should be on the effects of the measure, not on the constitutional status of the authority from which it originates. Moreover, critics point out that the State aid rules are addressed to States and that the Treaty does not contemplate the existence of regional authorities:[16] while it may be the case that many important powers have shifted from the national to the sub-national level, this state of affairs should find recognition in a treaty amendment rather than through a novel approach which, in attempting to accommodate a pressing political need, may result in exonerating measures that have a potentially damaging impact on competition.

In order to evaluate this criticism, it is necessary to consider whether the presence of autonomy really does make a difference in terms of anti-competitive effects; whether, in other words, genuine autonomy rules out the existence of an impact on competition equivalent to the impact that would potentially arise from a measure enacted by a region that lacks such autonomy, or from a regionally circumscribed measure enacted by a central government. Consider the hypothetical example of a region of a Member State where nearly all the country's financial services industry is clustered. Suppose that the central government decided to confer on that region autonomous status and to provide it with tax and spend powers, and that such powers were exercised autonomously, without interference from central government. Suppose, moreover, that the region set its tax rate at a significantly lower level than the national equivalent. Imagine, also, that the region was able to rely on its low tax rate to draw to its jurisdiction undertakings operating in the financial sector from other countries. On the strength of this effect, the region would be able to afford the decision to set the tax rate without any transfers from central government. On the *Azores* approach, this region would be regarded as sufficiently autonomous and its corporate tax rate would not constitute State aid.

What, then, is the difference between this scenario, where the region enjoys full autonomy, and cases where such autonomy is missing? The Court's answer is that the key lies in the fact that, in the autonomy scenario, undertakings operate under a political and economic environment that is separate from the national framework. If a region exercises its fiscal powers under institutional and procedural autonomy, and does not receive cross-subsidies or transfers from the State, its decisions in the fiscal sphere only affect the infrastructure and business environment in which undertakings operate. That is because, under autonomy,

[15] B Kurcz, 'How Selective is Selectivity? A Few Thoughts on Regional Selectivity' (2007) 66 *CLJ* 313; J Winter, (Case Note) (2008) 45 *CML Rev* 183.

[16] Eg Winter, (Case Note) (n 15).

a region must take political responsibility for *individual* decisions and accept the financial consequences of reductions in fiscal revenue.[17] In doing so, the region needs to devise means of absorbing the budget effects of its fiscal policy decisions. It might, for instance, reduce spending on infrastructure, or on public services. In a region that lacks autonomy, the responsibility for such decisions and/or their financial consequences may be shouldered by other regions and/or by the central government. Thus, undertakings that are subject to taxation in an autonomous region operate in a different economic environment to undertakings that live in the rest of the country: they may have lower corporate taxation but, as a result, may not benefit from the same level of public spending as occurs in other parts of the country.

The crucial assumption in *Azores* seems, therefore, to be that genuine autonomy creates a distinct *economic space*, such that the relationship in terms of economic space between an autonomous region and the Member State of which it is part is equivalent, mutatis mutandis, to the relationship between *different* Member States.[18] Just as the comparison between undertakings operating in different national regulatory regimes is deemed irrelevant,[19] the comparison between undertakings operating under an autonomous region and undertakings operating in other parts of the country becomes devoid of relevance. The fundamental reason behind this assumption is that a genuinely autonomous tax regime creates separate cost structures for undertakings. Moreover, the absence of cross-subsidies means that undertakings in other parts of the country are not affected by the fiscal decisions taken by the authorities in the autonomous region. Conversely, in the absence of financial autonomy, a decision taken by the regional authorities may have implications for undertakings located in other parts of the country (as the transfer is funded by central government).

The argument based on economic space and autonomy runs into several problems, however. First of all, the economic space in which undertakings operate does not necessarily coincide with the jurisdiction of the tax authority. Undertakings that are subject to corporation tax in one Member State are likely to operate beyond regional borders and may in fact conduct most of their business outside those borders. In the absence of adequate mechanisms to allocate profits among different corporation tax jurisdictions, it may well be that undertakings that effectively operate within the same economic space gain a competitive edge because of the autonomous status of the regions in which they are domiciled for tax purposes. Secondly, while the absence of financial transfers is an essential requirement for a region to be regarded as genuinely autonomous, the *UGT-Rioja* ruling makes

17 The point was made by the UK government in *Azores* (n 2) and referred to by the Court at para 68.

18 The term 'economic space' is borrowed from A Hughes Hallett and D Scott, 'Scotland: A New Fiscal Settlement', Centre for Dynamic Macroeconomic Analysis Working Paper Series, 10/09, www.st-andrews.ac.uk/economics/CDMA/papers/wp1009.pdf. The Court uses the term 'reference framework'.

19 For the reasons illustrated above.

plain that the requirement applies exclusively to the specific tax measure under consideration. Since the financial autonomy test focuses on the individual decision and on direct links between a transfer and the decision, any type of indirect compensation will fall through the net. Given that the Court does not go as far as to require comprehensive economic and financial autonomy, its test does not rule out indirect compensation mechanisms. For instance, the test does not rule out the possibility that lower taxation may in the long term result in a budget deficit and may, eventually, involve a bail-out by the central government.[20] Of course, Member States may be able to eliminate ex ante indirect transfers or compensation mechanisms, and to introduce safeguards designed to reduce the likelihood of bail-outs.[21] But the *Azores* approach does not compel them to do so.

B. The Constitutional Dimension

To this point, close analysis of the *Azores* jurisprudence has concluded that the test advanced by the Court is not as far reaching as to exclude the risk of distortions of competition caused by regional tax measures. This analysis, however, has, so far, neglected the constitutional dimension of this case law. The fundamental question that needs to be considered here is whether the constitutional status of regional autonomy is only relevant as an element in the selectivity test, or whether the existence of a constitutional dimension also colours the Court's approach to the problem in a more general sense.

As seen above, in *UGT-Rioja*, Advocate General Kokott expressed the view that the *Azores* ruling struck the right balance between, on the one hand, the obligation, under Article 4(2) TEU, to respect national constitutional identities and, on the other, the principle that Member States are barred from pleading internal constitutional reasons to escape the application of EU law. The Court, while following the Advocate General's advice in large part, did not mention Article 4(2) TEU. This is not the first instance in which the Court has not shared an Advocate General's enthusiasm for this provision.[22] Yet, it may be wondered whether, in

[20] Sub-national governments often act as if under a 'soft budget constraint': they are inclined to spend and/or borrow excessively and disinclined to tax at the appropriate level. See generally G Eskeland and J Litvack (eds), *Fiscal Decentralization and the Challenge of Hard Budget Constraints* (Cambridge, MIT Press, 2003). For a recent example of this phenomenon, see V Mallet and J Ford, 'Zapatero warns on regional spending' *Financial Times*, 16 January 2011.

[21] For instance, by adopting similar solutions to those proposed in Hughes Hallett and Scott, 'Scotland: A New Fiscal Settlement' (n 18).

[22] See Advocate General Poiares Maduro's Opinion in Case C-213/07 *Michaniki* [2008] ECR I-9999, paras 31–33. See also the Opinion of Advocate General Ruiz-Jarabo Colomer in C-205/08 *Umweltanwalt von Kärnten v Kärntner Landesregierung* [2009] ECR I-11525, para 47. There are, nonetheless, a couple of instances in which the Court has referred to the provision. In Case C-473/93 *Commission v Luxembourg* [1996] ECR I-3207, the Court recognised that Article 4(2) TEU (which was, at the time, Article F(1) TEU) could, in principle, justify a derogation from the free movement provisions, but rejected that justification in the case at hand. And see, more recently, in relation to Article 21

this particular area of EU law, the omission may actually inhibit an exhaustive justification from being provided for the significant leap away from EU law orthodoxy taken in *Azores*. In effect, the adoption of a Member State's jurisdiction as the natural reference framework for the selectivity test flows naturally from the structure of the Treaty, which assumes that regulatory or tax jurisdictions are drawn along national lines and that the relevant economic space in which undertakings operate is the national territory. In the absence of a compelling economic argument to overcome the fact that regions, as far as the definition of State aid is concerned, are irrelevant, and in the absence of reasons inherent to State aid law that justify such a move, the constitutional argument offered by Advocate General Kokott may provide the basis for a normative justification.

Arguably, only once it is accepted that EU law should be interpreted in such a way as to avoid encroaching upon national constitutional identities, does the *Azores* test acquire a coherent shape. The starting point is the tension between Article 4(2) TEU and Article 107 TFEU. A strict interpretation of the definition of State aid would prevent asymmetrically devolved regions from exercising the power to tax, or would prescribe that Member States introduce precise and detailed arrangements in order to exclude the possibility of indirect transfers or future bail-outs. The latter solution appears to be disproportionate, however—it would be extremely difficult to police, and would severely constrain the choices open to Member States in pursuing tax decentralisation. The opposite solution, to give regional authorities carte blanche in matters of taxation, would be equally undesirable as it would present a high risk of abuse and would leave the door open to potential distortions of competition. Instead, the balance struck by the Court in *Azores* constrains Member States in order to minimise distortions and, at the same time accepts, to a certain extent, the risk that some distortions may occur. But these side-effects are necessary in order to maintain the effectiveness of State aid policy, while showing deference towards a core feature of national constitutional identity.[23]

This interpretation may appear to resonate with the arguments of a certain strand of constitutional pluralism, which holds that, in the presence of competing claims to normative authority, which are equally valid from the perspective of the legal orders from which they each emanate, the Court should explore new

TFEU, Case C-208/09 *Sayn-Wittgenstein* [2010] ECR I-0000. The *Omega* judgment, which, however, does not contain any reference to Article 4(2) TEU, is often cited as an example of sensitivity towards domestic constitutional identity: Case C-36/02 *Omega* [2004] ECR I-9609. For discussion, see LFM Besselink, 'National and constitutional identity before and after Lisbon' (2010) 6 *Utrecht Law Review* 36; T Konstadinides, 'Constitutional Identity as a Shield and as a Sword: The European Legal Order within the Framework of National Constitutional Settlement' (2010–2011) 13 *Cambridge Yearbook of European Legal Studies* 195; A von Bogdandy and S Schill, 'Overcoming Absolute Primacy: Respect for National Constitutional Identity under the Lisbon Treaty' (2011) 48 *CML Rev* 1417.

23 Besselink, 'National and constitutional identity before and after Lisbon' (n 22) believes that the obligation stemming from Article 4(2) TEU may concern the core of national constitutional identity rather than any constitutional provision.

means of avoiding conflicts between constitutional orders.[24] Yet, while a loose association with the broad ideas of constitutional pluralism may be legitimate in respect of Advocate General Kokott's reasoning, the language of the Court does not lend itself to such an interpretation. Granted, the Court cannot be expected to adopt the academic vernacular of constitutional pluralism; but it can reasonably be expected to make use of existing normative tools, namely Article 4(2) TEU, in order to provide its reasoning with greater openness and coherence. There is little doubt that the avoidance of conflict with national constitutional identities ranks high among the Court's priorities. After all, the Court created, over the years and well before the explosion of interest in constitutional pluralism, a number of juridical devices designed to compose potentially conflicting EU and national claims: one need only think of the doctrine of mandatory requirements, or the creation of an EU doctrine of fundamental rights as general principles drawn from national constitutional traditions and from the European Convention on Human Rights. And while much of the constitutional pluralist's attention has been directed towards the resolution of hypothetical conflicts arising from major ruptures in constitutional dialogue between the EU and its Member States, as Davies has argued, there is much to commend to the idea that the legal reasoning employed in avoiding conflicts between constitutional systems in those day-to-day situations in which they are more likely to arise should be articulated more openly.[25] Perhaps, as far as the *Azores* jurisprudence is concerned, Article 4(2) TEU holds the key to such openness.

2. THE SHIFTING SCOPE OF TAX COMPETITION

The shift in the definition of the relevant reference framework is predicated, as seen before, on the recognition of the autonomous region as the relevant economic space. There are important implications that turn on this new relevance of autonomous regions. For, while the system of State aid law prescribes a rigid separation between the prohibition of State aid and the compatibility of its justifications, such that policy considerations are expected to feature only in the latter stage, the very prohibition of State aid has nonetheless served as a powerful policy tool in the Commission's efforts to curb harmful tax competition. A redefinition of the boundaries of the concept of selectivity along regional lines carries with it, therefore, a redefinition of the space in which tax competition may take place. This section examines, first, the background to the Commission's policy on tax competition and the role of State aid in this connection, and then goes on to consider the significance of the *Azores* case law for this policy.

[24] See in particular G Davies, 'Constitutional Disagreement in Europe and the Search for Pluralism', Eric Stein Working Paper 1/2010, www.papers.ssrn.com/sol3/papers.cfm?abstract_id=1559323.

[25] Ibid.

The starting point in the debate on tax competition is the idea that, when economic factors are able to move across jurisdictions, decisions regarding the allocation or the level of the tax burden influence businesses' choice of location; governments therefore deliberately engage in a process of mutual rivalry aimed at attracting or retaining the establishment of business activities within their respective jurisdictions. In this light, businesses are seen as consumers to whom governments offer a choice of different combinations of tax and public goods' provision. Much as in competition among undertakings, rivalry focuses on price or on the quality of the product offered (respectively the tax system and the public goods): certain States may opt for a low-tax competitive strategy; others may decide to compete on the quality of the provision of public goods.

Different schools of thought have emerged in relation to the assessment of the impact of tax competition. One view holds that tax competition acts as a powerful and positive constraint on politicians' tendency to pursue their own self-interest by exerting a downward pressure on taxation and public spending—competition, on this view, represents a means of disciplining governments whose fiscal appetite is at odds with the general welfare of society.[26] On this view, governments' recourse to taxation is an expression of their desire to increase their own powers (the Leviathan argument) and/or of pressures from particular interest groups. Competition among governments may reduce the influence of these interests and yield outcomes that better match the preferences of those who choose a jurisdiction on the basis of the combination of the level of taxation and level of public service provision that it has to offer. Tax competition is, according to such a view, 'an objective to be sought in its own right'.[27]

Opponents of this view argue that the use of fiscal measures to influence the choice of business location creates negative cross-border externalities. Not only are governments severely limited in their powers to deploy fiscal policy to stimulate domestic growth and to pursue redistributive goals, but national electorates are also prevented from being able to exercise effective influence over their governments' fiscal policies.[28] When governments compete on corporate taxation, the argument goes, the outcome is a generalised downward pressure on corporate taxation levels (a 'race to the bottom'), even in States that would not necessarily share the same preference on the relative allocation of the tax burden as those States that initiated the 'race to the bottom'. In other words, lowering the tax burden for undertakings may not always be linked to a clear strategy aimed at attracting relocation; it may—rather—be a move dictated by necessity rather than by choice. The move may be a response to aggressive competitive strategies on the part of other States. Yet, a generalised reduction in tax rates may only be

[26] G Brennan and JM Buchanan, *The Power to Tax: Analytical Foundations of a Fiscal Constitution* (Cambridge, Cambridge University Press, 1980) ch 9.

[27] Ibid 186.

[28] HW Sinn, *The New Systems Competition* (Oxford, Wiley-Blackwell, 2003); FW Scharpf, *Governing in Europe: Effective and Democratic?* (Oxford, Oxford University Press, 1999).

sustainable if accompanied by a reallocation of the fiscal burden from mobile to less mobile economic factors.

Both of these views agree on the proposition that competition among jurisdictions leads to a 'race to the bottom'. The so-called 'new economic geography' literature questions, however, the extent and inexorability of such an effect.[29] The level of taxation, according to this literature, may not necessarily be a decisive factor in influencing location. An exodus of corporations towards a low tax jurisdiction may not be inevitable. Other factors that may be more powerful than tax rates in determining location choices ('agglomeration forces', in the language of new economic geography) may in effect have a defining impact on such decisions, as industrial activity tends to agglomerate in countries that have a widespread presence of advanced economic activity.[30] The design of corporate taxation differs accordingly: larger States with more advanced economies tend to have higher tax rates, whereas smaller States with less developed economies are more likely to gain from aggressive tax competition.[31]

There is a significant European dimension to the debate on tax competition, which raises issues that lie at the heart of European integration. A crucial feature of this debate is the link between taxation and national democratic sovereignty. The delicate nature of such a link is reflected in the unanimity requirement for legislation to be introduced in the fiscal area.[32] Although attempts to introduce harmonising legislation in the field of direct taxation have emerged periodically, all such attempts have floundered in the absence of unanimous agreement among the Member States. In the 1990s, however, partly as a result of the growing salience of subsidiarity, the Commission changed its stance on the matter. Plans to harmonise corporate taxation were put on ice, leaving the Member States fully in control of their tax systems,[33] while the focus of Community intervention was placed on major distortions of competition. This proved more attractive to the Member States, given the difference in views among them as to the appropriate level and scope of intervention in the field. The increase in interdependence, amplified in the European context by the removal of obstacles to the free flow of

[29] Eg R Baldwin and P Krugman, 'Agglomeration, Integration and Tax Harmonisation' (2004) 48 *European Economic Review* 1.

[30] This may explain why a country such as Germany, which has one of the highest levels of corporate taxation among industrialised countries, is also very successful in attracting foreign direct investment.

[31] The examples of Ireland, the Baltic States and Cyprus appear to confirm this. However, some point out that tax is not the only factor in attracting businesses to these jurisdictions. Among the 'agglomeration factors' that have facilitated foreign direct investment in Ireland, Krugman emphasises the high level of education of its workforce. P Krugman, 'Good News from Ireland: A Geographical Perspective' in A Gray (ed), *International Perspectives on the Irish Economy* (Dublin, Indecon, 1998) 38–53.

[32] Article 114(2) TFEU and Article 115 TFEU.

[33] There is, however, an important (ongoing) project to establish a Common Consolidated Corporate Tax Base (CCCTB). In 2004, the Commission set up a working group made up of national experts to formulate technical solutions to be elaborated in a directive based on Article 115 TFEU. www.ec.europa.eu/taxation_customs/taxation/company_tax/common_tax_base/index_en.htm.

economic factors and, in particular, by the liberalisation of capital movements, coupled with the adoption of the European single currency, which eliminated monetary policy as a means of achieving comparative advantage,[34] increased the tendency of Member States to acquire or consolidate their competitive edge through taxation and exacerbated the distortions caused by these strategies.[35] In this environment, while some Member States (plainly, those that stood to gain from tax competition) opposed any move towards coordination in the tax area, others (those that perceived tax competition as a threat) called for decisive intervention at supranational level.[36]

The Commission's new approach, which focused on 'harmful tax competition', was therefore an attempt to mediate between apparently irreconcilable positions. In December 1997, agreement was reached in the ECOFIN Council on the three areas that the Commission had highlighted as deserving greater coordination: business taxation; withholding taxes on cross-border interest and royalty payments between companies; and taxes on savings. In the first area, the finance ministers passed a resolution in respect of a Code of Conduct on business taxation and the Commission undertook to publish guidelines on the application of State aid to business taxation.[37] In the other two areas, the Commission was asked to issue proposals for directives. The Code of Conduct on business taxation, a soft law instrument, provided for a roll-back of existing measures and a 'stand-still' commitment (a commitment, that is, to refrain from introducing any such measures in the future). Both were, of course, voluntary commitments. Subsequently, a Code of Conduct Group was established in order to identify the tax measures that may fall within the scope of the Code of Conduct for business taxation. In a report of November 1999, the Group identified 66 tax measures with harmful features.[38] Finally, in June 2003, the Council reached an agreement on adopting the Code of Conduct.[39] Alongside the adoption of the Code, the Commission undertook to publish guidelines on the application of Articles 107 to 109 TFEU to measures relating to direct business taxation and expressed commitment to 'the strict application' of the State aid rules.[40]

Interestingly, State aid became an effective means of achieving clout against the Member States in negotiations leading to the adoption of the Code of Conduct.[41] In fact, because of the (partial) overlap between the Code and the State aid rules,

[34] Within the 'euro-zone'.

[35] Though the constraints associated with the Growth and Stability Pact, which requires Member States to converge around criteria aimed to achieve price stability and to contain their budget deficit, also act as a brake on Member States' ambitions to pursue competitiveness through fiscal means.

[36] C Radaelli and US Kraemer, 'Governance Areas in EU Direct Tax Policy' (2008) 46 *Journal of Common Market Studies* 315.

[37] Conclusion of the ECOFIN Council Meeting Concerning Taxation Policy [1998] OJ C 2/1.

[38] 40 in EU Member States, three in Gibraltar and 23 in dependent or associated territories.

[39] The Code remains a soft law instrument.

[40] Code of Conduct, para J.

[41] For an early assessment see W Schön, 'Taxation and State Aid in the European Union' (1999) 36 *CML Rev* 911.

the latter could be said to have achieved through legal obligation part of what was to be achieved, according to the Code of Conduct, through voluntary cooperation.[42] Moreover, the pressure exerted through the State aid investigations is widely acknowledged to have acted as a 'hard law stick' in inducing Member States to reach agreement on the Code of Conduct.[43] As the Commission itself recognised in its 2004 report on State aid relating to business taxation, the application of the State aid rules in parallel with the work on the Code of Conduct had 'facilitated the conclusion of an agreement on the Code of Conduct'.[44] This relationship may be seen at play in the Commission's decision-making practice in the field of corporate taxation, which became particularly intense between 2001 and 2003, during which time investigations were launched against 15 different aid measures across 12 Member States, all of which were found to fall within Article 107(1) TFEU.[45]

While some commentators have encouraged the use of State aid as a 'majoritarian' means of dealing with the lack of the necessary unanimous consensus for harmonisation, others have stigmatised this practice as a form of tax harmonisation by stealth.[46] A third group has questioned the effectiveness of the use of State aid as a means of dealing with harmful tax competition. The application of State aid in such a function may, they argue, turn out to be counterproductive, as it may encourage Member States to replace preferential regimes with generally applicable low tax regimes thus creating a more serious distortion than the original one.[47]

[42] Radaelli and Kraemer, 'Governance Areas in EU Direct Tax Policy' (n 36).

[43] The expression is used by W Bratton and J McCahery, 'Tax Coordination and Tax Competition in the European Union: Evaluating the Code of Conduct on Business Taxation' (2001) 38 *CML Rev* 677. According to Radaelli and Kraemer, 'different modes of governance have been used strategically to reinforce each other in the same governance arena. Some Member States have not liked it and argued that the Commission could not demand agreement on a soft learning process within the code and at the same time dangle the Damocles' sword of the Treaty-based State aid procedure on the recalcitrant governments. But this is precisely what the Commission's political strategy was trying to achieve.' ibid 328.

[44] 'Commission Report on the Implementation of the Notice on the Application of the State Aid Rules to Measures Relating to Business Taxation' (2004) C434 of 9/2/2004 www.ec.europa.eu/competition/state_aid/studies_reports/rapportaidesfiscales_en.pdf.

[45] Ibid.

[46] From the former camp, Scharpf argues that 'if there are good reasons to use legal, rather than political, processes for the control of State aids, these would also support the use of the same kinds of procedures for controlling the temptations of unfair regulatory competition', FW Scharpf, 'Democratic Legitimacy under Conditions of Regulatory Competition: Why Europe Differs from the United States' in K Nicolaidis and R Howse (eds), *The Federal Vision* (Oxford, Oxford University Press, 2000) 355. From the latter camp, F Nanetti and G Mameli, 'The Creeping Normative Role of the EC Commission in the Twin-Track Struggle Against State Aids and Harmful Tax Competition' (2002) 11 *EC Tax Review* 185; A Fantozzi, 'The Applicability of State Aid Rules to Tax Competition Measures: A Process of *de Facto* Harmonization in the Tax Field?' in W Schön (ed), *Tax Competition in Europe* (Amsterdam, IBFD, 2003) 121–32. A more nuanced view is expressed in CHJI Panayi, 'State Aid and Tax: The Third Way?' (2004) 32 *Intertax* 283.

[47] M Keen, 'Preferential Regimes Can Make Tax Competition Less Harmful' (2001) 54 *National Tax Journal* 757; a similar argument is made by G Meussen, 'Fiscal Support Measures and Harmful Tax Competition' (2000) 9 *EC Tax Review* 152. The Irish 'manufacturing relief' scheme could be described as an example of this phenomenon. The scheme provided for a preferential corporate tax rate of 10% in favour of undertakings in the manufacturing industry in Ireland. In its infancy, the scheme was considered to be lawful: the Commission initially raised no objections to it, as it considered the

If State aid is an effective tool in the pursuit of the Commission's policy against harmful tax competition, that tool may have been blunted by the *Azores* jurisprudence. The potential effect of the *Azores* test is to shift the space for tax competition from the inter-State to the infra-State level. One may see this as a natural consequence of tax decentralisation, and some may even regard this as a positive development: proponents of tax competition will argue that it results in a more efficient allocation of business across regions; its detractors may argue, instead, that such tax competition may lead to an unequal distribution of wealth across regions and may ultimately threaten the bond of solidarity among regions. Yet, given the well-known agglomeration effects that arise where certain industries are clustered around a circumscribed geographic area, there is a real danger that regional autonomy could be used to replicate similar states of affairs to those that the Commission's application of the State aid rules had attempted to bring to an end. Instead of singling out certain economic sectors for competitive tax measures, Member States may well choose to go down the regional autonomy route to achieve the same effect. Nonetheless, the *Azores* test contains some form of safeguard against the excesses of strategic decision-making, as the requirement for regions to bear the financial consequences of their decisions in tax matters could act as a disincentive for regions to engage in aggressive competitive tactics, and should, to an extent, prevent Member States from providing regions with the funds that would allow such tactics to be exploited.

3. CONCLUSION

At a time when, as a consequence of the banking and euro-zone crises, public finances are, in a number of Member States, under severe strain, and fiscal retrenchment is the order of the day, the debate on self-government and fiscal autonomy is necessarily coloured by the prevailing economic climate. In this state of affairs, tensions between different levels of governance are exacerbated. EU institutions are often perceived to be at odds with national democracies, as they exert a strong influence over domestic economic policy decisions, particularly in the euro-zone.[48] Moreover, indirect transfers from countries with stronger

measure to have a general scope and, hence, to fall outside the scope of Article 107(1) TFEU; nor did it raise any objections when, in 1990, the Irish government notified its intention to extend this rate until 2010. It was only in 1998, in light of the events that set the Code of Conduct process in motion, that the Commission decided that the Irish manufacturing relief scheme was to be regarded as aid (albeit existing rather than new aid). Subsequently, the Commission negotiated with Ireland the phasing out of the existing scheme and its replacement with a general corporate tax with a 12.5% rate on trading income and a 25% rate on other income. See Commission 'Proposal for appropriate measures under Article 93(1) of the EC Treaty concerning Irish corporation tax' [1998] OJ C 395/09.

48 On which see F Scharpf, 'Monetary Union, Fiscal Crisis and the Preemption of Democracy' in LSE 'Europe in Question' Discussion Paper Series No 36/2011, www2.lse.ac.uk/europeanInstitute/LEQS/LEQSPaper36.pdf.

finances towards countries with weaker finances are a cause of great concern for public opinion in the former countries. Similar tensions are mirrored within individual Member States, as governments attempt to rein in public spending by exercising closer control over financial decisions taken at decentralised level.

These tensions are the result of the direct and indirect connections between different economic and political spaces. Thus, fiscal profligacy in, say, Catalonia is no longer exclusively a Spanish problem but, as a result of economic and monetary union, becomes a European issue. Similarly, Northern Ireland's plan to introduce a corporate tax rate to match the Republic of Ireland's rate, if it ever materialises, is not simply a matter that concerns the UK alone, but raises issues of comparative advantage within the EU. To complicate matters further, since fiscal autonomy is often enshrined in national constitutional structures, interactions between different economic and political spaces may also be regarded as interactions between different constitutional spaces.

State aid is part of this picture. The significance of the line of case law developed since the *Azores* ruling is that it brings about a fundamental shift in the definition of the relevant economic space in State aid law from the exclusively national to the sub-national level. Yet, as this chapter has shown, that case law takes on a distinctly constitutional flavour as the internal constitutional structures of the Member States, their constitutional spaces, become integral to the State aid test where fiscal autonomy is concerned. There is no doubt that, as a matter of EU constitutional law, the internal constitutional structures of the Member States should be given due weight; yet, as this chapter has argued, a more open and explicit articulation of the role played by national constitutional identities in the Court's reasoning would help to justify an otherwise problematic jurisprudential stance.

Finally, even if the legal definition of the scope of Article 107(1) TFEU cannot explicitly take account of the Commission's commitment to preventing harmful tax competition, the effect of the case law on this issue is to frame the scope of tax competition within the EU and within the Member States. Plainly, if the scope of Article 107(1) TFEU permits different corporate tax regimes to co-exist within individual Member States, the potential for arbitrage increases. The *Azores* test, the rationale of which is to ensure that decentralised corporate tax regimes are grounded in local economic realities and are not merely a means of circumventing the State aid provisions, is—arguably—not watertight. It is not unthinkable that Member States, in their efforts to operate aggressive tax competition strategies, effect, without falling foul of the State aid provisions, indirect transfers in the direction of decentralised governments so as to compensate for lower tax rates. Perhaps this is the price to be paid for the recognition of the fact that even this segment of the EU's economic law does not exist in a constitutional vacuum.

7

Funding Public Services

The State aid dimension of public service provision is a relatively recent phenomenon. Its emergence during the last decades of the twentieth century is a result of momentous shifts in economic ideology and of the resulting processes of privatisation and liberalisation that have radically changed the way in which public services are delivered.[1] Direct provision by Member States is no longer the dominant model, and public service tasks have often become amalgamated with commercial activities. However, much as privatisation and liberalisation typically lead to new forms of regulatory intervention, the (partial) eclipse of the role of the State as direct provider of public services has gradually led to the creation of new regulatory tools aimed at safeguarding the public interest.[2] State support to undertakings charged with Public Service Obligations (PSOs), or providing Services of General Economic Interest (SGEIs) is among these tools.[3]

This chapter examines the extent to which State aid law constrains national regulatory autonomy in relation to public services, and the extent to which that autonomy has prompted the Court to redefine the concept of State aid. These questions matter not only to State aid, but also to the European economic constitution as a whole, as answers to them have profound consequences on the way in which the EU's legal order structures the relationship between market and nonmarket concerns. If the notion of a social market economy is to have any bite, public services are natural candidates for a re-balancing of EU internal market law. In order to examine these questions, however, it will be necessary to trace with some degree of detail the evolution of State aid law relating to SGEI-funding. The chapter will then assess the overall picture emerging from this evolution by examining three questions: how far State aid law impacts on the Member State's

[1] M Freedland and S Sciarra (eds), *Public Services and Citizenship in European Law* (Oxford, Clarendon Press, 1998); T Prosser, *The Limits of Competition Law* (Oxford, Oxford University Press, 2005); E Szyszczak, *The Regulation of the State in Competitive Markets in the EU* (Oxford, Hart Publishing, 2007) ch 1; W Sauter, 'Services of General Economic Interest and Universal Services in EU Law' (2008) 33 *EL Rev* 167.

[2] See generally, S Picciotto, 'Liberalization and Democratization: The Forum and the Hearth in the Era of Cosmopolitan Post-Industrial Capitalism'(2000) 63 *Law and Contemporary Problems* 157; T Prosser, 'Public Service Law: Privatization's Unexpected Offspring' (2000) 63 *Law and Contemporary Problems* 63.

[3] The two terms (PSOs and SGEI) are used interchangeably here, unless the context demands otherwise. On the confusion in the case law between the two concepts see L Hancher and P Larouche, 'EU Regulation of Network Industries and Services' in P Craig and G de Búrca (eds), *The Evolution of EU Law*, 2nd edn (Oxford, Oxford University Press, 2011) 762.

autonomy in defining and organising SGEIs; how far it is possible to separate the question of funding from questions concerning the nature and structure of SGEIs; how far this case law impacts on the separation between market participation and market regulation which previous chapters have taken to be central to understanding the evolution of State aid law.

1. SERVICES OF GENERAL ECONOMIC INTEREST

References to public services were already present in the Treaty of Rome, which contained safeguards in favour of undertakings performing SGEIs,[4] and in sector-specific legislation.[5] However, the movement towards stronger buttresses for such services, and towards a (more precise) collocation within EU law of the concept that encapsulates them, began when the expansion of the internal market increasingly came to be perceived as a threat to the viability of national welfare regulation.[6] For years, internal market law had left this area of national regulatory competence virtually untouched, whilst focusing predominantly on domestic trade regulation through the lens of the free movement of goods provisions, and on the anti-competitive practices of undertakings.[7] This was consistent with the underlying assumption that the Member States would embrace trade integration while remaining free to develop and expand their domestic welfare systems, through public intervention and through regulation.[8] This state of affairs, which

[4] Namely Article 86(2) EC, now 106(2) TFEU ('Undertakings entrusted with the operation of services of general economic interest or having the character of a revenue-producing monopoly shall be subject to the rules contained in this Treaty, in particular to the rules on competition, in so far as the application of such rules does not obstruct the performance, in law or in fact, of the particular tasks assigned to them. The development of trade must not be affected to such an extent as would be contrary to the interests of the [Union])' and, with regard to transport, Article 73 EC, now 93 TFEU ('Aids shall be compatible with this Treaty if they meet the needs of coordination of transport or if they represent reimbursement for the discharge of certain obligations inherent in the concept of a public service').

[5] Council Regulation 1191/69 on action by Member States concerning the obligations inherent in the concept of a public service in transport by rail, road and inland waterway [1969] OJ L156; Council Regulation 1107/70 on the granting of aids for transport by rail road and inland waterway [1970] OJ L130, which was repealed by Regulation 1370/2007 of the European Parliament and Council on public passenger transport services by rail and road [2007] OJ L315.

[6] The term 'welfare' is used here in a very broad sense, to encompass social welfare legislation and the regulation of public services (including utilities). Utilities may be regarded as falling within this broad definition of 'welfare' because of the public element that permeates them. For a similar use of the term see D Damjanovic and B De Witte, 'Welfare Integration through EU Law: The Overall Picture in the Light of the Lisbon Treaty' in U Neergaard, R Nielsen and L Roseberry (eds), *Integrating Welfare Functions into EU Law* (Copenhagen, DJØF Forlag, 2009).

[7] See JHH Weiler, 'The Constitution of the Common Market Place: Text and Context in the Evolution of the Free Movement of Goods' in P Craig and G de Búrca (eds), *The Evolution of EU Law*, 1st edn (Oxford, Oxford University Press,1999) 360.

[8] See R Gilpin, *The Political Economy of International Relations* (Princeton, Princeton University Press, 1987); L Tsoukalis, *The New European Economy Revisited* (Oxford, Oxford University Press, 1997) 22. See also A Milward, *The European Rescue of the Nation State*, 2nd edn (London, Routledge, 2000).

underpinned the three post-war decades of economic growth, gradually came to an end with the progressive 'infiltration'[9] of internal market law into national welfare systems, including public services.[10] Increasingly, areas that previously had been seen in an altogether different light came to be characterised as 'markets' and to be subject to the EU's economic law. Competition law was instrumental towards the liberalisation of large sections of national welfare (in a broad sense), namely public utilities.

Yet, throughout this process, the EU did not, and could not, fully embrace a view of the market as an all encompassing imperative. It could not do so because of the existence of Article 106(2) TFEU, a provision which prevented nonmarket concerns from being treated as an afterthought along the path to market integration. The latter, being the result of a compromise between very distant positions, contained a number of grey areas,[11] and the absence of a definition of SGEIs, coupled with the lack of a clear indication of the relative hierarchy between market and nonmarket values within the Treaty provided the ingredients for some 'hard cases'. Throughout the evolution of its case law on Article 106(2) TFEU the Court never directly addressed the question of the content of SGEIs. As Buendía Sierra points out, it has avoided expressly denying a service the status as SGEI.[12] In *BUPA*, a case that will be examined in some detail below, the General Court has conceded that 'there is no clear and precise regulatory definition of the concept of an SGEI mission'.[13] In the absence of harmonisation, the Court defers to national definitions of SGEIs, providing minimum criteria the respect of which offers the focus of the Commission's review limited to manifest error of assessment.[14]

The other fundamental question, to which the Court has devoted far greater attention, is whether, in instances of conflict, SGEIs supersede, or merely derogate

[9] The term is borrowed from S Giubboni, *Social Rights and Market Freedom in the European Constitution: A Labour Law Perspective* (Cambridge, Cambridge University Press, 2006) who attributes its first use in this context to G Lyon-Caen, 'L'Infiltration du Droit du Travail par le Droit de la Concurrence' [1993] *Droit Ouvrier* 313.

[10] A number of interconnected factors created the conditions for this change: first, the radical shift in economic ideology, partly caused by the prolonged period of economic crisis and readjustment of European industries which took place between the 1970s and the mid-1980s; secondly, the rigid constraints on public spending arising from the commitments in the Maastricht Treaty's conditions for EMU; thirdly, the challenges to national monopolies, especially in the field of public utilities, brought by private undertakings, which, by exploiting the potential economies of scale offered by the liberalisation of national markets, sought to increase their competitiveness in a setting of increasing international interdependence. A Héritier, 'The Politics of Public Services in European Regulation' Max Planck Institute for Research on Collective Goods No 2001/1, www.papers.ssrn.com/sol3/papers.cfm?abstract_id=269314.

[11] On the genesis of this provision and on the background to it see J Buendía Sierra, *Exclusive Rights and State Monopolies under EC Law* (Oxford, Oxford University Press, 1999).

[12] JL Buendía Sierra, 'Article 86' in J Faull and A Nickpay (eds), *The EC Law of Competition*, 2nd edn (Oxford, Oxford University Press, 2007) 630. On occasion, the Court's scrutiny over the definition has been of a more enquiring nature. In *Enirisorse*, the Court found the definition of the PSO to be excessively broad, Joined Cases C-34/01 to C-38/01 *Enirisorse SpA v Ministero delle Finanze* [2003] I-14243.

[13] Case T-289/03 *BUPA v Commission* [2008] ECR II-81, para 165.

[14] Case T-106/95 *FFSA v Commission* [1997] ECR II-229, para 192; T-17/02 *Fred Olsen* [2005] ECR II-2031 para 215.

from, internal market law. The Court's interpretation of the provision has evolved from carving a restrictive role for SGEIs in relation to internal market law towards an approach which, arguably, puts the two sets of interests on an axiological par.[15] Yet, there are references, scattered around in these judgments, to the language of derogation, thus allowing the opposite view to be taken.[16] The Court reiterates the claim that Article 106(2) TFEU should be interpreted narrowly, which of course leads one to believe that it recognises the priority of competition over SGEIs. In *Air Inter*,[17] the General Court held that the implication of a strict interpretation was that it was not sufficient for the performance of SGEIs to be 'simply hindered or made more difficult', but proof would have to be furnished of the fact that the application of competition law would obstruct the performance in law or in fact of the particular task assigned to it, and that proof entailed rejecting less restrictive means of fulfilling the public interest tasks (proportionality in the strict sense). Nonetheless, these cases appear to be isolated instances of a strict interpretation of proportionality, as the majority of judgments tend to adopt a more lenient version of the test, placing the emphasis on necessity rather than on proportionality in its narrow sense (the existence of less restrictive alternatives).[18] According to Baquero, the test consists in 'a technique to assess whether regulatory measures connected to services of general interest are indeed in the general interest or whether they pursue private interests.'[19] The test thus formulated bears the advantage of being 'less intrusive' than a strict proportionality test, and 'allows the Court to preserve a margin of appreciation for public authorities and to respect the legitimacy of democratic processes and legislation'.[20]

[15] To say that the market and nonmarket interests *are* on the same level as a matter of principle does not amount to a claim that the two sets of values are left unchanged by the proportionality test carried out by the Court, as the outcome of such a test entails a certain degree of sacrifice of the interests involved. Plainly, the evaluation of the outcome will turn on one's views as to relative weight that market and public interest considerations *should* be given. Baquero Cruz argues that, in its Article 106(2) TFEU case law, the Court does not rely on proportionality and therefore does not carry out a balancing of competing interests, as that operation would give excessive weight to competition. The Court relies, instead, on a necessity rather than a strict proportionality test and regards competition and SGEIs as having equal weight. J Baquero Cruz, 'Beyond Competition: Services of General Interest and European Community Law' in G de Búrca (ed), *EU Law and the Welfare State—In Search of Solidarity* (Oxford, Oxford University Press, 2005) 197. On the wider theme of market and nonmarket concerns in relation to scope of competition law see N Boeger, 'Solidarity and EC competition law' (2007) 32 *EL Rev* 319.

[16] See Buendía Sierra, 'Article 86' (n 12).

[17] Case T-260/94 *Air Inter* [1997] ECR II-997.

[18] Buendía Sierra, 'Article 86' (n 12) and Sauter, 'Services of General Economic Interest and Universal Services in EU Law' (n 1) argue that different variants of the proportionality test apply to different regulatory contexts and that the strictness of the test is correlated to the exercise of its regulatory competence by the EU. Baquero Cruz, 'Beyond Competition: Services of General Interest and European Community Law' (n 15), instead, appears to prefer a uniform approach to proportionality, and argues that the Court's case law does not actually concern proportionality. See also, L Hancher, 'Community, State and Market' in P Craig and G de Búrca (eds), *The Evolution of EU Law*, 1st edn (Oxford, Oxford University Press, 1999).

[19] Baquero Cruz, 'Beyond Competition: Services of General Interest and European Community Law' (n 15) 197.

[20] Ibid.

While one may regard the Court's approach to the assessment of SGEIs in relation to competition law as a satisfactory compromise, the desultory attention exhibited by the Court to the *definition* of SGEI has undoubtedly left a gap in our understanding of how the EU interprets such services. The Member States' willingness to emphasise the significance of SGEIs within the EU, and, arguably, to reject the prevalence of the law of the internal market over SGEIs was sanctioned by the Amsterdam Treaty's introduction of Article 16 TEC (now Article 14 TFEU), a provision which, however, did not offer a concrete basis for EU action in the field.[21] At the same time, the Commission began to reflect on the meaning of such services and to set out its views on the matter. That reflection did not, however, culminate in legally binding definitions; instead, the matter continued to be confined to policy documents exhibiting a considerable degree of vagueness.[22] The decade of constitutional revision has produced a new provision on SGEIs: Article 14 TFEU, which replaces Article 16 TEC, lays down a *specific legislative competence* aimed at establishing the principles and setting the conditions to enable SGEIs to fulfil their missions.[23] At the same time, a Protocol on services of general interest (SGIs) was added to the Lisbon Treaty, which uses SGIs as an umbrella to cover both SGEIs and 'non-economic services of general interest' (NESGIs).[24] The emphasis in the protocol seems to be on discretion and

[21] Article 16 TEC read: 'without prejudice to Articles 73, 86 and 87, and given the place occupied by services of general economic interest in the shared values of the Union as well as their role in promoting social and territorial cohesion, the Community and the Member States, each within their respective powers and within the scope of application of this Treaty, shall take care that such services operate on the basis of principles and conditions which enable them to fulfil their missions'. Article 36 of the Charter of Fundamental Rights reads as follows: '[t]he Union recognises and respects access to services of general economic interest as provided for in national laws and practices, in accordance with the Treaties, in order to promote the social and territorial cohesion of the Union'. For different views on the significance of Article 16 TEC see: L Flynn, 'Competition Policy and Public Services in EC Law after the Maastricht and Amsterdam Treaties' in D O'Keefe and R Twomey (eds), *Legal Issues of the Amsterdam Treaty* (Oxford, Hart Publishing, 1999); M Ross, 'Article 16 EC and Services of General Interest: From Derogation to Obligation?' (2000) 25 *EL Rev* 22; E Szyszczak, 'Public Service Provision in Competitive Markets' [2001] *Yearbook of European Law* 35; J Baquero Cruz, 'Beyond Competition: Services of General Interest and European Community Law' (n 15); M Krajewski, 'Providing Legal Clarity and Securing Policy Space for Public Services Through a Legal Framework for Services of General Economic Interest: Squaring the Circle?' (2008) 14 *European Public Law* 377.

[22] Commission, 'Communication on services of general economic interest' COM (1996) 443; Commission, 'Communication on services of general economic interest in Europe' COM (2000) 580 final; Commission, 'Green Paper on services of general interest, COM (2003) 270; Commission, 'White Paper on services of general interest', COM (2004) 374; Commission, 'Communication on social services of general interest in the EU', COM (2006) 177; Commission, 'Communication on services of general interest, including social services of general interest: a new European commitment', COM (2007) 725.

[23] Article 14 TFEU adds to Article 16 EC the following sentence: '[t]he European Parliament and the Council, acting by means of regulations in accordance with the ordinary legislative procedure, shall establish these principles and set these conditions without prejudice to the competence of Member States, in compliance with the Treaties, *to provide, to commission and to fund such services*'.

[24] The term 'non-economic services of general interest' is also used in the services directive in order to exclude such services from its scope. See Article 2(2)(a) Directive 2006/123/EC of the European Parliament and of the Council of 12 December 2006 on services in the internal market [2006] OJ L376/36.

regulatory diversity in relation to SGEIs and, as to NESGIs, on ring-fencing such services from the Treaty.[25]

Even from this bird's eye overview of the evolution of the concept of SGEIs/SGIs, and discounting the multitude of 'grey areas' that emerge from it, it is possible to detect the emergence of two key features. First, it seems no longer doubtful that the EU now treats these services as central to the economic constitution: SGEIs may no longer be seen as an obstruction to the realisation of the internal market but have become an integral part of the project. The second feature to emerge is that the *domestic* interests that shape the concept of SGEIs/SGIs gain recognition *as a matter of EU law* among the 'shared values of the Union' and limit the scope for an EU-based review of national choices concerning the organisation of such services.

2. COMPENSATION FOR PUBLIC SERVICE OBLIGATIONS

The debate canvassed so far is of direct relevance to the concept of State aid. In fact State aid and SGEIs are mutually dependent concepts: on the one hand, the debate on SGEIs has undoubtedly been shaped by the intrusion of State aid law into public service provision; on the other, the concept of SGEIs has played a vital role in the process of re-defining the notion of State aid. Before turning to these points, however, it is useful to sketch out the evolution of case law on compensation for the performance of PSOs, and to refer to the main tenets emerging from the Commission's policy in this regard.

A. The 'State Aid' and 'Compensation' Approaches

In its infancy, the jurisprudence on this issue was dominated by two sharply contrasting views. One side of the argument held that the funding of SGEIs should fall within the definition of State aid, but also allowed for the possibility that such funding could benefit from an exemption based on Article 106(2) TFEU, which would follow a similar logic to the one displayed in the exemptions in Article 107(3) TFEU. The upshot of this position was that the notification and stand-still obligations would be triggered regardless of the existence of compensation. The 'State aid' position (as it has come be known) was briefly outlined in *Banco Exterior de España*,[26] in which the Court explained that a measure which

[25] It is unclear, however, whether the partial overlap of language between Article 14 TFEU and Article 2 of the Protocol should be attributed any meaning. Whilst the former refers to the competence of the Member States 'to provide, to commission and to *fund*' SGEIs, the Protocol refers to the competence 'to provide, commission and *organise*' NESGIs.

[26] Case C-387/92 *Banco Exteriór de España v Ayuntamiento de Valencia* 387/92 [1994] ECR I 877.

the Spanish government had defended as being justified by its public interest purpose fell within Article 107(1) TFEU, albeit suggesting that Article 106(2) TFEU could come into play. Advocate General Lenz attempted to shed some light on the relationship between Article 106(2) TFEU and Articles 107 and 108 TFEU: in his view, the public mission derogation could not apply at the outset, since Article 106(2) TFEU 'sets the framework for the review of EU-law criteria for the safeguarding of *Community* interests' (emphasis added).[27] This interpretation was later confirmed in the General Court's jurisprudence, which further explored the interaction between Article 106(2) TFEU and Article 107(1) TFEU. In *FFSA*,[28] the measure in question was a tax concession granted by the French legislator to the national Post Office (La Poste) as a means to compensate La Poste for the extra-costs incurred in fulfilling its statutory obligation to provide a universal postal service. The General Court had no doubt that this legislation should fall squarely within the scope of Article 107(1) TFEU, as it gave La Poste a financial advantage with regard to its competitors which were subject to the stricter fiscal regime. However, the wording of Article 106(2) TFEU and, in particular, the expression 'in so far as the application of those rules … does not obstruct the performance of the particular tasks' entailed that, provided that the conditions for the application of Article 106(2) TFEU were met, a measure caught by article 107(1) TFEU could nevertheless be considered to be compatible with the internal market.[29]

The State aid approach was reversed by the CJEU in *Ferring*, which introduced the so-called 'compensation approach'.[30] The case concerned a French law granting a tax exemption to wholesale distributors of pharmaceutical products,[31] in consideration for the wholesaler's PSOs.[32] Ferring, a pharmaceutical company, brought an action before a French court claiming that the law gave rise to State aid—a reference followed shortly thereafter. The Court relied on *ADBHU*,[33] a ruling on the compatibility with the State aid provisions of an indemnity for undertakings carrying out the collection and disposal of waste oils, which was provided for in the 'Waste Oils' Directive,[34] where it had found that the indemnity

27 Ibid para 71.

28 Case T-106/95 *Fédération française des sociétés d'assurances (FFSA) v Commission of the European Communities* [1997] ECR II-229.

29 The same approach was followed in Case T-46/97 *SIC-Sociedade Indipendente de Comunicaçao v Commission* [2000] ECR II-2125.

30 Case C-53/00 *Ferring v ACOSS* [2001] ECR I-9067.

31 Council Directive 92/25/EEC, on the wholesale distribution of medicinal products for human use OJ 1992 L 113/1 allowed Member States to impose PSOs on wholesale distributors of pharmaceuticals, provided that these tasks could be regarded as warranted on grounds of public health protection and were proportionate in relation to this objective.

32 Which consisted in: keeping a permanent stock of medicinal products comprising at least nine-tenths of all forms of medicines sold in France, satisfying all needs of regular customers for at least two weeks, guaranteeing delivery of every medicine sold in the distribution area within 24 hours of receipt of an order.

33 Case 240/83 *Procureur de la République v Association de défense des brûleurs d'huiles usagées* [1985] ECR 531.

34 Council Directive (EEC) 75/439 on the Disposal of Waste Oils [1975] OJ L194/23.

consideration for the services performed by the collection or disposal undertakings and therefore fell outside the definition of State aid.[35] The Court held that, provided that there was a *necessary connection* between the exemption and the additional costs incurred, the wholesalers could not be deemed to enjoy any *real* advantage.[36]

What is remarkable about this judicial *revirement* is that the compensation issue was shifted back from the compatibility stage to the threshold stage. As Advocate General Léger, one of the sharpest critics of *Ferring*, pointed out,[37] the ruling potentially had 'considerable repercussions for the Commission's policy on State aid.'[38] He recalled that in recent years the Commission had undertaken a wide-ranging review of the policy to be adopted with regard to SGEIs and had committed itself to exploring ways in which it could increase legal certainty and transparency in the field. Instead, in *Ferring*, the Court had 'rendered pointless the efforts taken by the competent authorities to define Community policy in the area of public sector financing'.[39]

Many commentators remarked on the increased potential for abuse that *Ferring* opened up: it was clear that Member States would be tempted to use compensation for PSOs as a disguise for distortive measures.[40] Moreover, the Court did not proffer any indication of how the equivalence between the compensation and the extra costs deriving from PSOs was to be assessed. However, the ruling also appeared to increase the risk of recovery of compensation measures based on errors of judgement regarding the measure's immunity from Article 87(1). *Ferring* no doubt represented a safeguard against EU interference into the organisation of national public services, but the blanket approach followed by the Court meant that, in the absence of equivalence between compensation and the costs arising from SGEI provision, and given the unavailability of an Article 106(2) TFEU defence, the measure would be doomed.

[35] ADBHU concerned judicial review of a piece of Community legislation rather than a State aid case in the proper sense. In its judgment in *ADBHU* the Court had simply confirmed that the balance struck by the Community legislature between State aid and environmental protection was the appropriate one.

[36] Ibid para 27.

[37] In both of his Opinions for *Altmark*, the Advocate General advised the Court to overrule the judgment Opinion of Advocate General Léger delivered on 19 March 2002 for Case C-280/00 *Altmark Trans GmbH, Regierungspräsidium Magdeburg v Nahverkergesellschaft Altmark GmbH* [2003] ECR I-7747; and Opinion delivered on 14 January 2003 for the same case.

[38] Ibid para 94. See also D Grespan, 'An Example of the Application of State Aid Rules in the Utilities Sector in Italy' (2002) 3 Competition Policy Newsletter 17, which is cited by Advocate General Léger's second Opinion.

[39] Ibid para 98.

[40] C Rizza, 'The Financial Assistance Granted by Member States to Undertakings Entrusted with the Operation of a Service of General Economic Interest' in A Biondi and P Eeckhout (eds), *The Law of State Aid in the European Union* (Oxford, Oxford University Press, 2003) 67–84; P Nicolaides, 'Distortive Effects of Compensatory Aid Measures: A Note on the Economics of the *Ferring* Judgement' (2002) 6 *European Competition Law Review* 313. For an isolated voice in favour of *Ferring*, see A Bartosch, 'The Relationship between Public Procurement and State Aid Surveillance—The Toughest Standard Applies?' (2002) 39 *CML Rev* 551.

B. *Altmark* and Beyond

As expected, *Ferring* triggered references from national courts seeking clarification on the application of the Court's 'equivalence test'.[41] The matter was finally settled by the full Court in *Altmark*.[42] The Court appears to have been partially influenced, rather than by the Advocate General assigned to the case, by the opinion of Advocate General Jacobs, who handed down his conclusions in another case which raised the issue of compensation for PSOs. In *GEMO*, in fact, the Advocate General had suggested a compromise between the State aid and compensation approaches. In cases where a clear and manifest link between the financing and the PSOs imposed could be established, *Ferring* would continue to apply. Where instead such a quid pro quo relationship was not clear-cut from the outset, the State aid approach would come into play. The Advocate General added that a way to establish the existence of a quid pro quo would be to assign the PSOs and their respective funding through public procurement procedures.

Such views found partial acceptance in the Court's ruling in *Altmark*, which went considerably further.[43] At first, the Court appeared to confirm the *ADBHU/Ferring* line of jurisprudence, as it held that no real advantage, and therefore no State aid, was involved where a State measure counted as compensation for the services provided by the recipient undertakings in their discharge of PSOs. However, it went on to add four stringent cumulative conditions (the fourth of which consisted of two alternatives):

a) the recipient undertaking was to be subject to *clearly defined* PSOs;
b) the compensation 'parameters' were to be 'established in advance in an objective and transparent manner' in order to avoid conferring an advantage in favour of the recipient undertaking over competing undertakings;
c) the level of compensation could not exceed what was necessary to cover wholly or partially the costs incurred in the discharge of PSOs, taking into account the relevant receipts and a reasonable profit for discharging these;
d) there was to be *either* i) selection through a public procurement procedure, *or* ii) compensation based 'an analysis of the costs which a *typical undertaking*, well run and adequately provided with means of transport so as to be able to meet the necessary public service requirements would have to bear in fulfilling those obligations'.[44]

[41] Joined Cases C-34/01 to C-38/01 *Enirisorse v Amministrazione delle Finanze* [2003] ECR I-14243; Case C-126/01 *Ministre de l'économie, des finances et de l'industrie v GEMO SA* [2004] ECR I-13769.

[42] Case 280/00 *Altmark Trans GmbH, Regierungspräsidium Magdeburg v Nahverkergesellschaft Altmark GmbH* [2003] ECR I-7747.

[43] Six Member State intervened: Germany and Spain were in favour of maintaining *Ferring* in place; Denmark, France, the Netherlands and the UK were for Advocate General Jacobs' *GEMO* approach.

[44] Case 280/00 *Altmark Trans GmbH, Regierungspräsidium Magdeburg v Nahverkergesellschaft Altmark GmbH* (n 42) paras 89–92.

The *Altmark* conditions seemed to be far stricter than the ones established in *Ferring*.[45] The fact that the parameters for compensation were to be established in advance meant that a law such as the one at issue in *Ferring*, which introduced a tax on direct sales by pharmaceutical laboratories to restore (a posteriori) the competitive balance that had been altered by the imposition of PSOs on wholesalers, would have failed the *Altmark* test. Moreover, it was clear that the wholesalers were not chosen after a public procurement procedure; it was also unlikely that the compensation contained in the tax would be compatible with a cost-benchmarking criterion.[46]

C. A Retreat from *Altmark*?

The Commission's post-*Altmark* practice was characterised by widespread reliance on Article 106(2) TFEU, probably to a greater extent than the Court had envisaged.[47] This state of affairs, according to critics, was the result of the Commission's exceedingly narrow reading of the *Altmark* criteria and of the lack of integration between *Chronopost* and *Altmark*.[48] In *Chronopost*,[49] a case decided a few weeks before *Altmark*, the central problem was whether a monopolist operating under the universal service obligation to maintain the postal network throughout the national territory should, as the General Court had held, charge its subsidiary a price for the use of its network that reflected the price that a benchmark private undertaking not operating in the reserved sector would, under normal market conditions, charge its subsidiary. The CJEU rejected this benchmark, as, it held, a private undertaking would never have created a network equivalent to the universal postal network, given the fixed costs and the obligations involved. In the absence of a suitable comparator, the costs to be taken into account in verifying the absence of an advantage in the price paid to La Poste were to be those verifiable costs that La Poste had actually incurred.

There have been attempts to reconcile the two judgments. Some have argued that the two rulings are unrelated, as the issue at the heart of *Chronopost* was the

[45] Case C-53/00 *Ferring v ACOSS* (n 30).

[46] For a follow-up on *Ferring*, see Case C-526/04 *Laboratoires Boiron* [2006] ECR I-7529 a preliminary ruling arising from an action brought by a pharmaceutical laboratory to obtain repayment of tax on direct sales which had funded the aid in question. The Court found that the applicant was to be able to plead the State aid character of the tax in order to obtain repayment of the charge on the grounds that at least one of the *Altmark* conditions was not fulfilled.

[47] The General Court has confirmed that, in laying down the *Altmark* conditions, the Court had not intended to render Article 106(2) TFEU redundant with respect to the assessment of the *compatibility* with the internal market of SGEI-financing, Case T-354/05 *TFE1* [2009] ECR II-471, para 135.

[48] For an overview of Commission decisions post-*Altmark* see A Renzulli, 'Services of General Economic Interest: The Post-*Altmark* Scenario' (2008) 14 *European Public Law* 399; E Szyszczak, '*Altmark* Assessed' in Szyszczak, E (ed), *Research Handbook on State Aid* (Cheltenham, Edward Elgar, 2011).

[49] Joined Cases C-83/01P, C-93/01P and C-94/01P *Chronopost and others v Ufex and others* [2003] ECR I-6993.

'economic status of the postal network' rather than the presence of a PSO, and the Court, having acknowledged the impossibility of a comparison with a purely commercial operation, 'applied a market benchmark' to evaluate the degree of fit with normal market conditions.[50] Others have, instead, acknowledged the direct relevance of *Chronopost* to PSO compensation. As Von Danwitz puts it, *Chronopost* reflects a balance between the competing objectives of a rigorous application of the State aid rules and the protection of public service tasks; in the absence of an appropriate comparator, State aid control may only be based on available parameters.[51] Bartosch has claimed that the apparent tension between the two rulings could be resolved by considering *Chronopost* as a *lex specialis* with respect to the general framework laid down in the *Altmark* ruling.[52] The latter author, however, has lamented the Commission's 'unimaginative' interpretation of *Altmark* in relation to *Chronopost*. Where the Commission found that a public tender was not available, in the absence of a suitable comparator, its assessment automatically shifted to the compatibility stage (under Article 106(2) TFEU). It is only at the latter stage that the flexibility displayed in *Chronopost* would play its part, and the existing costs, rather than hypothetical ones, would be taken into consideration. Appeals to revise the *Altmark* benchmarking requirement in the light of *Chronopost* have so far gone unheeded.[53]

Alongside *Chronopost*, the General Court's *BUPA* ruling is the most significant development in this area since *Altmark*.[54] One of the striking features of the ruling is the level of detail in which the application of the *Altmark* conditions was reviewed; remarkably, the review focused on criteria that the Commission decision, which pre-dated *Altmark* and was based on the *Ferring* approach, had not considered. The case is worthy of note also for its subject-matter, the organisation of private health insurance, which had never before been examined in the light of *Altmark*.

BUPA (a private health insurance company) brought an annulment action against a Commission decision not to raise objections in relation to an Irish 'risk equalisation scheme' (RES) relating to the private medical insurance (PMI) market.[55] Before the health insurance system was liberalised, the Voluntary Health Insurance Board (VHI) was the only operator in Ireland to be licensed by the

[50] A Biondi, 'The Financing of Services of General Economic Interest' in T Tridimas and P Nebbia (eds.) *EU Law for the 21st Century* (Oxford, Hart Publishing, 2005) 268; A Renzulli, 'Services of General Economic Interest: The Post-*Altmark* Scenario' (n 48).

[51] 'Although', he adds, 'the standard might not have been written with the precision of a textbook in business administration' A von Danwitz, 'The Concept of State Aid in Liberalised Sectors' (2008) EUI Working Paper 28.

[52] A Bartosch, 'Compensation for Public Service Obligations: Post-*Altmark* Remarks' in M Sánchez Rydelski, *The EC State Aid Régime: Distortive Effects Distortive Effects of State Aid on Competition and Trade* (London, Cameron May, 2006) 55. See also, T Mueller, 'Efficiency Control in State Aid and the Power of Member States to Define SGEIs' (2009) 4 *European State Aid Quarterly* 39.

[53] A Sinnaeve, 'State Financing of Public Services: The Court's Dilemma in the *Altmark* Case' [2003] *European State Aid Law Quarterly* 351.

[54] Case T-289/03 *BUPA v Commission* (n 13).

[55] Commission decision concerning the establishment of a risk equalisation scheme (RES) in the Irish health insurance market State aid N 46/2003 [2003] OJ C186/16.

Minister for Health. The process of liberalisation was accompanied by the introduction of the RES, which provided for compensation to be paid by insurers with a low risk profile in favour of insurers with a higher risk profile effected through a levy collected and distributed by the Health Insurance Authority. As a result of this mechanism, the market incumbent, VHI, was at the receiving end of the scheme, whilst more recent market entrants, such as BUPA (the appellant), were net contributors to the RES. In its decision not to raise objections, the Commission, applying *Ferring*,[56] found the scheme to represent compensation for the discharge of SGEIs by PMI insurers and therefore not to constitute aid under Article 107(1) TFEU or that, alternatively, it could be declared compatible with the common market under Article 106(2) TFEU. It seemed clear to the Commission that the Irish regulations imposed PSOs on all PMI insurers consisting in: a) an 'open enrolment requirement', that is, the obligation to offer PMI contracts regardless of age, sex or health status of the persons applying for a policy; b) a 'lifetime cover requirement' which meant that cover could not be discontinued when the policy-holders became old or sick; c) a 'community rating' mechanism whereby the same premium would apply to all policy-holders for the same type of product irrespective of their health status, age or sex; d) a requirement to ensure minimum quality standards in PMI products.

In bringing its action against the decision, BUPA claimed, among other things, that the Commission had misapplied Articles 107(1) TFEU and 106(2) TFEU, and had erred in law in failing to examine the legality of the RES under Articles 86(1) EC and 106(2) TFEU. In particular, BUPA claimed that the scheme was incapable of satisfying the *Altmark* conditions. The General Court agreed with the applicant that *Altmark* should be taken to apply to the case at hand;[57] however, the General Court added that, given the circumstances of the case, it was appropriate 'to apply the criteria formulated in *Altmark*, in accordance with the spirit and the purpose which prevailed when they were laid down, in a manner adapted to the particular facts of the present case'.[58] Its analysis of the concept of SGEIs, within the context of the first *Altmark* condition, was equally cautious:

> It must be made clear that in Community law and for the purposes of applying the EC Treaty competition rules, there is no clear and precise regulatory definition of the concept of an SGEI mission and no established legal concept definitively fixing the conditions that must be satisfied before a Member State can properly invoke the existence and protection of an SGEI mission, either within the meaning of the first *Altmark* condition or within the meaning of [Article 106(2) TFEU].[59]

Relying on its Article 106(2) TFEU case law, the Court held that, given the discretion that the Member States enjoyed in defining SGEIs, any such definition could

[56] Case C-53/00 *Ferring v ACOSS* (n 30) which was good law at the time of the decision.

[57] Even if the decision had been issued before the judgment was delivered, as *Altmark* had not set any temporal limitations to its effects.

[58] Case T-289/03 *BUPA v Commission* (n 13) para 160.

[59] Ibid para 165.

only be questioned by the Commission in the event of manifest error.[60] The Member State's prerogative in defining the SGEIs was confirmed by the absence of specific EU competences in that field and by the tenor of Article 14 TFEU which referred to the EU's and the Member States' duty to act in the field of SGEIs 'each within their respective powers'. This was all the more so in an area such as health care, where the EU enjoyed only limited powers under Article 168(1) and (5) TFEU. However, the General Court went on to add, EU law was to ensure that the SGEI mission satisfied 'certain minimum criteria common to every SGEI mission', that is, the entrustment by an act of the public authority and the universal and compulsory nature of the mission, both of which the Member State had to prove to be present in the case at hand.[61]

The applicant had argued that, rather than laying down an SGEI, the Irish legislation imposed normal regulatory constraints on all PMI undertakings without there being entrustment of a mission by an act of the public authority. The Court replied that the entrustment of public interest goals could be effected not only by coupling an SGEI mission with the conferral of an exclusive or special right on an undertaking but also by imposing an SGEI on all undertakings. Moreover, the Irish legislation was an act of a public authority which created and defined 'a specific mission consisting in the provision of PMI services in compliance with PMI obligations'.[62] The fact that PMI services covered only a section of the population did not detract from the universal character of such services nor did the fact that the PMI was complementary or supplementary to the public healthcare system prevent the mission imposed on PMI providers from being considered as compulsory, as the PMI insurers were required to offer the service on the market.

Moving on to the second *Altmark* condition, the General Court rejected the applicant's claim that the compensation under the RES was not carried out in accordance with predetermined criteria which were objective and transparent. Contrary to what the applicants had argued, the regulator did not have discretion over the determination of the compensation. However, the Court added that even if that discretion did exist it would not be contrary to the *Altmark* criterion. Again, relying on its case law on Article 106(2) TFEU, the General Court held that the Member State had discretion not only in defining an SGEI but *also in determining the compensation for the costs* which entailed an assessment of complex economic facts.

As to the third *Altmark* condition, the necessity and proportionality of the compensation, the General Court, again, reiterated its caveats concerning the Member State's discretion, the Commission's limited review of that discretion, and the resulting limits on the judicature's review of the Commission's decisions. BUPA had argued that the Commission had misapplied the necessity and

[60] The Court relied on Case T-17/02 *Fred Olsen v Commission* [2005] ECR II-2031, para 216, 'and the case law cited therein', ie, Case T-106/95 *FFSA and Others v Commission* [1997] ECR II-229, para 99.

[61] Case T-289/03 *BUPA v Commission* (n 13).

[62] Ibid para 182.

proportionality test. In coming to the conclusion that compensation was necessary, the Commission had ignored the fact that PMI insurers could protect their profitability by adopting commercial strategies consisting in refusing new members over the age of 65, or imposing long waiting periods on the sick, and were in a position to adjust contractual terms and differentiate premiums according to risks. As to the proportionality of compensation, the applicant contended that there was no specific link between the RES compensations and the actual costs incurred by the PMI providers in complying with their SGEI obligations.

The General Court found that the applicant had not demonstrated how the premiums could be adjusted, given the open enrolment and community rating obligations; moreover, the possibility of refusing cover for those over 65 was limited in practice, as that possibility was confined to those who had not previously subscribed to the PMI cover and the deferral of cover for the sick was limited in time. As to the proportionality of the scheme, the General Court acknowledged that there was no direct relationship between the premiums paid by insurers and the compensation payments under the RES, as the latter system was not intended to compensate additional costs associated with a specific PMI service, 'but only to equalise the additional burdens' that insurers with a negative risk profile had to bear.[63] However, the equalisation of burdens was essential to ensuring the intergenerational solidarity which lay behind the obligations imposed on the PMI operators and to compensate the additional burdens that those obligations entailed.

The General Court felt it necessary to point out that the operation of the RES system was 'radically different' from that of the compensation systems at stake in *Ferring* and *Altmark*, which entailed that it could not 'strictly fulfil the third *Altmark* condition, which requires that it be possible to determine the costs occasioned by the performance of an SGEI obligation'.[64] However, it added, the quantification of the additional costs by means of a comparison between the actual risk profile of a PMI insurer and an average market risk profile in light of the amounts paid by all PMI insurers subject to the RES was 'consistent with the purpose and the spirit of the third *Altmark* condition', as the compensation was calculated on the basis of elements which were 'specific, clearly identifiable and capable of being controlled'.[65]

The complainant had also claimed that the Commission had not taken into account the receipts and a reasonable profit that could arise from the provision of PMI services. The General Court emphasised, again, the peculiarities of the Irish scheme which warranted a 'modified' version of the *Altmark* approach. There was no correlation between the costs arising from the risk profile and the receipts, as the costs that the RES took into account were not directly linked to the provision of an SGEI, there was no need to take into consideration the receipts obtained for PMI services. What is more, a strict application of the third *Altmark* condition

[63] Ibid para 235.
[64] Ibid para 237.
[65] Ibid.

would amount to calling in question Ireland's choice to establish the RES system, which took no account of the receipts and profits of the PMI insurers and which was designed to ensure the proper functioning of a PMI market subject to the PMI obligations. 'However', the Court added 'neither the purpose nor the spirit of the third *Altmark* condition' required that receipts be taken into account in a system of compensation which operated independently of receipts.[66]

The General Court concluded its examination of the pleas based on *Altmark* by considering whether the costs compensated under the RES were those of an efficient undertaking, as required by the fourth condition in that judgment. According to the General Court, that comparison was unnecessary, as, unlike the compensation measure at issue in *Altmark*, the RES payments were not determined solely on the basis of the costs incurred by the undertakings that received compensation, but also on the basis of the costs of insurers that contributed to the scheme without benefiting from it, as the payments were not intended to compensate for an identified cost relating to the supply of a PMI service. The General Court added that the Commission was, nonetheless, required to establish that the compensation did not cover costs that arose from the inefficiency of the PMI providers and, on that front, it was satisfied that the Commission had sufficiently demonstrated that the compensation scheme was neutral with regard to the efficiency of the PMI operators.

D. The Commission Packages

The Commission's practice was complemented in 2005 with a set of measures, the so-called *Altmark* package, otherwise known as the 'Monti-Kroes' package, which attempted to clarify the conditions set out in *Altmark* and to reduce the administrative burden on both the Member States and the Commission. It did so through an amendment to the Transparency Directive, a Decision based on Article 106(2) TFEU which created a de minimis rule, and a Framework on the application of Article 106(2) TFEU to funding of SGEIs.[67] The purpose of the Decision was to allay concerns arising from the retroactive application of *Altmark*, by exempting from notification those measures that complied with the first three

[66] Ibid para 241.

[67] Commission Decision 2005/842/EC on the application of Article 86(2) of the EC Treaty to State aid in the form of public service compensation granted to certain undertakings entrusted with the operation of services of general economic interest [2005] OJ L312/67; Community framework for State aid in the form of public service compensation [2005] OJ C297/04; Commission Directive 2005/81/EC of 28 November 2005 amending Directive 80/723/EEC on the transparency of financial relations between Member States and public undertakings as well as on financial transparency within certain undertakings [2005] OJ L312/47, later codified, together with all other amendments to the original directive, by Directive 2006/111/EC on the transparency of financial relations between Member States and public undertakings as well as on financial transparency within certain undertakings [2006] OJ L318/17.

of the *Altmark* criteria, while introducing an alternative to the strict efficiency test envisaged by the CJEU. The Framework applied to compensation which fell foul of the *Altmark* requirements and was not eligible under the conditions set out in the Decision; its purpose was to provide guidance as to the application of Article 106(2) TFEU at the compatibility stage. In amending the Transparency Directive, Directive 2005/81 required all undertakings that received compensation for PSOs and that carried out other (non PSO-related) activities to keep separate accounts for its public service activities, regardless of whether or not they received State aid. The significance of the amendment resided in the need, which arose after *Altmark*, to ensure the monitoring of funding flows of undertakings which were relieved from the burden of notification.

At the end of 2011, as a result of the realisation that, even after the Monti-Kroes package, many grey areas had remained, and after a consultation exercise on the review of its first package, the Commission introduced a new set of measures. The new package comprises of four measures: a Communication, which seeks to flesh out the *Altmark* criteria;[68] a Decision, which applies only to certain categories of SGEIs (social services), and sets out the conditions under which compensation for PSOs can be exempted from notification on the basis of Article 106(2) TFEU;[69] a new Framework for assessing large compensation amounts granted to operators outside the social services field, which determines stringent conditions (which include public procurement procedures) under which State aid may be authorised under Article 106(2) TFEU;[70] and, finally, a proposal for a de minimis Regulation in the field of SGEIs.[71]

In approaching the matter of defining SGEIs, the Commission emphasises the Member States' competence in this area in the absence of EU legislation. However, it adds that 'it would not be appropriate to attach specific public service obligations to an activity which is already provided or can be provided satisfactorily and under conditions, such as price, objective quality characteristics, continuity and access to the service, consistent with the public interest, as defined by the State, by undertakings operating under normal market conditions'.[72] Nonetheless, the Commission's assessment of whether a service can be provided by the market is limited to checking whether the Member State has made a manifest error. The Commission also considers that for the services to be classified as SGEIs they must be addressed to

[68] Commission, 'Communication on the application of the European Union State aid rules to compensation granted for the provision of services of general economic interest' [2012] OJ C8/4.

[69] Commission Decision of 20 December 2011 'on the application of Article 106(2) of the Treaty on the Functioning of the European Union to State aid in the form of public service compensation granted to certain undertakings entrusted with the operation of services of general economic interest' [2012] OJ L7/3.

[70] Commission, 'Communication—European Union framework for State aid in the form of public service compensation' (2011) [2012] OJ C8/15.

[71] Commission, 'Communication—Approval of the content of a draft for a Commission Regulation on de minimis aid for the provision of services of general economic interest' [2012] OJ C8/23.

[72] Commission, 'Communication on the application of the European Union State aid rules to compensation granted for the provision of services of general economic interest' (n 68) para 48.

citizens or be in the interest of society as a whole.[73] As to the entrustment of the PSOs, the Commission does not require specific formalities, thus allowing for domestic regulatory diversity, yet it adds that the entrustment act should indicate: (a) the content and duration of the public service obligations; (b) the undertaking and, where applicable, the territory concerned; (c) the nature of any exclusive or special rights assigned to the undertaking by the authority in question; (d) the parameters for calculating, controlling and reviewing the compensation; and (e) the arrangements for avoiding and recovering any overcompensation.

As to the obligation to establish compensation parameters in advance, the Communication makes it clear that there is no requirement for compensation to be calculated on the basis of a specific formula, provided that the parameters are clear from the outset. The Commission requires, where the undertaking is offered a reasonable profit as part of its compensation, that the entrustment act establish the criteria for calculating such a profit. What the Commission means by reasonable profit is, instead, specified in relation to the third *Altmark* condition, which concerns the absence of over-compensation. In the Commission's view, reasonable profit means the rate of return on capital that would be required by a typical company considering whether or not to provide the SGEI for the whole duration of the period of entrustment, taking into account the level of risk. The level of risk depends on the sector concerned, the type of service and the characteristics of the compensation mechanism. The rate should be determined where possible by reference to the rate of return on capital that is achieved on similar types of public service contracts under competitive conditions (for example, contracts awarded under a tender). In sectors where there is no undertaking comparable to the undertaking entrusted with the operation of the SGEI, reference can be made to comparable undertakings situated in other Member States, or, if necessary, in other sectors, provided that the particular characteristics of each sector are taken into account. In determining what constitutes a reasonable profit, the Member States may introduce incentive criteria relating, in particular, to the quality of service provided and gains in productive efficiency. Efficiency gains cannot be achieved at the expense of the quality of the service provided.[74]

As to the fourth *Altmark* condition, the Communication clarifies the types of tender procedures that are acceptable and which are not, and which types of award criteria are deemed to comply with Article 107(1) TFEU. While Member States are not prevented from relying on qualitative award criteria, or imposing qualitative standards on public service providers, the award is to be based on the most economically advantageous offer. Crucially, the Commission has shed some light on the meaning of the second limb of the fourth *Altmark* condition, the cost benchmarking condition. The gist is that the meaning of 'well-run' undertaking is not to be found in an abstract benchmark, but should be sensitive to con-

[73] Ibid para 50.
[74] Ibid para 43.

text, (eg by taking into account the fact that different sectors have different cost structures). Here too, the Commission makes allowances for qualitative requirements. In fact, in relation to the benchmarking condition ('Member States can also use analytical ratios relating to the quality of supply as compared with user expectations'). And, importantly, the Commission adds that 'an undertaking entrusted with the operation of an SGEI that does not meet the qualitative criteria laid down by the Member State concerned does not constitute a well run undertaking even if its costs are low'.[75]

3. DEFINING SGEIS

One of the fundamental questions regarding SGEIs and State aid is the degree of scrutiny to which the classification of certain activities as SGEIs by Member States is subject as a matter of EU law. It has been argued by some that the *Altmark* approach, compared to the State aid approach, brings about an intensified review of the national definitions of SGEIs.[76] For instance, in *FFSA*, the General Court held that, in the absence of EU rules on the matter, the Commission was not entitled to question the content of the PSOs or the 'expediency of the political choices' made by the national authorities in this regard.[77] *Altmark*, instead, the argument goes, has provided the means for EU law to intrude into domains that the State aid approach had largely left to national discretion, and the Court has shown itself eager to exploit this opportunity. According to this view, the (post-*Altmark*) ruling in *GEMO* supports this claim, as the Court found that the actual provision of a service rather than the compensation for such service constituted aid.[78]

Yet, the idea that *Altmark* results in a higher-intensity review of national definitions of SGEIs seems to be undermined by the recent case law, in particular by the *BUPA* ruling, which sends a strong signal in the opposite direction. As seen before, the General Court roundly dismissed the argument that SGEIs should be regarded as an EU concept.[79] It held that EU law bows to national conceptions of public service and leaves it to the Member State to identify which tasks to attribute to that notion. At the same time, however, the General Court did go on to examine, admittedly in an eminently light-touch fashion, minimum criteria the observance of which would form the focus of EU level scrutiny.[80]

[75] Ibid para 72.

[76] E Gromnicka, 'Services of General Economic Interest and State Aids Regime: Proceduralisation of Political Choices?' (2005) 11 *European Public Law* 429.

[77] Case T-106/95P *FFSA* [1997] ECR II-229, para 192.

[78] See also Case T-157/01 *Danske Busvognmænd v Commission* [2004] II-917.

[79] An idea that had been circulating in the literature for some time. See eg Buendía Sierra, 'Article 86' (n 12).

[80] M Ross, 'A Healthy Approach to Services of General Economic Interest? The BUPA Judgment of the Court of First Instance' (2009) 34 *EL Rev* 127, 131.

Arguably, a more searching inquiry into the basis of the public service classification would have produced a rather different outcome.[81] Consider, for instance, the issue of universal access. Not only did the General Court accept as falling within the definition of universal service a service with limited territorial or material coverage, or which was enjoyed by only a relatively limited group of users; it also allowed for the possibility that certain categories of higher risk users be excluded from the benefits of private medical insurance, if only for a few years, without such exclusion barring designation of the services as SGEIs. Moreover, the General Court accepted that services could be offered for profit and that 'luxury' services could fall within the definition of universal service.[82] Of course, had judicial review been based on provisions on minimum standards to apply as a basis for SGEIs, such practices would have been questionable. Yet the Court was faced with the opposite legal background: not only was there no EU legislation creating PSOs, or universal access obligations, but the matter concerned an area of competence such as health care, which is a predominantly national competence and of only residual and complementary EU competence.[83]

If it is granted that *BUPA* should be read against its own peculiar background, it is also true that the General Court's general approach, as far as the definition of SGEIs is concerned, does not conflict with earlier cases. Previous case law does not substantiate the claim that *Altmark* brings about an intensification of EU review of SGEIs. In *GEMO*, the Court did not question the *existence* or the *content* of an SGEI, nor the compensation for it, but pointed to a side-effect of the provision of the service, that is, to the fact that certain undertakings (farms and slaughterhouses) received a service free of charge funded through a levy on other undertakings (supermarkets). In other words, the SGEI was not at issue in the Court's judgment. The General Court's *Combus* ruling seems, at first sight, more relevant as an example of intensified judicial review of national reliance on an SGEI.[84] There the General Court rejected the Commission's view that the beneficiary of aid, a bus company (Combus), had been assigned a PSO. Yet closer inspection reveals that it is of equally scarce avail in substantiating this claim. There the General Court found that no *obligation*, beyond the contractual obligations that the undertaking in question had agreed to, had been imposed on Combus to further a specific public interest goal. Yet, the General Court did not reach beyond the level of review for manifest error of assessment required by the Court's Article 106(2) TFEU case law: under that case law, the fulfilment of contractual obligations under a public service contract would not amount to an act of entrustment, a condition that the Court has from an early date ascribed to Article 106(2) TFEU.[85]

81 W Sauter, 'Annotation of Case T-289/03 *BUPA v Commission*' (2009) 46 *CML Rev* 269.

82 Case T-289/03 *BUPA v Commission* (n 13) para 206.

83 Article 152 EC. See generally M Ross, 'A Healthy Approach to Services of General Economic Interest? The BUPA Judgment of the Court of First Instance' (n 80).

84 Case T-157/01 *Danske Busvognmænd v Commission* (n 77).

85 Case 127/73 *BRT v SABAM* [1974] ECR 313, para 15.

The Commission's powers of review in relation to SGEIs also appear to limit the extent to which the existence of a market failure may be considered to be a precondition.[86] The Commission has made it clear in its recent SGEI package that PSOs should be imposed only where the market, in the absence of regulation, is unable to satisfy the public interest. To illustrate this point, it uses the example of broadband, in relation to which it has provided clarification through a specific set of guidelines, the gist of which is that, where the private sector has already invested in broadband network infrastructure and is already providing competitive broadband services with adequate coverage, setting up parallel broadband infrastructure should not be considered as an SGEI.[87] However, it seems clear that the Commission does not intend this to be a stringent requirement—the standard is that of a manifest error. The fact that 'under normal market conditions' undertakings are unlikely to satisfy the demands that the public interest places on them seems a fairly straightforward point for Member States to make, especially given that the public interest is defined by the Member States themselves, and 'public' simply means that the services are 'addressed to citizens' or are provided 'in the interest of society as a whole'.[88]

The lack of normative grip of market failure is perhaps unsurprising. To require, as a matter of law, that public services be recognised as SGEIs only in the presence of a demonstrable market failure would be highly problematic. Certainly, Commission State aid policy makes frequent assumptions about market failures, and market failures are an analytical tool that the Commission employs in justifying State aid.[89] However, such assumptions are made in the context of analysing questions of compatibility under Article 107(3) TFEU, not in the context of defining the conditions for public measures to fall under Article 107(1) TFEU. The concept of market failure does not lend itself to the kind of objective definition that a legal threshold would require. One should not be oblivious to the fact that the *Altmark* test is, in principle, one that any public authority or domestic court should be able to carry out independently. Moreover, systematic recourse to the concept of market failure would contradict one of the fundamental principles that underlie recent developments within the field of SGEIs, the principle of subsidiarity. As seen before, the Protocol on Services of General Interest attached to the Lisbon Treaty strongly emphasises the latitude enjoyed by authorities in organising SGEIs. To question the reasons behind the rejection of the market as the provider of such services would amount to second-guessing national choices regarding SGEIs.

[86] On the link between SGEIs and market failures see Sauter, 'Services of General Economic Interest and Universal Services in EU Law' (n 1), Szyszczak, 'Public Service Provision in Competitive Markets' (n 21), Nicolaides, 'Distortive Effects of Compensatory Aid Measures: A Note on the Economics of the *Ferring* Judgement' (n 40).

[87] Commission, 'Communication on the application of the European Union State aid rules to compensation granted for the provision of services of general economic interest' (n 69) [49] and 'Community Guidelines for the application of State aid rules in relation to rapid deployment of broadband networks' [2009] OJ C 235/7.

[88] Ibid para 50.

[89] See generally, 'State Aid Action Plan—Less and better targeted State aid—a roadmap for State aid reform 2005–2009' COM (2005) 107 final, 7/6/2005.

A. State Aid and the Constitutional Relevance of Solidarity

If it is clear that SGEIs do not have an autonomous EU meaning, one may wonder whether they are actually a constitutional value. Solidarity may hold the clue. There are various levels at which the concept of may be understood. On a general level, the concept, which has increasingly gained currency both in the academic debate and within the institutional debate at EU level, evokes the set of social values that are generally juxtaposed to the values of the market.[90] On a more specific, yet connected, level, solidarity provides the rationale for the intensely problematic demarcation of the scope *ratione personae* of competition law. Besides being central to the definition of economic activity for the purpose of drawing the boundaries of the notion of undertaking,[91] solidarity is also prominent in the Commission's policy statements concerning the dividing line between 'services of general economic interest' and 'services of general interest'.[92] Alongside the use of solidarity as a feature of practical reasoning that informs discourse on the 'European model of society', there is a more 'operational' (though not uncontroversial) side to the concept which shapes judicial reasoning regarding *both the outer and the inner limits* of competition law. It allows us to determine not only when an activity should, in principle, be subject to competition law, but also when, and under which circumstances, competition and internal market law may be considered as a hindrance to the fulfilment of the task.[93]

Solidarity is undoubtedly a polymorphous concept, which possesses different meanings in correspondence with the different contexts in which it appears—in the Treaties, in the case law, in institutional policy statements, and in the literature.[94] At a basic level, though, it possesses two dimensions. First, it is a state of affairs in which Member States find themselves in as a result of integration: the Schuman declaration's reference to 'de facto solidarity', a situation that would result from the pooling together of resources between former enemies, alludes to

[90] For a discussion of both see M Ross, 'The value of solidarity in European public services law' in M Krajewski, U Neergaard and J van de Gronden, *The Changing Legal Framework for Services of General Interest in Europe—Between Competition and Solidarity* (The Hague, Asser Press, 2009).

[91] Joined Cases C-159/91 and C-160/91 *Poucet and Pistre* [1993] ECR I-637; Case C-244/94 *FFSA and Others* [1995] ECR I-4013; Case C-218/00 *Cisal* [2002] ECR I-691; Joined Cases C-264/01, C-306/01, C-354/01 and C-355/01 *AOK-Bundesverband and Others* [2004] ECR I-2493; Case C-205/03P *FENIN v Commission* [2006] ECR I-6295. See N Boeger, 'Solidarity and EC competition law' (n 15).

[92] It is to be noted, however, that the Commission tends to rely on the concept to distinguish between SGEIs and SGIs and to treat solidarity as a value which is central to the latter but not to the former, eg, Commission, 'White Paper on services of general interest' (n 22), or the 2007 'Communication on services of general interest, including social services of general interest: a new European commitment' (n 22).

[93] See Boeger, 'Solidarity and EC competition law' (n 15).

[94] For an in depth exploration of the various aspects of solidarity see the essays contained in M Ross and Y Borgmann-Prebil (eds), *Promoting Solidarity in the European Union* (Oxford, Oxford University Press, 2010).

this dimension.[95] Secondly, it is an inherently moral notion: it appears in Article 3 TEU, which sets out the objectives of the EU, all of which may be regarded as moral imperatives. The 'Solidarity' chapter in the Charter of Fundamental Rights, which covers areas as disparate as workers' rights, environmental protection and consumer protection, may be seen as a manifestation of this conception of solidarity. Yet, solidarity may have an operational aspect which arises from national contexts where it is formulated and given substance: solidarity, in other words, is intended as a bond between citizens of a Member State, rather than between different Member States, or between EU citizens. In the context of SGEIs, solidarity constitutes the distinctive trait of national traditions of public service which gains recognition at EU level. Yet, the Lisbon Treaty's reference to the social market economy, a system which centres around the values of solidarity, may reinforce the prominence of solidarity in EU law. As was noted earlier, the Lisbon Treaty itself has been receptive to calls towards constitutionalising 'solidarity'. This appears to be so, not only where general statements are concerned, but also at a more concrete level, where SGEIs and SGIs are concerned. Article 14 TFEU provides a footing for legislation to be enacted in the field of SGEIs, while making clear in the Protocol on SGIs that such legislation is to be informed by subsidiarity. Beyond the many issues of interpretation, there is no doubt that the move strengthens the view that the European economic constitution recognises nonmarket values as fundamental and sets corresponding outer and inner limits to the expansion and prevalence of competition and State aid law.[96]

The concept of solidarity, inter-generational solidarity in particular, undoubtedly played a central role in *BUPA* in characterising the obligations imposed on PMI providers as PSOs. However, as has been argued, the General Court's acceptance of the normative strength of arguments based on this concept in *BUPA* may also be seen as a 'potentially significant step towards reworking the European model of competition to include elements of solidarity'.[97] One may, of course, doubt whether the deferential approach to national choices regarding the definition of SGEIs displayed in *BUPA* extends beyond areas where inter-generational solidarity is not a central concern, or where national competences are not as closely guarded as in the health sector. This objection, it is submitted, may well be justified as far as the assessment of compensation is concerned, but, as has been argued here, *BUPA* does not appear to be a substantial retrenchment from the existing position regarding the *definition* of SGEIs, even if the post-*Altmark*

[95] Schuman declaration of 9 May 1950, www.europa.eu/abc/symbols/9-may/decl_en.htm.

[96] On the difficulties surrounding these provisions, see Krajewski, 'Providing Legal Clarity and Securing Policy Space for Public Services Through a Legal Framework for Services of General Economic Interest: Squaring the Circle?' (n 21). By *outer* limits we mean the limits to the scope of competition and State aid, and by *inner* limits we mean the limits to the full application of those provisions, namely those limits that already reside in Article 106(2) TFEU but which are, arguably, strengthened by the Lisbon Treaty.

[97] Ross, 'A Healthy Approach to Services of General Economic Interest? The BUPA Judgment of the Court of First Instance' (n 80) 140.

developments are taken into account. Perhaps, the conclusion to be drawn from *BUPA* is that, for the purpose of State aid law, SGEIs are, at the current state of development, requirements to which Member States ascribe special significance, a significance which the EU recognises and promotes as being a manifestation of its own values clustered under the label of solidarity, values to which EU law attaches no precise prescriptions. It is only where EU legislation intervenes to regulate a specific sector that SGEIs become endowed with an independent normative content and effect, which supersedes national definitions of public services, and which requires close EU scrutiny.[98] Moreover, more general legislation under Article 14 TFEU would also advance the EU dimension of solidarity. Yet, as the more recent regulatory intervention in this area demonstrates, the Commission prefers to keep a tight grip over the regulatory process by relying on its powers under Articles 106 and 107 TFEU, rather than allowing other institutions (the Council and the European Parliament) to play a part.

B. Evaluating Compensation

Most of the focus of the Commission and the Court in reviewing compensation for PSOs has been placed on vetting compensation mechanisms, rather than on reviewing the content of PSOs. However, it would be disingenuous to argue that the two exercises are unrelated. As a matter of fact, the view that *Altmark* intensifies scrutiny of SGEIs may, after all, turn out not to be unfounded if one considers the criteria that the Court has introduced in assessing the level of compensation for PSOs. Positions on different methods for assessing compensation are inextricably linked to views concerning the co-existence of nonmarket values alongside market mechanisms and the corresponding ordering of priorities.

The rationale of *Altmark*, some have argued,[99] is to draw a line between necessary compensation, which induces undertakings 'to increase their supply' of the services that entail extra costs, and unnecessary compensation, which covers costs arising from services that undertakings would offer even in the absence of compensation. This view indentifies the acid test for the necessity of compensation in the behaviour of the market players: if undertakings cease to perform a certain activity regarded as an SGEI unless the extra costs arising from it are financed by the State, it is clear that public funding is necessary; in the opposite case, such compensation will amount to State aid. The best way to avoid overcompensation

[98] This of course echoes Sauter's remarks, 'Services of General Economic Interest and Universal Services in EU Law' (n 1) with the important difference that the latter author believes that the analysis of market failures should constitute the starting point in any assessment of the public mission, whatever the intensity of review.

[99] P Nicolaides, 'The Economics of Services of General Economic Interest' in M Sánchez Rydelski, *The EC State Aid Régime: Distortive Effects of State Aid on Competition and Trade* (London, Cameron May, 2006) 575.

is therefore to auction the SGEI which will ensure that compensation is kept at the minimum level.

However, there are some fundamental objections to this approach. Reliance on public procurement threatens to 'undermine some of the central values associated with the provision of public services, notably trust and the use of co-operative rather than conflictual, or adversary, relations'.[100] Moreover, this method of selection of public service providers may lead to underinvestment, especially where the service is entrusted for a limited period of time and the public service provider is not able to predict if it will be able to bid successfully the next time the SGEI is put to tender. Furthermore, asymmetries in information among the various participants may cause undertakings to place unrealistic bids, which will then result in inadequate provision of the services, or to over-compensation.[101] Public procurement is also open to the objection that tenders may not always lead to compensation being set at the lowest level, given the risk of collusion between participants, or the risk of bias in favour of the incumbent(s).[102]

The alternative to public procurement, the benchmarking requirement, is also problematic. Naturally, the rationale of the benchmarking requirement is to provide an alternative to public procurement as a selection method, where this proves impossible or inadequate. Yet, in the recent past, the Commission read the fourth condition as being exclusively focused on efficiency; it, instead, allowed flexibility to set in where Article 106(2) TFEU comes into play. This approach may perhaps have been motivated by a concern with legal certainty and with the risk of abuse that a 'wider' reading of *Altmark* would engender. However, this is not the only possible reading of that condition. It is possible to read the benchmarking requirement as providing some flexibility for public authorities in contrast to the mechanistic nature of public procurement. The wording of the condition, arguably, lends itself to this interpretation. In fact, the Court in *Altmark* does not merely impose the *average* undertaking to be chosen as a benchmark, but specifies that such an undertaking should be 'well run and adequately provided with means so as to be able to meet the necessary public service requirements'. It does not seem far-fetched that in the context of public service provision that requirement should leave open some discretionary assessment as to the suitability of the undertaking to deliver 'high quality' public services. Both *Chronopost* and *BUPA* suggest that the EU Courts may be more eager to follow this line of approach.

The second reason why one may find the rigid application of *Altmark* to be unsatisfactory is that it posits a reductivist notion of SGEIs, which claims that

[100] T Prosser, 'Competition Law and Public Services: From Single Market to Citizenship Rights' (2005) 11 *European Public Law* 543, 562.

[101] H Cox, 'Questions About the Initiative of the European Commission Concerning the Awarding and Compulsory Competitive Tendering of Public Service Concessions' (2003) 74 *Annals of Public & Cooperative Economics* 7; O Mattisson and A Thomasson, 'The Strategic Process and its Impact on the Outcome of a Tender' (2007) 78 *Annals of Public & Cooperative Economics* 439.

[102] S Santamato and N Pesaresi, 'Compensation for Services of General Economic Interest: Some thoughts on the *Altmark* ruling', *Competition Policy Newsletter*, 1/2004, 17.

SGEI provision may be reconciled with the internal market by nudging SGEIs in the direction of the market. Member States retain their autonomy in designating certain activities as SGEIs, but are significantly constrained in the way in which they structure them: *Altmark* influences the decision as to how the SGEIs must be funded, but also the decision as to *who* should provide the service. Some have argued that this approach does not depart from the case law on Article 106(2) TFEU.[103] In particular, it has been argued that *Altmark* takes its cue from the requirement in that case law that SGEIs be delivered efficiently.[104] In *Glöckner*,[105] the Court held that a limitation of the full force of competition law would not be accepted if it were demonstrated that the undertakings charged with PSOs were unable to satisfy demand in relation to those services. The emphasis in *Altmark* on the condition that SGEIs be delivered 'at the least cost to the Community', and the role of efficiency in the selection of the SGEI provider seems, mutatis mutandis, to reproduce the approach of that case law.[106]

A fundamental assumption behind this position, however, is that it is possible to question the efficiency of SGEI providers without questioning SGEIs. That, however, may not always be the case. To confine national autonomy to the identification of tasks that are worth promoting and significantly constraining the choices as to how these tasks should be achieved seems to be a contradiction of EU law's commitment to subsidiarity in this sector. Moreover, it is not always possible to separate questions regarding the nature of SGEIs from questions regarding their provision and their funding. *BUPA* is an illustration of this. In the Irish health insurance system, the community rating system, which prohibited insurers from adjusting premiums or benefits according to consumers that subscribed to the same plan, was made possible by the introduction of the risk equalisation scheme (RES) which sought to neutralise differences in insurers' claims costs from different risk profiles. Clearly, without the RES the community rating would not have been achievable.

It is of course possible to argue, as Sauter does, that the General Court, in *BUPA*, could have been more searching in its analysis of the RES under the *Altmark* criteria. An ex post compensation based on actual costs does not provide an incentive for innovation and cost reduction.[107] More specifically, in an ex post compensation mechanism the costs are borne by competitors and the profits derived from efficiency are 'skimmed off', thus reducing incentives for genuine competition to emerge. However, this type of argument goes to the substance of the system. This is implicitly acknowledged by Sauter who argues that the system should provide 'incentives for efficient contracting and purchasing, investing in

[103] G Monti, *EC Competition Law* (Cambridge, Cambridge University Press, 2007) 490–91.
[104] Ibid.
[105] Case C-475/99 *Ambulanz Glöckner* [2001] ECR I-8089.
[106] Monti, *EC Competition Law* (n 103). It is worth noting that in *Glöckner* the Court focused on allocative efficiency, whereas the efficiency requirement in *Altmark* refers to productive efficiency.
[107] Sauter, 'Annotation of Case T-289/03 *BUPA v Commission*' (n 81).

quality, in multi-agency and multi-professional care and prevention' in order to drive down costs.[108] While these may be pertinent questions, it is hard to see how it is possible to address them without questioning the political choices effected by domestic policy makers.[109]

In recognising the impossibility of promoting the full force of competition in the Irish system without delving into the structure of the policy, the General Court has acknowledged the flexible nature of the outer limits of State aid law, in a manner which may appear to stem from the concept of 'obstruction' in the Article 106(2) TFEU case law: in this sense, the ruling may be taken to represent 'a carefully positioned reassessment of social and market priorities'.[110] Critics will regard the *BUPA* judgment as the analytically flawed relaxation of a test that would otherwise have produced politically uncomfortable outcomes. However, the judgment may not only be viewed as the adoption of a more flexible approach to *Altmark*, which is able to adapt to the peculiarities of the domestic regulatory context, but also as an approach that is better able to capture the renewed relevance of SGEIs. Whilst the Court's analysis of compensation issues may be criticised for its loose interpretation of the benchmarking requirement in the fourth *Altmark* condition, compensation issues are intensely related to the core of the organisation of SGEIs. In other words, EU interference in the way in which compensation is determined is inevitably an intrusion in the way in which Member States choose to structure their public services.

Perhaps *BUPA* represents the recognition that the *Altmark* orthodoxy, if left unaltered, would lead to politically and constitutionally unacceptable results. The intensely prescriptive nature of the *Altmark* solution, in fact, sits uneasily with the supporting role attributed to EU competence in the field of health care.[111] Of course, the free movement case law is a natural objection to this argument, as the EU Courts have not shied away from making inroads into national healthcare systems.[112] Yet, it is submitted, whilst the focus of the free movement health care case law is on individual claimants' eligibility to entitlements, and only indirectly on the structure of national health systems, applying the *Altmark* efficiency benchmark to the Irish scheme would have *directly* questioned some of the key assumptions behind the structure of the health insurance system in Ireland.

[108] Ibid 273.

[109] And, of course, all the more so in the field of health care.

[110] Ross, 'A Healthy Approach to Services of General Economic Interest? The BUPA Judgment of the Court of First Instance' (n.80) 131. See also A Biondi, '*BUPA v Commission*' (2008) *European State Aid Quarterly* 401.

[111] The constitutionally sensitive nature of this area of competence was famously exposed in Case C-376/98 *Germany v European Parliament and Council of the European Union* [2000] ECR I-8419.

[112] Case C-372/04 *R (on the application of Watts) v Bedford Primary Care Trust* [2006] ECR I-4325. Of course, this is not to underestimate the potential and actual effects of the free movement case law on national healthcare systems—it is beyond the scope of this chapter to consider these further. See, among others, G Davies, 'The Effect of Mrs.Watts' Trip to France on the National Health Service' (2007) 18 *Kings College Law Journal* 158.

BUPA exposes a fundamental tension between the efficiency-orientated assessment of compensation that emanates from *Altmark* and the recognition of national discretion in both the TFEU and, especially, in the Protocol on SGIs, which have strengthened the idea that the definition and funding of SGEIs is primarily a matter for Member States. The Protocol specifically refers to Member State competence, and to the 'wide discretion' enjoyed by national authorities in this respect. Admittedly, these provisions contain an ambiguity which *may* be read as an indication that the separation between definition and funding has made its way into the Treaty. In fact, on the one hand, Article 14 TFEU introduces a basis for legislation to set the conditions for financing SGEIs, but adds that such legislation 'shall establish these principles and set these conditions without prejudice to the competence of Member States, *in compliance with the Treaties*, to provide, to commission and *to fund* such services'. On the other hand, however, Article 1 of the Protocol recognises 'the essential role and the wide discretion of national, regional and local authorities in *providing, commissioning and organising* services of general economic interest as closely as possible to the needs of the users'. The different language may have been used to emphasise that while funding is an area that Member States retain as part of their competences, their discretion is limited by the Commission's scrutiny over compliance with the State aid provisions.

Nonetheless, there is no doubt that, all things considered,[113] the new provisions, combined with the *BUPA* jurisprudence, provide fertile ground for a more sophisticated approach to State aid and SGEIs, which is able to modulate the intensity of its review to reflect the nature of the competence that Member States exercise, but also to reflect the wide discretion that they enjoy in 'providing commission and organising' SGEIs. The crucial question will therefore be how far it is possible to review the competence to fund SGEIs without undermining the latter discretion. In its 2005 package, and to a greater extent in its 2011 package, the Commission displays sensitivity towards these concerns. Granted, the latest package is more restrictive than previous decision-making practice in the area in its interpretation of Article 106(2) TFEU to measures that fall within Article 107(1) TFEU, an approach which is justified on account of the distortive nature of large amounts of compensation and the multinational character of some the undertakings involved in SGEI provision.[114] Yet, at the same time, the package introduces greater flexibility in the interpretation of the *Altmark* conditions. As seen before, the Commission recognises that quality is an element of the selection process, both when a public procurement procedure is employed, and in relation to the benchmarking approach. With regard to the former, it strives to reconcile qualitative criteria with the requirements of public procurement, and in relation to the

113 Ie taking account of the lack of a constitutionally sanctioned 'wide discretion' in the field of SGEI-funding.

114 See Commission, 'Communication—European Union framework for State aid in the form of public service compensation' (n 70).

latter, it makes clear that qualitative criteria are intrinsic to the benchmark.[115] The strong formulation used with regard to the relevance of quality with respect to cost benchmarking is particularly significant. The Commission makes clear that benchmarking is not solely based on efficiency, and that low cost options do not always reflect public service values.

4. BEYOND THE MARKET PARTICIPANT—REGULATOR DICHOTOMY

In the *Kuipers* case,[116] which concerned a system of supplements paid to milk producers by the Netherlands' Milk Board, Advocate General Kokott suggested that the case law on state financing of SGEIs was based on the idea that such compensation did not fall within the scope of Article 107(1) TFEU, an idea which, she added, was 'ultimately merely an expression of the general principle that the law on aids does not apply to legal relationships in which a normal market consideration corresponds to a service', since 'a person who provides a service and obtains a normal market consideration in return is not a recipient of aid but rather operates on the market under conditions of normal competition'.[117] Taken literally, this statement appears to suggest that there is a market for SGEIs in which the performance of such services is remunerated at a price resulting from the interaction of supply and demand, and that, therefore, the case law in this area flows naturally from the application of the principles that come into play where Member States act as ordinary market participants. Such a view of things, however, does not appear to square with the evolution of what is a necessarily complex, and necessarily 'hybrid', case law arising from a reality in which market and regulation, the private and the public spheres, are intertwined to such an extent as to make the public/private dichotomy traced in the previous chapters appear inadequate. The evolution of the Court's case law in this area reflects an attempt, ungainly perhaps, but necessary, to adapt the interpretative tools of State aid law to an emerging and expanding phenomenon which neither the Treaty, nor the Court's earlier case law had envisaged. To regard this evolution as the expression of a constant principle in State aid law is to deny both the peculiarity of the underlying relationship that this case law seeks to capture, and the conceptual differences that mark out this case law from previous developments.

Yet there is another light in which to read Advocate General Kokott's remarks. In order for the compensation measure to fall outside the scope of Article 107(1) TFEU, some sort of *market equivalence* needs to be established. The idea behind

[115] Ibid para 72.

[116] Case C-283/03 *Kuipers* [2005] ECR I-4255 Opinion of Adovcate General Kokott.

[117] Ibid para 79. Unlike the Advocate General, the Court decided that it was unnecessary to answer the national Court's question concerning the Dutch system's compatibility with the State aid rules as it fell within the scope of Community rules on the common organisation of the market in the milk and milk products.

the *Altmark* test is in fact to attempt to reproduce as closely as possible the market paradigm, hence the preference for public procurement procedures and the alternative benchmark of the 'typical undertaking'. Some commentators regard this approach as a variant of the market operator test and therefore place it within that category.[118] Leaving aside taxonomy, the fundamental question concerns the extent to which market and nonmarket concerns come into play in the *Altmark* test and how this assessment compares to the one carried out in the context of the market operator principle.

At an abstract level, some degree of commonality among the two approaches emerges from the assumption, which both appear to subscribe to, that public, nonmarket, concerns should not be used as a façade behind which to hide anti-competitive arrangements between Member States and undertakings. The market operator principle requires the role of the State as public authority to be severed from its role as market participant, and prevents considerations that appertain to the former role to influence the assessment of actions taken in the latter. *Altmark* aims to achieve a similar *general* objective, but through significantly different means. *Altmark* requires compensation to cover only those costs that an efficient undertaking would incur, and to classify as State aid those costs that result from inefficiency as State aid.

However, in assessing whether or not a measure falls within Article 107(1) TFEU, the Court unequivocally (though impliedly) rejected the idea that public interest considerations were irrelevant to that exercise. On the contrary, those considerations were among the necessary conditions for a measure to fall outside the definition of State aid, as the first step in the assessment of compensation measures consisted in determining the existence of an SGEI and the entrustment of a PSO through an act of a public authority. The existence of public interest concerns, and the role of the State as a public authority were therefore crucial ingredients in addressing the State aid question.

Another source of difficulty arising from the Court's *Altmark* approach lies in the relationship between compensation measures and normal regulation. As seen in chapter five, State aid law takes for granted that undertakings are normally required to internalise the costs of regulation,[119] and any measure that relieves them of such costs is seen as creating a selective advantage, as regulation is treated as being within an undertaking's normal costs. Perhaps a way to reconcile the *Altmark* approach with the market operator test would be to argue that the imposition of tasks in the public interest is distinct from normal regulation. By imposing PSOs, the public authority steps outside the normal regulatory framework to create a semi-private relationship with the undertaking it entrusts with those

[118] M Hansen, A van Ysendyck and S Zuhlke, 'The Coming of Age of EC State Aid Law' (2004) 25 *European Competition Law Review* 202; and L Hancher, T Ottervanger and PJ Slot, *EC State Aids*, 3rd edn (London, Sweet and Maxwell, 2006) ch 3; E Sczyszczak, *The Regulation of the State in Competitive Markets in the EU* (n 1) ch 4.

[119] Case 173/73 *Italy v Commission* [1974] ECR 709.

tasks. In *BUPA*, the General Court appeared to follow a similar logical path as it distinguished PSOs from normal regulation, but did not suggest that the former should be ascribed to the State's commercial sphere. Instead, the General Court seemed to be referring to the fact that the obligations imposed on undertakings under the Irish scheme went beyond the demands that States ordinarily place on undertakings, the costs of which are expected to be shouldered by the undertakings themselves; in recognising the special nature of PSOs, the General Court implied that these represented *a particular form* of regulation.

It seems clear from what has been said that a nonmarket element is a necessary (though not sufficient) condition to rule out the application of Article 107(1) TFEU; without it, the transaction in question would not be able to withstand analysis in light of the State aid provisions.[120] Recognising the nonmarket element in PSOs does not necessarily mean, however, that compensation for such obligations should be regarded as having a non-economic character, as Advocate General Léger claimed in *Altmark*.[121] If the services have an economic element, denoted by the term 'Services of General *Economic* Interest', their compensation should be seen as partially falling within the scope of an economic exchange, even if such an exchange cannot be assimilated to a normal market exchange: the two alternative limbs of the fourth condition, the creation of a market through public procurement and the benchmarking of the SGEI provider's costs on a market-drawn comparator, bear this out. Recognising the economic element embedded in the definition of SGEIs allows us to take stock of developments in national economies which have led to the emergence of channels of public service delivery that straddle the public-private, State-market divide. Plainly, there is no room for clear-cut dichotomies in this field.

5. CONCLUSION

Public services are a testing ground for the post-Lisbon Treaty environment characterised by a greater responsiveness to the social dimensions of the market economy.[122] Unlike in the area examined in the previous chapter, the case for a recognition, as a matter of EU law, of constitutional concerns that act as a brake on negative integration finds explicit support in a number of legal sources. At a general level, it finds support in the constitutional values embedded in the notion of solidarity and in the objective of creating a social market economy. At a more explicit level it finds support in the specific legal provisions that recognise the

[120] Eg in Case T-157/01 *Danske Busvognmænd* (n 77).

[121] Advocate General Léger, Opinion delivered on 14 January 2003 for Case 280/00 *Altmark Trans GmbH, Regierungspräsidium Magdeburg v Nahverkergesellschaft Altmark GmbH* [2003] ECR I-7747.

[122] U Neergaard, 'Services of General Economic Interest under EU Law Constraints' in D Schiek, U Liebert, and H Schneider, *European Economic and Social Constitutionalism after the Treaty of Lisbon* (Cambridge, Cambridge University Press, 2011) 174–95.

importance of SGEIs as a matter of EU law. Given the predominantly national character of redistributive policies, one could simply characterise the interaction between economic integration and SGEIs as a tension between EU and domestic values. That interaction, however, is more complex and intriguing. The law on these issues is traversed by multiple tensions between market and nonmarket concerns, between the EU and the domestic level, but also between administrative discretion and constitutional principle. Granted, the self-satisfied and elusive rhetoric surrounding the so-called 'European model of society', often bandied about in policy documents in this area, fails to identify the specifically European (as opposed to domestic) dimension of public services. Yet, the legal interaction between competition and public services seems to have reached a level of sophistication which allows us to hazard the conclusion that this is an area in which EU law is beginning to display the conditions for national nonmarket concerns, in particular, considerations relating to the *quality* of public services, to be carefully integrated into the realisation of an efficient transnational market economy.

8

Conclusion

The chapters of this book have proceeded from the fundamental premise that, even in areas of low political salience, such as those areas that we normally associate with the economic constitution, questions regarding the legitimacy of European integration are pertinent questions. Answers to these questions turn on the ability of the Court to deliver the legal infrastructure of market integration without compromising nonmarket values that are deeply embedded in national political and constitutional systems. The focal concern of this book has been to attempt to explain what the law of State aid brings to this effort.

Much like the rest of internal market law, State aid law does not lend itself to labelling exercises. Yet, it possesses a set of distinctive traits that mark it out from other areas of internal market law. The distinctiveness of this policy emerges from a number of features that can be appreciated by examining the system of State aid control, and by dissecting the elements that make up the definition of State aid. In an overview of State aid policy as whole, chapter three has identified centralisation as the most prominent trait of this system of rules. The centralised nature and the centralising effect of this area of internal market law derive from the sharp demarcation between the definition of State aid and its possible policy justifications, and from the procedural consequences attached to this demarcation.

The reasons for centralisation, as far as State aid is concerned, are readily intelligible: cross-border externalities and commitment problems justify the particular limitation of sovereignty demanded by State aid law. Yet, what is remarkable is the degree to which State aid control, because of its centralised nature, impacts on national regulatory choices and on their realisation. State aid policy has been aptly characterised in the literature as a mixture of negative and positive integration. Not only does it prevent certain kinds of State aid altogether, it also prescribes procedures and mechanisms that allow State aid to be channelled towards objectives that the EU regards as worthy of being pursued. Naturally, the definition of State aid represents the negative side of integration, whereas the positive integration aspect is associated with the compatibility assessment carried out by the Commission. Yet, even the definition of State aid control contains strong regulatory elements, a fact which can be appreciated by looking back at each of the four chapters dedicated to the scope of Article 107(1) TFEU—the distinct regulatory nature and or effect of State aid is present in each of the areas that they cover. Chapter four has examined the legal treatment of State participation in market transactions. Under the market operator principle, States are required to conform to standards of behaviour drawn from the market. This is plainly an efficiency test. Yet, by requiring that market 'rationality' inform the decisions of public authorities, the market operator principle turns market standards into regulatory standards. Areas of activity that were previously unconstrained by legal standards become subject to fresh standards which, albeit deriving from the market, are mediated and formalised by the Commission and by the Court.

The effect of State aid may also be to prevent or limit deregulation. In cases concerning the significance of State aid to the regulatory capacity of the State, examined in chapters five and six, Member States are prevented from relaxing generally applicable standards. The thrust of the case law is that, if regulation is to apply in a prima facie asymmetrical fashion, asymmetry should prove to be inherent in the regulatory system, and should not result from a political or commercial choice to discriminate in favour of a certain undertaking, or economic sector. This approach to State aid, which centres around the selectivity test, is at its most contentious when applied to sub-national corporate taxation. A strict interpretation of the State aid rules would have implied that a geographically-circumscribed set of tax rules was to be regarded as selective. Yet, in *Azores* the Court introduced a test that allows the sub-national regulatory (tax) system to be treated as the appropriate reference framework. In doing so, it determined the parameters that any attempt to devolve fiscal powers now needs to take into account.[1] If, for instance, a new settlement for Scottish devolution was to come into existence, and if that settlement was to cover corporate taxation, it would necessarily have to respect the parameters set by the Court.

There is also no doubt that the case law on compensation for Public Service Obligations (PSOs) also has a distinct regulatory element to it. The combination of the *Altmark* criteria and of the Commission's subsequent packages on State aid and Services of General Economic Interest (SGEIs) provide detailed guidance both on the compensation mechanisms and on the selection of the public service provider.[2] The *Altmark* ruling prescribes two alternatives, public tenders and benchmarking, both of which complement or replace pre-existing domestic regulatory mechanisms or regulate previously unregulated territory.

If it is true that centralisation is the most prominent trait of State aid law, it is also true that each of the areas examined in this book reveal a tension between the naturally centralising nature of the definition of State aid, and a clear set of decentralising tendencies in the case law. The centralising nature of State aid control, as was argued, is associated with the precept that causes and aims, including policy considerations, are irrelevant to the definition of State aid and should therefore be ignored at that stage. However, the conceptual 'purity' that this precept implies has suffered infiltrations from a number of different public policy concerns that have partially eroded the monopoly of the Commission over public policy

[1] Case C-88/03 *Portugal v Commission (Azores)* [2006] ECR I-7115.

[2] Case 280/00 *Altmark Trans GmbH, Regierungspräsidium Magdeburg v Nahverkergesellschaft Altmark GmbH* [2003] ECR I-7747.

justifications. Decentralisation occurs insofar as decisions regarding questions of fit between national measures and the scope of Article 107(1) TFEU entail an assessment of the regulatory objectives of the measures under consideration; an assessment, that is, which would normally be regarded as the exclusive province of the Commission under Article 107(2) and (3) TFEU. Such decentralising impulses are seen at work in the context of the application of the material selectivity test, where the Court has developed the notion of a justification based on inherent features of the regulatory system. Decentralisation is also seen at work in the *Azores* line of case law, in which the question regarding geographical selectivity entails an assessment of the degree of institutional and constitutional autonomy enjoyed by the sub-national entity. Finally, decentralisation plays a significant part in the context of the State aid scrutiny of compensation for the fulfilment of public service tasks. In addition to setting in motion a process of re-regulation, the *Altmark* jurisprudence implies that the scope of Article 107(1) TFEU hinges, inter alia, on the existence of a public service mission, a domain that, as the Court and the Commission have confirmed, lies squarely within national competence.

Another fundamental feature of State aid law highlighted in this book is the existence of a dichotomy between cases involving State participation in the market and those concerning regulation. The two sets of situations give rise to radically different legal tests which, in turn, produce significantly different effects and raise disparate concerns. Given the emphasis on competitiveness, the fact that, in cases involving the State's participation in market transactions, State aid law relies on criteria that promote efficiency seems unremarkable. The idea behind the market operator test is that, in its dealings with the market, the State's actions should be governed by criteria that are liable to harden the budget constraints of undertakings. Yet, the market operator principle has given rise to the concern that the emphasis on market rationality may result in hollowing out the concept of a mixed economy, an economy, that is, in which the public and private sector co-exist alongside each other. This is a similar concern to the one examined in chapter two in relation to sections of free movement law, in which the breadth of scope of the internal market provisions, as interpreted in recent case law, was regarded as bearing the potential to engender a gradual erosion in varieties of capitalism. As far as State aid is concerned, the market operator principle does not, as such, prevent the survival of the entrepreneurial State. Nonetheless, the mechanisms that flow from the principle force a reconfiguration of the role of the State as market participant. State aid law does not force the State out of the market; it compels it to play by the rules of the market mediated through the market operator test. This reconfiguration, however, cannot be entirely without consequence: it has the capacity to cause greater convergence in the organisation of national capitalist systems.[3]

[3] To what extent this convergence is actually happening is an interesting empirical question which lies outside the scope of this research.

What is remarkable about State aid law, however, is the combination of an economically liberal orientation with a set of legal tools the effect of which is to curtail the freedom of Member States to engage in regulatory competition. Where Member States act as regulators, they are required to enact non-discriminatory, non-selective regulation. In itself, this aspect of State aid law is sufficient to reject claims that this part of internal market law conforms to a neo-liberal model of economic constitution. At the same time, however, the case law constitutes an attempt to cast a wide net on regulatory measures, while seeking to avoid subjecting all aspects of national regulation to State aid scrutiny. The tension between these two conflicting aspirations is reflected in the Court's jurisprudence on the inherent justification and on the State resources condition.

Part II has also identified difficulties in tracing the dividing line between activities that are subject to the market operator test and other activities. As explained in chapter four, to ascribe commercial significance to activities that are normally perceived as regulatory in nature is a questionable exercise. This is because the system of State aid is predicated on the assumption that undertakings operate in a regulatory environment, the costs of which they ordinarily internalise. Where the State alters this framework, it alters the competitive balance in favour of an undertakings or group of undertakings. However, the *Ryanair* and *EDF* case law appears to suggest that a partial shift away from this approach may be taking place.[4] In both cases, activities that the Commission had characterised as emanating from the State's regulatory or prerogative powers were deemed to be amenable to the market operator test. The impact of this new approach may amount to a change in the general orientation of State aid in relation to regulatory competition, the significance of which could be to encourage Member States to use regulation strategically.

Chapter two of this book identified the imperative of safeguarding non-economic values in the pursuit of market integration as being the main challenge of constitutional adjudication in the internal market. It was suggested that, through a teleological interpretation that strives to safeguard national constitutional domains and the pursuit by Member States of nonmarket values, the Court could achieve a more solid basis for its legitimacy. This is particularly true of areas in which non-economic values are recognised as a matter of EU primary law. Part III has addressed two areas in which this is the case: chapters six and seven examined, in particular, the significance of constitutional identity and of SGEIs respectively in shaping the recent evolution of the definition of State aid in the Court's case law. While the Court did not appear to rely on the relevance, as a matter of EU law, of national constitutional identity, it was argued in chapter six that an explicit reliance on Article 4(2) TEU would help to explain why criteria that appear to be alien to the logic of State aid law, such as institutional autonomy, have become, as a result of the Court's interpretation, part of the scope of Article 107(1) TFEU.

[4] Case T-196/04 *Ryanair* [2009] ECR II-3643; Case T-156/04 *Electricité de France* [2009] ECR II-4503; Case C-124/10 P *European Commission v Électricité de France and Others* (5 June 2012).

While the recognition of national constitutional identity in the definition of State aid in relation to regional autonomy would not make any practical difference to the formulation of the legal test applied in *Azores*, the Court's reasoning would acquire greater openness.

The situation is rather different where public services are concerned. As shown in chapter seven, the significance of SGEIs as a constitutional value is fully acknowledged in the definition of State aid. The combined effect of the EU Courts' case law and of the Commission's regulatory initiatives has meant that the current relationship between State aid and SGEIs is more balanced than was previously the case. One may regret that this relationship has not been addressed in the context of legislative measures designed to construct a European dimension of public services, and has, instead been mainly articulated in terms of safeguarding *domestic* public service values. However, in a context of limited powers, limited legitimacy and, necessarily, limited ambition, the current regulation of public service funding may be considered to be a genuine achievement.

Bibliography

Ahlborn, C and Berg, C, 'Can State Aid Control Learn from Antitrust? The Need for a Greater Role for Competition Analysis under the State Aid Rules' in Biondi, A Eeckhout, P and Flynn, J (eds), *The Law of State Aid in the EU* (Oxford, Oxford University Press, 2004) 41–67.

—— and Grave, C, 'Walter Eucken and Ordoliberalism: An Introduction from a Consumer Welfare Perspective' (2006) 2 *Competition Policy International* 197.

Akkermans, B and Ramaekers, E, 'Article 345 TFEU (ex Article 295 EC), Its Meanings and Interpretations' (2009) 15 *European Law Journal* 292.

Akman, P, 'Searching for the Long-Lost Soul of Article 82 EC' (2009) 29 *OJLS* 267.

Amato, G, *Antitrust and the Bounds of Power: The Dilemma of Liberal Democracy in the History of the Market* (Oxford, Hart Publishing, 1997).

Atanasiu, I, 'State Aid in Central and Eastern Europe' (2001) 24 *World Competition* 257.

Azoulai, L, 'The Court of Justice and the Social Market Economy: The Emergence of an Ideal and the conditions for its Realization' (2008) 45 *CML Rev* 1335.

Bacon, K, 'State Aids and General Measures' (1997) 17 *Yearbook of European Law* 269.

——, 'The Concept of State Aid: The Developing Jurisprudence in the European and UK Courts' (2003) 24 *European Competition Law Review* 54.

Baldwin, B, Scott, C and Hood, C, *A Reader on Regulation* (Oxford, Oxford University Press, 1998).

Baldwin, R and Krugman, P, 'Agglomeration, Integration and Tax Harmonisation' (2004) 48 *European Economic Review* 1.

Baquero Cruz, J, *Between Competition and Free Movement* (Oxford, Hart Publishing, 2002).

——, 'Beyond Competition: Services of General Interest and European Community Law' in de Búrca, G (ed), *EU Law and the Welfare State—In Search of Solidarity* (Oxford, Oxford University Press, 2005) 169–212.

Barca, F and Trento, S, 'State ownership and the evolution of Italian corporate governance' (1997) 6 *Industrial and Corporate Change* 533.

Barnard, C and Deakin, S, 'Market Access and Regulatory Competition' in Barnard, C and Scott, J (eds), *The Law of The Single European Market: Unpacking the Premises* (Oxford, Hart Publishing, 2002) 197–224.

Barnard, C, 'EU "Social" Policy: From Employment Law to Labour Market Reform' in Craig, P and de Búrca, G (eds), *The Evolution of EU Law*, 2nd edn (Oxford, Oxford University Press, 2011).

Bartosch, A, 'The Relationship between Public Procurement and State Aid Surveillance—The Toughest Standard Applies?' (2002) 39 *CML Rev* 551.

——, 'Compensation for Public Service Obligations: Post-*Altmark* Remarks' in Sánchez Rydelski, M, *The EC State Aid Régime: Distortive Effects Distortive Effects of State Aid on Competition and Trade* (London, Cameron May, 2006) 55.

——, 'Aid to Social Housing and European State Aid Control' (2007) *European Competition Law Review* 563.

——, 'Is there a Need for a Rule of Reason In European State Aid Law?' (2010) 47 *CML Rev* 729.

——, Case Note on EDF (2010) 9 *European State Aid Law Quarterly* 679.

Bator, FM, 'The Anatomy of Market Failure' (1958) 72 *Quarterly Journal of Economics* 351.

Baudenbacher, C and Bremer, F, 'European State Aid and Merger Control in the Financial Crisis—From Negative to Positive Integration' (2010) 1 *Journal of European Competition Law and Practice* 267.

Bertero, E and Rondi, L, 'Hardening the Soft Budget Constraint through "Upward Devolution" to a Supranational Institution: The Case of the European Union and Italian State-Owned Firms' in Sun, L (ed), *Ownership of Governance of Enterprises: Recent Innovative Developments* (London, Palgrave Macmillan, 2003) 124–58.

Besley, T and Seabright, P, 'The Effects and Policy Implications of State Aids to Industry: An Economic Analysis' (1999) 34 *Economic Policy* 13.

Besselink, LFM, 'National and constitutional identity before and after Lisbon' (2010) 6 *Utrecht Law Review* 36.

Bilal, S and Nicolaides, P, 'State Aid Rules: Do They Promote Efficiency?' in Bilal, S and Nicolaides, P (eds), *Understanding State Aid Policy in the European Community: Perspectives on Rules and Practice* (The Hague, Kluwer, 1999) 29–46.

Biondi, A and Eeckhout, P, 'State Aid and Obstacles to Trade' in Biondi, A, Eeckhout, P and Flynn, J (eds), *The Law of State Aid in the EU* (Oxford, Oxford University Press, 2004) 103–17.

——, —— and Flynn, J (eds), *The Law of State Aid in the European Union* (Oxford, Oxford University Press, 2004).

——, 'The Financing of Services of General Economic Interest' in Tridimas, T and Nebbia, P (eds), *EU Law for the 21st Century* (Oxford, Hart Publishing, 2005) 268.

——, 'Some Reflections on the Notion of "State Resources" in European Community State Aid Law' (2007) 30 *Fordham International Law Journal* 1426.

——, '*BUPA v Commission*' (2008) *European State Aid Quarterly* 401.

—— and Farley, M, 'The Relationship between State Aid and the Single Market' in Szyszczak, E (ed), *Research Handbook on State Aid* (Cheltenham, Edward Elgar, 2011) 277–92.

Blauberger, M, 'From Negative to Positive Integration?' (2008) Max Planck Institute for the Study of Societies Discussion Paper 08/4.

Boeger, N, 'Solidarity and EC competition law' (2007) 32 *EL Rev* 319.

Bovens, M, 'New Forms of Accountability and EU Governance' (2007) 5 *Comparative European Politics* 104.

Von Bogdandy, A and Schill, S, 'Overcoming Absolute Primacy: Respect for National Constitutional Identity under the Lisbon Treaty' (2011) 48 *CML Rev* 1417.

Bohm, F, Eucken, W and Grossmann-Doerth, H, 'The Ordo Manifesto of 1936' in A Peacock and H Willgerodt (eds), *Germany's Social Market Economy: Origins and Evolution* (London, Macmillan, 1989) 15–26.

Brothwood, M, 'The Commission Directive on Transparency of Financial Relations between Member States and Public Undertakings' (1981) *CML Rev* 207.

Bratton, W and McCahery, J, 'Tax Coordination and Tax Competition in the European Union: Evaluating the Code of Conduct on Business Taxation' (2001) 38 *CML Rev* 677.

Brennan, G and Buchanan, JM, *The Power to Tax: Analytical Foundations of a Fiscal Constitution* (Cambridge, Cambridge University Press, 1980).

Buendía Sierra, JL, *Exclusive Rights and State Monopolies under EC Law* (Oxford, Oxford University Press, 1999).

——, 'Article 86' in Faull, J and Nickpay, A (eds), *The EC Law of Competition*, 2nd edn (Oxford, Oxford University Press, 2007) 630.

—— and Smulders, B, 'The Limited Role of the "Refined Economic Approach" in Achieving the Objectives of State Aid Control: Time for Some Realism' in Buendia Sierra, JL and others, *Liber Amicorum Francisco Santaolalla Gadea* (The Hague, Kluwer, 2008) 1–26.

Cahill, D, (ed), *The Modernisation of EU Competition Law Enforcement in the EU* (Cambridge, Cambridge University Press, 2004).

Cini, M and McGowan, L, *Competition Policy in the European Union* (Basingstoke, Macmillan, 1998).

Craig, P, 'Constitutions, Constitutionalism and the European Union' (2001) 7 *European Law Journal* 125.

Coppi, L, 'The Role of Economics in State Aid Analysis and the Balancing Test' in Szyszczak, E (ed), *Research Handbook on State Aid* (Cheltenham, Edward Elgar, 2011) 64–90.

Cox, H, 'Questions About the Initiative of the European Commission Concerning the Awarding and Compulsory Competitive Tendering of Public Service Concessions' (2003) 74 *Annals of Public & Cooperative Economics* 7.

Criscuolo, A, 'The State in a Liberal Market Economy: A Private Investor and Creditor or a Public Authority' (1999) 24 *EL Rev* 525.

Daintith, T, 'The Techniques of Government' in Jowell, J and Oliver, D (eds), *The Changing Constitution* (Oxford, Clarendon Press, 1994).

Damjanovic, D and De Witte, B, 'Welfare Integration through EU Law: The Overall Picture in the Light of the Lisbon Treaty' in Neergaard, U, Nielsen, R and Roseberry, L (eds), *Integrating Welfare Functions into EU Law* (Copenhagen, DJØF Forlag, 2009).

von Danwitz, A, 'The Concept of State Aid in Liberalised Sectors' (2008) EUI Working Paper 28.

Dashwood, A, '*Viking* and *Laval*: Issues of Horizontal Direct Effect' (2007–2008) 10 *Cambridge Yearbook of European Legal Studies* 525.

——, 'Article 308 and the Outer Limit of Expressly Conferred Community Competence' in Barnard, C and Odudu, O (eds), *The Outer Limits of European Union Law* (Oxford, Hart Publishing, 2009).

Davies, A, 'One Step Forward, Two Steps Back? The *Viking* and *Laval* Cases in the ECJ', (2008) 37 *Industrial Law Journal* 126.

Davies, G, 'The Effect of Mrs. Watts' Trip to France on the National Health Service' (2007) 18 *Kings College Law Journal* 158.

——, 'Constitutional Disagreement in Europe and the Search for Pluralism', Eric Stein Working Paper 1/2010.

Davies, P, 'Market Integration and Social Policy in the Court of Justice' (1995) 24 *Industrial Law Journal* 49.

Deardorff, AV, 'The Economics of Government Market Intervention, and its International Dimension' in Bronkers, M and Quick, R (eds), *New Directions in International Economic Law* (The Hague, Kluwer, 2000) 71–84.

Devroe, W, 'Privatizations and Community Law: Neutrality versus Policy' (1997) 34 *CML Rev* 267.

Dewatripont, M and Seabright, P, '"Wasteful" Public Spending and State Aid Control' (2006) 4 *Journal of the European Economic Association* 513.

Di Bucci, V, 'Quelques Aspects Institutionnels du Droit des Aides d'État' in Buendia Sierra, JL and others, *Liber Amicorum Francisco Santaolalla Gadea* (The Hague, Kluwer, 2008) 43–64.

Di Via, L, *Antitrust e Diritti Sociali: Contributo ad una Teoria dell'Abuso del Diritto* (Napoli, Edizioni Scientifiche Italiane, 2004).

Dyson, K and Featherstone, K, *The Road to Maastricht: Negotiating Economic and Monetary Union* (Oxford, Oxford University Press, 2009).

Eleftheriadis, P, 'The Idea of a European Constitution' (2007) 27 *OJLS* 1.

——, 'The Structure of European Union Law' (2009–2010) 12 *Cambridge Yearbook of European Legal Studies* 121.

Eskeland, G and Litvack, J (eds), *Fiscal Decentralization and the Challenge of Hard Budget Constraints* (Cambridge, MIT Press, 2003).

Eucken, W, *Grundsätze der Wirtschaftspolitik* (Tübingen, Francke und Mohr, 1952).

Fantozzi, A, 'The Applicability of State Aid Rules to Tax Competition Measures: A Process of *de Facto* Harmonization in the Tax Field?' in W Schön (ed), *Tax Competition in Europe* (Amsterdam, IBFD, 2003) 121–32.

Farley, M, 'The Role of Economics-based Approaches when Analysing Effects on Trade and Distortions of Competition after *Wam*' (2010) *European State Aid Law Quarterly* 369.

Fingleton, J, Ruane, F, Ryan, V, 'Market Definition and State Aid Control' [1999] 3 *European Economy* 65.

Flynn, L, 'Competition Policy and Public Services in EC Law after the Maastricht and Amsterdam Treaties' in O'Keefe, D and Twomey, R (eds), *Legal Issues of the Amsterdam Treaty* (Oxford, Hart Publishing, 1999).

Follesdal, A and Hix, S, 'Why There is a Democratic Deficit in the EU: A Response to Majone and Moravcsik' (2006) 44 *Journal of Common Market Studies* 533.

Fox, E, 'State Aids Control and the Distortion of Competition—Unbundling "Distortion"' *Annual Proceedings Fordham Corporate Law Institute Conference*, 28th vol (The Hague, Kluwer, 2001) 91.

Freedland, M and Sciarra, S (eds), *Public Services and Citizenship in European Law* (Oxford, Clarendon Press, 1998).

Friederiszick, HW, Röller, L-H, Verouden, V, 'European State Aid Control: An Economic Framework' in Buccirossi, P (ed), *Advances in the Economics of Competition Law* (Cambridge Mass., MIT Press, 2008) 625–69.

Friend, M, 'State Guarantees as State Aid: Some Practical Difficulties' in Biondi, A, Eeckhout, P and Flynn, J (eds), *The Law of State Aid in the European Union* (Oxford, Oxford University Press, 2004) 231–45.

Gerber, DJ, 'Constitutionalising the Economy: German Neo-Liberalism, Competition law and the 'New' Europe' (1994) 42 *American Journal of Competition Law* 25.

——, *Law and Competition in Twentieth Century Europe: Protecting Prometheus* (Oxford, Oxford University Press, 2001).

Gerner-Beuerle, C, 'Shareholders between the Market and the State. The VW Law and other Interventions in the Market Economy' (2012) 49 *CML Rev* 97.

Gilliams, H, 'Stress Testing the Regulator: Review of State Aid to Financial Institutions after the Collapse of Lehman' (2011) 36 *EL Rev* 3.

Gilpin, R, *The Political Economy of International Relations* (Princeton, Princeton University Press, 1987) 355.

Giubboni, S, *Social Rights and Market Freedom in the European Constitution: A Labour Law Perspective* (Cambridge, Cambridge University Press, 2006).

Goldschmidt, N and Wohlgemuth, M, 'Social Market Economy: Origins, Meanings and Interpretations' (2008) 19 *Constitutional Political Economy* 261.

Greaves, R, 'Autonomous Regions, Taxation and EC State Aids Rules' (2009) 34 *EL Rev* 779.

Gromnicka, E, 'Services of General Economic Interest and State Aids Regime: Proceduralisation of Political Choices?' (2005) 11 *European Public Law* 429.

Grossman, E, 'Europeanization as an Interactive Process: German Public Banks Meet EU State Aid Policy' (2006) 44 *Journal of Common Market Studies* 325.

Gröteke, F and Kerber, W, 'The Case of Ryanair—EU State Aid Policy in the Wrong Runway?' (2004) 55 *ORDO* 313.

Gyselen, L, 'The Substantive Legality Test Under Article 81(3) EC Treaty—Revisited in Light of the Commission's Modernization Initiative' in von Bogdandy, A, Mavroidis, PC and Mény, Y (eds), *European Integration and International Co-ordination: Studies in Honour of Claus-Dieter Ehlermann* (The Hague, Kluwer Law International, 2002).

Hall, PA and Soskice, D (eds), *Varieties of Capitalism: The Institutional Foundations of Comparative Advantage* (Oxford, Oxford University Press, 2001).

Hancher, L, 'The Public Sector as Object and Instrument of Economic Policy' in T Daintith (ed), *Law as an Instrument of Economic Policy* (Berlin, De Gruyter, 1988) 165–80.

—— Hancher, L, 'State Aids and Judicial Control in the European Community' (1994) 4 *European Competition Law Review* 134.

——, 'Community, State, and Market' L Hancher, 'Community, State and Market' in Craig, P and de Búrca, G (eds), *The Evolution of EU Law*, 1st edn (Oxford, Oxford University Press, 1999).

——, 'Towards a New Definition of a State Aid under European Law' (2003) 2 *European State Aid Law Review* 365.

——, 'Towards an Economic Analysis of State Aids' (2005) 3 *European State Aid Quarterly* 23.

——, Ottervanger, T and Slot, PJ, *EC State Aids*, 3rd edn (London, Sweet and Maxwell, 2006).

—— and Larouche, P, 'EU Regulation of Network Industries and Services' in Craig, P and de Búrca, G (eds), *The Evolution of EU Law*, 2nd edn (Oxford, Oxford University Press, 2011) 643–781.

Hansen, M, van Ysendyck, A and Zuhlke, S, 'The Coming of Age of EC State Aid Law' (2004) 25 *European Competition Law Review*_202.

Harlow, C, *Accountability in the European Union* (Oxford, Oxford University Press, 2002).

Hartley, T, *Constitutional Problems of the European Union* (Oxford, Hart Publishing, 1999).

Hawk, B, 'System Failure: Vertical Restraints and EC Competition Law' (1985) 32 *CML Rev* 973.

Héritier, A, 'The Politics of Public Services in European Regulation' Max Planck Institute for Research on Collective Goods No 2001/1.

Hildebrand, D and Schweinsberg, A, 'Refined Economic Approach in European State Aid Control—Will it Gain Momentum?' (2007) 30 *World Competition* 449.

Hofmann, H, 'Negotiated and non-negotiated administrative rule-making: the example of EC competition policy' (2006) 43 *CML Rev* 153.

Höpner, M and Schäfer, A, 'Polanyi in Brussels? Embeddedness and the Three Dimensions of European Economic Integration' (2010) Max-Planck-Institut für Gesellschaftsforschung Working Paper 10/8.

—— and ——, 'A New Phase of European Integration: Organised Capitalisms in Post-Ricardian Europe' (2010) 33 *West European Politics* 344.

Hughes Hallett, A and Scott, D, 'Scotland: A New Fiscal Settlement', Centre for Dynamic Macroeconomic Analysis Working Paper Series, 10/09.

Joerges, C, 'What is Left of the European Economic Constitution' (2005) 30 *EL Rev* 431.

——, 'A Renaissance of the European Economic Constitution?' in Neergaard, U, Nielsen, R and Roseberry, L (eds), *Integrating Welfare Functions into EU Law* (Copenhagen, DJØF Forlag, 2009).

Keen, M, 'Preferential Regimes Can Make Tax Competition Less Harmful' (2001) 54 *National Tax Journal* 757.

Kelemen, D, 'The Political Foundations of Judicial Independence in the European Union' (2012) 12 *Journal of European Public Policy* 43.

Kleiner, T, 'Modernization of State Aid Policy' in Szyszczak, E (ed), *Research Handbook on State Aid* (Cheltenham, Edward Elgar, 2011) 1–27.

Köhler, M, 'New Trends Concerning the Application of the Private Investor Test' (2011) 10 *European State Aid Law Quarterly* 21.

Konstadinides, T, 'Constitutional Identity as a Shield and as a Sword: The European Legal Order within the Framework of National Constitutional Settlement' (2010–2011) 13 *Cambridge Yearbook of European Legal Studies* 195.

Kornai, J, 'The Soft Budget Constraint' (1986) 39 *Kyklos* 3.

——, Maskin, E and Roland, G, 'Understanding the Soft Budget Constraint' (2003) 41 *Journal of Economic Literature* 1095.

Krajewski, M, 'Providing Legal Clarity and Securing Policy Space for Public Services Through a Legal Framework for Services of General Economic Interest: Squaring the Circle?' (2008) 14 *European Public Law* 377.

Krugman, P, 'Good News from Ireland: A Geographical Perspective' in A Gray (ed), *International Perspectives on the Irish Economy* (Dublin, Indecon, 1998) 38–53.

Kumm, M, 'The Jurisprudence of Constitutional Conflict: Constitutional Supremacy in Europe before and after the Constitutional Treaty' (2005) 11 *European Law Journal* 262.

Kurcz, B and Vallindas, D, 'Can General Measures be ... Selective? Some Thoughts on the Interpretation of a State Aid Definition' (2008) 45 *CML Rev* 159.

Lawson, C, 'The Theory of State-Owned Enterprises in Market Economies' (1994) 8 *Journal of Economic Surveys* 283.

Lenaerts, K, 'Constitutionalism and the Many Faces of Federalism' (1990) 38 *American Journal of Comparative Law* 205.

López, H, 'General Thought on Selectivity and Consequences of a Broad Concept of State Aid in Tax Matters' (2010) 9 *European State Aid Law Quarterly* 807.

Lubbig, T and von Merveldt, M, '*Stardust Marine*: Introducing Imputability into State Aid Rules-Plain Sailing into Calm Seas or Rowing Back into Shallow Waters?' (2003) 24 *European Competition Law Review* 629.

Lyon-Caen, G, 'L'Infiltration du Droit du travail par le Droit de la Concurrence' [1993] *Droit Ouvrier* 313.

McGowan, L, 'Europeanization Unleashed and Rebounding: Assessing the Modernization of EU Cartel Policy' (2005) 12 *Journal of European Public Policy* 986.

Poiares Maduro, M, *We The Court: The European Court of Justice and the European Economic Constitution* (Oxford, Hart Publishing, 1998).

——, 'Interpreting European Law: Judicial Adjudication in a Context of constitutional Pluralism' (2007) 1 *European Journal of Legal Studies*.

——, 'Courts and Pluralism' in Dunloff, JL and Trachtman, JP (eds), *Ruling the World?* (Oxford, Oxford University Press, 2009) 356–79.

Maier, M and Werner, P, 'Review of *AEM Spa v Autorità per l'Energia Elettrica e per il Gas*' (2005) 4 *European State Aid Quarterly* 657.

Majone, GD, 'The Rise of the Regulatory State in Europe' (1994) 17 *West European Politics* 77.

——, *Dilemmas of European Integration* (Oxford, Oxford University Press, 2005).

Marenco, G, 'The Birth of Modern Competition Law in Europe' in von Bogdandy, A Mavroidis, PC and Mény, Y (eds), *European Integration and International Co-ordination: Studies in Honour of Claus-Dieter Ehlermann* (The Hague, Kluwer Law International, 2002) 279–304.

Martinico, G, 'Complexity as the "Efficient Secret" of the European Constitution: an Alternative (Explanatory) Proposal' (2011) EUI Max Weber Working Paper 1/11.

Mattisson, O and Thomasson, A, 'The Strategic Process and its Impact on the Outcome of a Tender' (2007) 78 *Annals of Public & Cooperative Economics* 439.

Menon, A and Weatherill, S, 'Transnational Legitimacy in a Globalising World: How the European Union Rescues its States' (2008) 31 *Western Union Politics* 397.

Mertens de Wilmars, J, 'Réflexions sur les méthodes d'interprétation de la Cour de justice des Communautés européennes' (1986) *Cahiers de Droit Européen* 5.

Meussen, G, 'Fiscal Support Measures and Harmful Tax Competition' (2000) 9 *EC Tax Review* 152.

Milward, A, *The European Rescue of the Nation State*, 2nd edn (London, Routledge, 2000).

Moravcsik, A, 'In Defense of the "Democratic Deficit". Reassessing Legitimacy in the European Union' (2002) 40 *Journal of Common Market Studies* 603.

Monti, G, 'Article 81 and Public Policy' (2002) 39 *CML Rev* 1057.

——, *EC Competition Law* (Cambridge, Cambridge University Press, 2007).

Moran, M, 'Understanding the Regulatory State' (2002) 32 *British Journal of Political Science* 391.

Morijn, J, 'Balancing Fundamental Rights and Common Market Freedoms in Union Law: *Schmidberger* and *Omega* in the Light of the European Constitution' (2006) 12 *European Law Journal* 15.

Mortelmans, K, 'Towards convergence in the application of the rules on free movement and competition?' (2001) 28 *CML Rev* 613.

Mueller, T, 'Efficiency Control in State Aid and the Power of Member States to Define SGEIs' (2009) 7 *European State Aid Quarterly* 39.

Nanetti, F and Mameli, G, 'The Creeping Normative Role of the EC Commission in the Twin-Track Struggle Against State Aids and Harmful Tax Competition' (2002) 11 *EC Tax Review* 185.

Neergaard, U, 'Services of General Economic Interest under EU Law Constraints' in Schiek, D, Liebert, U and Schneider, H, *European Economic and Social Constitutionalism after the Treaty of Lisbon* (Cambridge, Cambridge University Press, 2011) 174–95.

Nicol, D, *The Constitutional Protection of Capitalism* (Oxford, Hart Publishing, 2010).
Nicolaides, P, 'Distortive Effects of Compensatory Aid Measures: A Note on the Economics of the *Ferring* Judgement' (2002) 6 *European Competition Law Review* 313.
——, 'Markets and Words: the Distortive Effect of Government Pronouncements' (2005) 26 *European Competition Law Review* 119.
——, 'The Economics of Services of General Economic Interest' in Sánchez Rydelski, M (ed), *The EC State Aid Régime: Distortive Effects of State Aid on Competition and Trade* (London, Cameron May, 2006) 575.
—— and Rusu, IE, 'Editorial: The Conflicting Roles of State Aid Control: Support of Financial Institutions versus Safeguarding the Internal Market' (2010) 17 *Maastricht Journal of European and Comparative Law* 223.
——, 'State Aid, Advantage and Competitive Selection: What Is a Normal Market Transaction? (2010) 10 *European State Aid Law Quarterly* 65.
—— and Rusu, IE, 'Private Investor Principle: What Benchmark and Whose Money?' (2011) 10 *European State Aid Law Quarterly* 237.
Nic Shuibhne, N, 'Annotation of Case C-76/05 *Schwarz and Gootjes-Schwarz* v. *Finanzamt Bergisch Gladbach*' (2008) 45 *CML Rev* 771.
——, 'Margins of Appreciation: National Values, Fundamental Rights and EC Free Movement Law' (2009) 34 *EL Rev* 230.
——, 'The Resilience of EU Market Citizenship' (2010) 47 *CML Rev* 1597.
Odudu, O, *The Boundaries of EC Competition Law* (Oxford, Oxford University Press, 2005).
——, 'Economic Activity as a Limit to Community Law' in Barnard, C and Odudu, O (eds), *The Outer Limits of European Union Law* (Oxford, Hart Publishing, 2009) 225–43.
——, 'Are State-Owned Health-Care Providers Subject to Competition Law?' (2011) 32 *European Competition Law Review* 231.
Ogus, A, *Regulation: Legal Form and Economic Theory* (Oxford, Oxford University Press, 1994).
Ojo, M, 'The Changing Role of Central Banks and the Role of Competition in Financial Regulation during (and in the Aftermath of) the Financial Crisis' (2011) 17 *European Law Journal* 513.
Oliver, P, 'Competition and Free Movement: Their Place in the Treaty' in Nebbia, P and Tridimas, T (eds), *Competition Law for the 21st Century* (Oxford, Hart Publishing, 2004).
——, 'Of Trailers and Jet Skis: Is the Case Law on Article 34 Hurtling in a New Direction?' (2011) 33 *Fordham International Law Journal* 1423.
Panayi, CHJI, 'State Aid and Tax: The Third Way?' 32 *Intertax* 283.
Parish, M, 'On the private investor principle' (2003) 28 *EL Rev* 70.
Picciotto, S, 'Liberalization and Democratization: The Forum and the Hearth in the Era of Cosmopolitan Post-Industrial Capitalism' (2000) 63 *Law and Contemporary Problems* 157.
Plender, R, 'Definition of Aid' in Biondi, A, Eeckhout, P and Flynn, J (eds), *The Law of State Aid in the European Union* (Oxford, Oxford University Press, 2003).
Prechal, S and de Vries, S, 'Seamless Web of Judicial Protection in the Internal Market?' (2009) 34 *EL Rev* 5.
Prete, L, 'State Aid Reform: Some Reflection on the Need to Revise the Notice on Guarantees' (2006) 29 *World Competition* 421.

Prosser, T, *Nationalised Industries and Public Control* (Oxford, Blackwell, 1986).
——, 'Public Service Law: Privatization's Unexpected Offspring'(2000) 63 *Law and Contemporary Problems* 63.
——, 'Competition Law and Public Services: From Single Market to Citizenship Rights' (2005) 11 *European Public Law* 543.
——, *The Limits of Competition Law* (Oxford, Oxford University Press, 2005).
Radaelli, C and Kraemer, U, 'Governance Areas in EU Direct Tax Policy' (2008) 46 *Journal of Common Market Studies* 315.
Renzulli, A, 'Services of General Economic Interest: The Post-*Altmark* Scenario' (2008) 14 *European Public Law* 399.
Riley, A, 'EC Antitrust Modernisation: The Commission Does Very Nicely—Thank you!' [2004] *European Competition Law Review* 604.
Ringe, W-G, 'Sparking Regulatory Competition in European Company Law—The Impact of the *Centros* Line of Case-Law and its Concept of "Abuse of Law"' in de la Feria, R and Vogenauer, S, *Prohibition of Abuse Law—a New General Principle of EU Law* (Oxford, Hart Publishing, 2010) 107–26.
——, 'Company Law and Free Movement of Capital' (2010) 69 *CLJ* 378.
Rizza, C, 'The Financial Assistance Granted by Member States to Undertakings Entrusted with the Operation of a Service of General Economic Interest' in Biondi, A and Eeckhout, P (eds), *The Law of State Aid in the European Union* (Oxford, Oxford University Press, 2003) 67–84.
Roberti, GM, *Gli Aiuti di Stato nel Diritto Comunitario* (Padova, CEDAM, 1997).
Rodger, B, 'State Aid—A Fully Level Playing Field?' [1999] *European Competition Law Review* 251.
Ross, M, 'State Aids: Maturing into a Constitutional Problem' (1995) 15 *Yearbook of European Law* 79.
——, 'State Aids and National Court: Definitions and Other Problems—A Case of Premature Emancipation?' (2000) 37 *CML Rev* 401.
—— Ross, M, 'Article 16 EC and Services of General Interest: From Derogation to Obligation?' (2000) 25 *EL Rev* 22.
——, 'The Value of Solidarity in European Public Services Law' in Krajewski, M, Neergaard, U and van de Gronden, J, *The Changing Legal Framework for Services of General Interest in Europe—Between Competition and Solidarity* (The Hague, Asser Press, 2009).
——, 'A Healthy Approach to Services of General Economic Interest? The BUPA Judgment of the Court of First Instance' (2009) 34 *EL Rev* 127.
—— and Borgmann-Prebil, Y (eds), *Promoting Solidarity in the European Union* (Oxford, Oxford University Press, 2010).
Rossi-Maccanico, PP, 'Gibraltar and the Unsettled Limits of Selectivity in Fiscal Aids' (2009) *European State Aid Law Quarterly* 63.
Rubini, L, 'The Elusive Frontier: Regulation under State Aid Rules' (2009) 8 *European State Aid Law Quarterly* 277.
——, *The Definition of Subsidy and State Aid* (Oxford, Oxford University Press, 2009).
Sally, R, *Classical Liberalism and International Economic Order* (London, Routledge, 2002).
Sauter, W, 'The Economic Constitution of the European Union' (1998) 4 *Columbia Journal of European Law* 27.
——, 'Services of General Economic Interest and Universal Services in EU Law' (2008) 33 *EL Rev* 167.

—— Sauter, W, 'Annotation of Case T-289/03 *BUPA v Commission*' (2009) 46 *CML Rev* 269.
Scharpf, FW, *Governing in Europe: Effective and Democratic?* (Oxford, Oxford University Press, 1999).
——, 'Democratic Legitimacy under Conditions of Regulatory Competition: Why Europe Differs from the United States' in K Nicolaidis and R Howse (eds), *The Federal Vision* (Oxford, Oxford University Press, 2000) 355.
——, 'The Double Asymmetry of European Integration' Max-Planck-Institut für Gesellschaftsforschung Working Paper 09/12.
——, 'Monetary Union, Fiscal Crisis and the Preemption of Democracy' in LSE 'Europe in Question' Discussion Paper Series No 36/2011.
Schepel, H, 'Delegation of Regulatory Powers to Private Parties Under EC Competition Law' (2002) 39 *CML Rev* 31.
——, 'Constitutionalising the Market, Marketising the Constitution, and to Tell the Difference: On the Horizontal Application of the Free Movement Provisions in EU Law' (2012) 18 *European Law Journal* 177.
Schiek, D, Liebert, U, Schneider, H, (eds) *European and Social Constitutionalism after the Treaty of Lisbon* (Cambridge, Cambridge University Press, 2011).
Schön, W, 'Taxation and State Aid in the European Union' (1999) 36 *CML Rev* 911.
Schütte, M, 'The Definition of State Aid' in Sánchez Rydelski, M (ed), *The EC State Aid Régime: Distortive Effects of State Aid on Competition and Trade* (London, Cameron May, 2006).
Sciarra, S, 'Diritto del Lavoro e Regole della Concorrenza in Alcuni Casi Esemplari della Corte di Giustizia Europea' (2000) 2 *Il Diritto del Mercato del Lavoro* 587.
——, 'Viking and Laval: Collective Labour Rights and Market Freedoms in the Enlarged EU' (2007–2008) *Cambridge Yearbook of European Legal Studies* (Oxford, Hart Publishing, 2008) 563–80.
Scott, C (ed), *Regulation* (Aldershot, Ashgate, 2002).
Semmelmann, C, 'The European Union's Economic Constitution under the Lisbon Treaty: Soul-Searching among Lawyers Shifts the Focus to Procedure' (2010) 35 *EL Rev* 516.
Simonsson, I, 'Privatisation and State Aid—Time for a New Policy' (2005) 26 *European Competition Law Review* 460.
Sinn, HW, *The New Systems Competition* (Oxford, Wiley-Blackwell, 2003).
Sinnaeve, A, 'State Financing of Public Services: The Court's Dilemma in the *Altmark* Case' (2003) 2 *European State Aid Law Quarterly* 351.
Slotboom, M, 'State Aid in Community Law: A Broad or Narrow Definition?' (1995) 20 *EL Rev* 289.
Smith, MP, 'Who Are the Agents of Europeanisation? EC Competition Policy and German Public Law Banks' (2001) EUI Working Paper 2001/39.
——, *States of Liberalization* (New York, State University of New York Press, 2005).
Snell, J, 'Economic Aims as Justifications for Restrictions on Free Movement' in Schrauwen, A (ed), *The Rule of Reason: Rethinking another Classic of EC Legal Doctrine* (Groningen, Europa Law Publishing, 2004).
——, 'Varieties of Capitalism and the Limits of European Economic Integration' (2010–2011) 13 *Cambridge Yearbook of European Legal Studies* 415.
Somek, A, 'Equality and Constitutional Indeterminacy: An Interpretative Perspective on the European Economic Constitution' (2001) 7 *European Law Journal* 17.
Spaventa, E 'From *Gebhard* to *Carpenter*: towards a (non-)Economic European Constitution' (2004) 41 *CML Rev* 743.

——, 'The Outer Limit of the Treaty Free Movement Provisions: Some Reflections on the Significance of *Keck*, Remoteness and *Deliège*' in Barnard C and Odudu, O (eds), *The Outer Limits of European Union Law* (Oxford, Hart Publishing, 2009) 245–71.
——, 'Federalisation Versus Centralisation: Tensions in Fundamental Rights Discourse in the EU' in Dougan, M and Currie, S, *50 Years of the European Treaties: Looking Back and Thinking Forward* (Oxford, Hart Publishing, 2009) 343–64.
Stein, E, 'Lawyers, Judges and the Making of a Transnational Constitution' (1981) 75 *American Journal of International Law* 1.
Streit, M and Mussler, W, 'The Economic Constitution of the EC from "Rome" to "Maastricht"' (1995) 1 *European Law Journal* 5.
Szyszczak, E, 'Public Service Provision in Competitive Markets' [2001] *Yearbook of European Law* 35.
Szyszczak, E, *The Regulation of the State in Competitive Markets in the EU* (Oxford, Hart Publishing, 2007).
—— (ed), *Research Handbook on State Aid* (Cheltenham, Edward Elgar, 2011).
Töpler, F and Butler, J, 'Proceed with Care: Purchasing Companies with Potential State Aid Liabilities' (2004) 25 *European Competition Law Review* 421.
Townley, C, *Article 81EC and Public Policy* (Oxford, Hart Publishing, 2009).
Tridimas, T, 'Terrorism and the ECJ: Empowerment and Democracy in the EC Legal Order' (2009) 34 *EL Rev* 103.
Tsoukalis, L, *The New European Economy Revisited* (Oxford, Oxford University Press, 1997).
Verhoeven, A, 'Privatisation and EC Law: is the European Commission "Neutral" with respect to Public versus Private Ownership of Companies?' (1996) 45 *International and Comparative Law Quarterly* 861.
Weatherill, S, *Law and Integration in the European Union* (Oxford, Oxford University Press, 1995) 272.
——, 'Compulsory Notification of Draft Technical Regulations: The Contribution of Directive 83/189 to the Management of the Internal Market' [1996] *Yearbook of European Law* 129.
——, 'Recent Case Law Concerning the Free Movement of Goods: Mapping the Frontiers of Market Deregulation' (1999) 36 *CML Rev* 51.
——, 'A Case Study in Judicial Activism in the 1990s: The Status Before National Courts of Measures Wrongfully Un-notified to the Commission' in O'Keefe, D (ed), *Liber Amicorum Slynn* (The Hague, Kluwer Law International, 2000).
——, 'The Commission's Options for Developing EC Consumer Protection and Contract Law: Assessing the Constitutional Basis' (2002) 13 *European Business Law Review* 497.
——, 'Supply and Demand for Internal Market Regulation: Strategies, Preferences and Interpretation' in Nic Shuibhne, N (ed), *Regulating the Internal Market* (Cheltenham, Elgar, 2006).
Weiler, JHH, 'The Transformation of Europe' (1991) 100 *Yale Law Journal* 2403.
——, 'The Constitution of the Common Market Place: Text and Context in the Evolution of the Free Movement of Goods' in Craig, P and de Búrca, G (eds), *The Evolution of EU Law*, 1st edn (Oxford, Oxford University Press, 1999) 360.
——, 'A Constitution for Europe? Some Hard Choices' (2002) 42 *Journal of Common Market Studies* 563.
Werner, P, 'Fiscal State Aid' (2006–2007) 9 *Cambridge Yearbook of European Legal Studies* 481.

Whish, R and Bailey, D, *Competition Law*, 7th edn (Oxford, Oxford University Press, 2012).

Winter, J, (Case Note) (2008) 45 *CML Rev* 183.

Wishlade, F, *Regional State Aid and Competition Policy in the European Union* (The Hague, Kluwer, 2003).

Wyatt, D, 'Horizontal Effect of Fundamental Freedoms and the Right to Equality after *Viking* and *Mangold*, and the Implications for Community Competence' (2008) 48 *Croatian Yearbook of European Law & Policy* 1.

Wyatt, D, 'Community Competence to Regulate the Internal Market' in Dougan, M and Currie, S (eds), *50 Years of European Treaties: Looking Back and Thinking Forward* (Oxford, Hart Publishing, 2009).

Index